CENTER
SQUARE

CENTER SQUARE

THE PAUL LYNDE STORY

JOE FLORENSKI AND STEVE WILSON

Advocate BOOKS

MANUFACTURED IN THE UNITED STATES OF AMERICA.

THIS TRADE PAPERBACK ORIGINAL IS PUBLISHED BY ADVOCATE BOOKS,
AN IMPRINT OF ALYSON BOOKS,
P.O. BOX 4371, LOS ANGELES, CALIFORNIA 90078-4371.
DISTRIBUTION IN THE UNITED KINGDOM BY TURNAROUND PUBLISHER SERVICES LTD.,
UNIT 3, OLYMPIA TRADING ESTATE, COBURG ROAD, WOOD GREEN,
LONDON N22 6TZ ENGLAND.

FIRST EDITION: AUGUST 2005

05 06 07 08 09 ✳ 10 9 8 7 6 5 4 3 2 1

ISBN 1-55583-793-X
ISBN-13 978-1-55583-793-8

LIBRARY OF CONGRESS CATALOGING-IN-PUBLICATION DATA
   WILSON, STEVE, 1970-
      CENTER SQUARE : THE PAUL LYNDE STORY / BY STEVE WILSON AND JOE
FLORENSKI.—1ST ED.
     ISBN 1-55583-793-X; ISBN-13 978-1-55583-793-8
     1. LYNDE, PAUL. 2. ACTORS—UNITED STATES—BIOGRAPHY.
   PN2287.L96 W55 2004
   792.02'8'092—DC22   2004047662
   [B]

CREDITS
COVER PHOTOGRAPHY BY FROM HULTON ARCHIVE.
COVER DESIGN BY MATT SAMS.

INTRODUCTION

In 1960, Paul Lynde had every reason to be happy. After years of obscure toil following his initial Broadway splash in *New Faces of 1952,* he'd dazzled audiences as Harry MacAfee, the put-upon parent of a rock-crazed teenager in *Bye Bye Birdie.* The hit musical had given Paul lots of exposure and already led to offers in film and television. Finally, his career seemed headed in the right direction.

So confident must Paul have been in his prospects that when he learned a friend had invited theatrical producer Hal Prince to her party, he begged himself onto the guest list. He couldn't pass up the chance to tell the man who helped create *The Pajama Game, Damn Yankees,* and *West Side Story* how much he admired his work (and no doubt encourage him to keep Paul in mind for future projects). At the party Paul had one cocktail too many, and whatever he originally meant to tell Prince fell out of his head. Instead of approaching Prince politely, he backed the man into a corner and gave him the sort of verbal beating that was his specialty when he was wasted. The next morning Paul realized what he had done and pleaded with the hostess for a chance to apologize to his victim. He got himself invited to another party…and ended up drunkenly eviscerating Prince all over again.

As we began our research, we saw Paul dealing with most

things in his life as he had dealt with Prince—simultaneously seeking and spurning what he desired. He wanted people to like him, but he trashed them to their faces. He spoke reverently of his hometown but fled it the first chance he got. He exhausted himself rehearsing and reworking comedy material, but usually despised the end product. He longed for lasting love but resigned himself to renting it by the hour.

Reading between the lines of Paul's relatively scant press coverage—mostly fluff pieces in forgotten TV magazines and unflattering bits in the gossip rags of the era—it became clear that Paul's impulse to crave and reject left him miserable. Hearing the stories (and Paul Lynde impersonations) of friends, coworkers, casual flings, and the assorted fanatics his fame attracted, we came to understand that Paul had several reasons to be angry.

A child of the Depression, Paul dreamed of fame and riches as an escape from an intolerant small town in the Midwest. The celebrities he watched on the movie screen every Saturday afternoon epitomized everything he wanted to be. He longed to follow in their footsteps—not those of his father, a onetime county sheriff and full-time butcher.

His obesity—the product of an overindulgent mother who plied him with food—didn't deter the starstruck teen. A born performer who needed attention, Paul made himself the sort of class clown who knows how to fight back with barbed wit as a defense against taunts. By the time he reached high school, he had a tight-knit circle of friends, a girlfriend named Marilyn, and a secure future at the family butcher shop, but he cast it all aside to study theater at Northwestern University.

Popular (if a little feared) on campus and adored (if not taken too seriously) onstage, Paul enjoyed in college the acceptance he'd always craved. He even found a few brothers in his fraternity who liked men the same way he did, but Paul wasn't ready to fully embrace his queerness. Perhaps most surprisingly to us, Paul still hadn't quite made up his mind about being with men or women: At college, he still pined for his high school sweetheart.

Paul's heady days as a big man on campus made the harshness of New York City that much harder for him to bear. He often found socializing and partying more interesting than auditioning. Not long into this halfhearted effort to make it on Broadway, word came from home that the remains of his war-hero brother had been identified, a tragedy compounded by the deaths in quick succession of his mother and father. A wedding announcement from Marilyn a year later didn't help either.

Depressed and penniless without his father's wallet to bail him out, Paul scraped by at odd jobs and nerve-wracking work as a nightclub comic before he talked his way into the cast of *New Faces of 1952*. The musical revue, which spawned a cast recording, national tour, and wide-screen movie, gave Paul a few good years of work as a TV comedian and Broadway director. But when the exposure petered out, he found himself and his shattered ego relegated to late-night TV and high-end dinner theater.

Paul increasingly took solace in the bottle, which only made matters worse. After the male *New Faces* dancer he dated tired of his abuse and left him, he turned to sleazy relationships with hustlers and other lowlifes. His work suffered to the point that he froze up in stage fright one night during a simple summer stage production.

Bye Bye Birdie saved his professional life, but it didn't improve his bad attitude. Then again, Paul's bitterness also made him a very funny man. If he weren't mad about something, he wouldn't have been Paul Lynde. The same fury that fired his comedy—and brought him more money than most character actors ever see—also kept him from enjoying what he had. He always wanted to move beyond the "funny uncle" roles, but his odd persona hemmed him in. Manic, hardwired for snideness, and with his conflicted sexuality worn prominently on his sleeve, Paul just wasn't leading-man material. Even as Paul loudly trashed the entertainment industry for relegating him to the role of a wacky costar, he took all the work it sent his way. The most glittering of these consolation prizes—his gig hashing out prepared "zingers" on *Hollywood Squares*—gave Paul a steady paycheck and became (to his unending annoyance) the source of his greatest recognition. Although he wouldn't live to appreciate the honor, his work on *Squares* also became the prototype for later gay entertainers to follow.

For this reason more than any other, we knew Paul deserved a biography. Too often our favorite comedian has been dismissed as a campy relic of a less-liberated time, a view that overlooks Paul's great, if accidental, achievement: getting away with being gay on TV on an almost daily basis for more than a decade.

Until Paul, gay characters on TV and film were mainly homophobic stereotypes. Ernie Kovacs made some ABC executives nervous in the 1950s whenever he played Percy Dovetonsils, a lisping, tiger print–wearing fruit who recited poetry from lace-lined books. A few years later, Jonathan Winters came on Jack Paar's talk show as "The Voice of Spring," wearing a suit and satyr horns:

"I bring you some little goodies from the forest," the lisping comic told the host.

"You've been on Third Avenue is where you've been," Paar shot back.

While screen legend Rock Hudson acted hetero until the very end, complete with a sham marriage, and beloved pianist Liberace sued the press for questioning the brand of manhood that compelled him to perform in sequined hot pants, Paul put on no such charade. He went the bold route of being his flamboyant, wise-cracking, crypto-closeted, caftan-clad self. Well before Billy Crystal played a gay man on *Soap*—and aeons before *Will & Grace* and *Queer Eye for the Straight Guy*—this fairy forefather's arch and bitchy wit snuck regular doses of the queer world into that bastion of intolerance, the American living room. Paul showed TV viewers that a gay man could deliver the jokes, not just be the butt of them. Paul titillated a naïve public by dancing right at the threshold of the closet, infusing his lines with an undercurrent of queer sexual frustration. In the process, he helped make homosexuality more palatable to the unwitting housewives and children who simply saw him as a stylish, funny man. To a generation of young gays and lesbians, he presented a role model of sorts, even if some would later brush him aside as a self-loathing queen. But these latter-day critics fail to see the trail he blazed. He refused to be ashamed of who he was (or perhaps he was just too tired to hide it).

Even so, Paul never saw his game show throne as a seat of liberation—just an increasingly abhorrent dead end. Constantly angry and juiced up, he ran afoul of the law, his friends, and even his alma mater, which banned him from campus. By the time Paul finally quit drinking, most of his work had dried up as well, and he only had a short time left to enjoy sobriety.

In the end, though he compromised himself in many ways to snatch at the stardom Hollywood kept dangling in his face, Paul never changed who he was—for which we, as undying fans, are eternally grateful. His life serves as a reminder of how far that sort of tenacity will get you in an industry that values artifice above all else. Paul was a lot of things, but no one could accuse him of being a phony.

CHAPTER 1

BIG QUEEN ON CAMPUS

"Mother indulged me."

The 1920s into which Paul Edward Lynde was born hardly roared with the rest of the country. Paul's hometown of Mount Vernon, Ohio, with a population just north of 9,000 when Calvin Coolidge sat in the White House, still set aside space on its downtown streets for horse-drawn wagons. The people there preferred whistling "Dixie," the minstrel song written by native son Dan Emmett, to most hits of the Jazz Age.

Hoy Lynde, a third-generation Ohioan, had lived in this quaint burg since just before the turn of the century. In 1916, he married Sylvia Bell Doup, a fourth-generation Buckeye herself, who stayed home with the kids as he worked his way up from deliveryman to head of the meat department at Pitkin's Provision Store. Their first daughter, Grace, arrived a year after Hoy's and Sylvia's marriage. Their second, Helen, came two years later, followed by sons Richard in 1920 and Coradon— whom everyone called Cordy—in 1923. On June 13, 1926, a week after the couple's aluminum anniversary milestone, Sylvia bore at home their fifth child, Paul, whom they named after a family friend.

In the familiar dynamic, Paul's mother nurtured and his father disciplined. Hoy spared the rod, but he could strike a threatening pose when he wanted to keep his kids in line. "Dad had a nice even disposition—he was mad all the time," Paul once joked. The son learned how to work Hoy for his own gain. "I was frightened of Dad, but I could get anything I wanted out of him by going through my mother. He worshipped her. I wasn't afraid of my mother, but she always thought I was silly. 'Oh Paul,' she'd say, 'you're so silly. You just do whatever you want to do.'"

Hoy supported his large brood—and continued the long Lynde tradition of public service—by replacing the ailing deputy sheriff of Knox County in early 1925. Nearly four years later—in November 1928, when Paul was 2—Hoy followed in his father's footsteps by winning election as sheriff in a near Republican sweep of county offices. The position included housing as a perk—at the county jail. The troublemakers and lowlifes Hoy incarcerated lived behind bars in the back of the building, and the Lynde family moved into an apartment at the front. Though the Lyndes only lived there during Hoy's consecutive two-year terms, Paul liked to tell people he grew up in prison.

Later, when Paul wasn't recalling his childhood as "the happiest time of my life," he was blowing off Mount Vernon as a place he wanted to leave "as soon as I could crawl." Ohio seemed like a very small place to a boy who had been obsessed with money and fame since he saw his first movies.

Assuming he had to be rich before he could be famous, young Paul told fantastic lies about his imaginary wealth, bragging of his show horses, waving to passing cars from the steps of a mansion as though he lived there, and making loud demands like "Where's my gold bathrobe?" He got hooked on movies after seeing *Ben Hur* on an outing with the nuns who watched over him while his mother recovered from an illness after the birth of Johnny, the sixth and final Lynde offspring. On reaching school age, Paul spent every Saturday at one of the two movie theaters in town. He liked most every star on the bill, though he particularly enjoyed the antics of the chubbier half of screen team Laurel and Hardy. His father, who preferred Will Rogers, had to fish his movie-crazed son out of the darkened theaters by flashlight almost every weekend.

Performing was one of the few ways for Paul to stand out as an otherwise average kid at the tail end of a formidable pecking order. Richard, the oldest, was the star athlete. Cordy was the brain. Johnny was the baby. Paul was the self-described "nothing." Friends remember Paul being particularly close to Helen and Cordy, though those two didn't necessarily know how relate to a brother who thought nothing of dressing up as a circus fat lady for backyard shows or parading up and down a friend's driveway in an old dress from the attic.

Paul found his first real audience, he once quipped, as the "Kirsten Flagstad of Ohio," singing and even touring the country with his church choir. He dreamed of becoming an opera singer and earned scholarships to attend summer music school, but his golden throat gave out during puberty and would be good for little else other than musical theater.

At the age of ten, Paul came down with peritonitis, an illness that inflames the wall of the abdomen. In those days, the disease could be fatal, but Paul pulled through. He then spent nearly a year bedridden and at the mercy of his overindulgent mother, who brought comfort food to her enfeebled son anytime she left the kitchen. Packing on the pounds, Paul developed a dysfunctional love affair with overeating that hounded him for the rest of his life.

The Lyndes rarely threw out leftovers—not because of the Depression but because Paul and his mother polished off anything still on the table. Lacking other ways to relate to each other, the two found a common link in food. As a snack, Paul sometimes wolfed down a dozen or so sandwiches spread with bologna, sweet pickles, peanuts, and mayonnaise.

Paul returned to elementary school 100 pounds heavier and suffered the inevitable insults from other kids. To shield himself from taunts of "tubby" and "lard-ass," Paul embraced the proud tradition of fat kids everywhere and became a clown. With an attitude. Paul's "macabre sense of humor," as friend Mark Kinney described it, didn't always go over well. When Paul's teacher told the "silly goose" that she would throw herself out the window if he didn't behave, Paul ran to the window and hurled it open. After a friend's mother admonished Paul to behave himself or go home, Paul observed loudly in front of her, "Gee, your mom's feisty today." At a football game, Paul rushed to the side of an injured player being carried off the field, spat on him, and yelled in his face, "Quitter!"

When he hit his teens, Paul worked weekends and summers at the Lynde Meat Market, which Hoy opened in 1937. Paul only took the job to please his father, but he found unexpected artistic stimulation dressing chickens and hawking meat. Though Paul hated yanking heads and feathers off poultry (his friends nicknamed him "Chicken Plucker"), the unsavory work inspired his trademark horrified wince. Likewise, taking orders put him in close contact with the Midwestern types he would later lampoon in his act.

Relishing having an audience on the other side of the counter, Paul pushed products with a mixture of blunt honesty and hammy patter that kept the customers coming back. "His father had this one man who worked for him, an assistant, for a hundred years, and when Paul was there all the man did was laugh. He could never get anything done," recalls childhood friend Barbara Shamansky, now Barbara Blashek. Another friend, Jacques Everhart, has said that Hoy showed some humor of his own at the counter. When a customer ordered a rump roast, Hoy would lay Shorty, the assistant, across the block, grab a saw, and pretend to shave off a piece of his ass.

Together, father and son formed an impressive selling team, and Paul basked in his father's pride. Hoy told Paul that he was far and away the best salesman of all his sons. Though they bonded over meat, Paul found Hoy's career embarrassing and called him a "cattle surgeon." Later, in college, when asked about his father's profession, Paul told people Hoy was "in business" and changed the subject.

Weighing over 200 pounds when he started ninth grade at Mount Vernon High School in 1940, Paul played off his girth with charming self-effacement. His senior yearbook picture sports a quote from Seneca leader Red Jacket: "A well-governed appetite is a great part of liberty." Resembling, in his words, a "teenage Edward Arnold" or "Kate Smith's niece," Paul managed to become as popular as an obese kid with mediocre academic skills and no athletic prowess could expect to be. He surrounded himself with other students of middling social standing who appreciated his sassy sense of fun. As ringleader, Paul spearheaded monkeyshines like selling friends' household furniture when their parents were out of town or improvising characters while draped in tablecloths at dance clubs and other public places.

Paul claimed he endured his teenage years "sans a belt or a love life," but in truth he dated Marilyn Surlas, a girl he had met in junior high. She had two things he admired most: wealth and an acid wit. Her father, a Greek immigrant, co-owned the Alcove, a popular restaurant in town where Paul and his friends hung out after school. Paul and Surlas spent endless hours making each other laugh. Paul started attending services at her Episcopal church, and she had to stifle her snickers when he made faces and gestures at her from his spot in the choir. "She was a good straight man for him," Blashek says. "She had a great sense of humor."

Paul's girlfriend witnessed a side of him few others saw. He wrote her sensitive love letters when he went away to summer music school and dropped his unrelenting jolliness when they were alone. "He appeared to be very outgoing, but underneath he was rather shy," says Surlas, known today as Marilyn Organ. She broke it off with Paul on occasion, but they always got back together. "Paul was very serious [about us]," she says. "I guess with me it was on and off." In his own inimitable way, Paul told her he planned to marry her: "With my looks and your charm, we could have wonderful children." Whenever he brought up matrimony, Surlas put off the subject and told him they'd talk about it later.

Paul participated in a respectable number of school activities, but he found his true niche in the drama club. Though his poundage relegated him to supporting parts, school plays further whet his appetite for stardom. "You could just see that it was part of his makeup," Everhart has said. "He was a good actor but not in the leading roles, and I think that goes back to the weight problem."

Speech teacher and play director Ruth Domigan Truxall suggested Paul study drama at Northwestern University in Evanston, Illinois, where she had taken some graduate courses. Paul claimed he chose to go there for romantic reasons. "I guess I thought if I couldn't be anything else, I could be funny and that would impress my girl," he said.

Paul's parents may have had misgivings about their son attending school out of state, but they didn't stand in his way. "After a high school show," Paul said, "Mother used to say to me, 'I like that pretty girl next to you.' I'd say, 'What about me?' She'd wave me aside, saying, 'Oh, you're so silly.' She thought show business was something I'd get over when I got good sense."

With his two oldest sons off fighting the war, Hoy couldn't see why Paul would refuse taking over the family business to pursue pipe dreams. Nonetheless, he agreed to pay Paul's tuition. "My father didn't oppose," Paul said. "He just didn't believe. It was simply too far beyond his experience."

By 1944, the year Paul matriculated, Northwestern University had established itself as one of the top drama schools in the country, serving as a springboard for scores of talented kids, among them Tony Randall, the anal half of TV's *The Odd Couple*, and Charlton Heston, movie Moses and gun guru. Paul attended school at the same time as Jean Hagen, Oscar-nominated for her work in *Singin' in the Rain,* and Patricia Neal, Oscar winner for *Hud.* Among Paul's fellow freshmen, he made fast friends with Cloris Leachman, who would go on to film and TV fame, and Charlotte Lubotsky, who would adopt the stage name Charlotte Rae and earn her greatest fame as Mrs. Garrett on the long-running sitcom *The Facts of Life.*

Paul and Rae made a habit of dropping by Leachman's boarding house. Young, talented, and bored, the kids expended their look-at-me energy on an old piano in the sitting room. Paul composed "songs" like "The Dying Indian," a single chord dirge he played with his index fingers as he warbled "Oooo-yeee-ooo-yeee—oooo—aaaaa!" They soon began improvising whole operas for a regular Saturday afternoon audience of students. "It was always spontaneous," Leachman says. "We sort of ran the school. I don't mean we were in any way leaders.... What were we? It was just our little band of cutter-uppers."

Like so many undergrads, Paul seized on college as an opportunity to transform himself. He did his best to live up to his idealized image of what a college man should be. In photos from the period, he almost always wears a tie, a blazer, and a very self-satisfied look on his face, carrying himself like a well-fed member of the leisure class. He stretched the truth about his family's wealth, casting Mount Vernon as some sort of country estate that he roamed as a squire. When

Barbara Blashek enrolled at Northwestern a year behind him, he worried she'd expose his exaggerations.

To his roommate, fellow drama major Basil Cross, Paul often spoke ad nauseam about Put-in-Bay, a tony island resort in Lake Erie where all *the* families kept summer houses; Kenyon College, a private institution near Mount Vernon where all *the* families sent their children (including Paul Newman, who went there during the years Paul attended school in Illinois); and Marilyn Surlas, *the* girl. Paul made his high school sweetheart out to be more beautiful than a Hollywood starlet and praised her for her drollery.

"Did you date Marilyn, or was she just the one you wanted to be most like?" Cross asked Paul one night after getting his fill of this nostalgic jabber.

"You just wouldn't understand," Paul snapped back.

Actually, Cross had a better chance of understanding than Paul initially realized. Cross had come to terms with being gay before college—not that he was about to reveal this secret to anyone when such an admission could get him expelled from school or worse. If Paul acknowledged his own gay leanings, he likely hadn't acted on them, and he wasn't going to tell Cross about them either. Instead, he continued to write and call Surlas and implored her to visit. She never did.

Despite his ongoing devotion to Marilyn, Paul had no qualms about seeing other girls, if only platonically. He almost always brought a date—usually Rae—to a party or dance. With so many women waiting for their own sweethearts to return home, dating during wartime was often more social than serious. Many students went out in groups and paired off mostly for convenience, a setup that let Paul mull over Marilyn and men without anyone questioning his preference for either.

From the day he aced his first acting class assignment by inventing an overzealous health department official who decried necking, petting, and "Lady Nicotine, gun moll of venereal disease," the big kid from small Mount Vernon finally found an appreciative audience—as long as he kept them laughing. In class one day, Paul offered a convincing Macbeth until, as if physically unable to stay serious, he smugly delivered one of Shakespeare's lines as only Paul Lynde would. He ruined the scene but sent everyone into hysterics.

In another class, Paul's built-in goofiness drew more laughs when he tried to read the nose speech from *Cyrano de Bergerac*. Though he had to finish the recitation in the professor's office, the demoralizing episode hipped the faculty to his natural gift for humor, and he immediately found himself cast as the former football player in *The Male Animal*. For the rest of his college career, Paul landed a steady stream of supporting parts in school productions, even beating out an influx of returning G.I.s for a choice role in *The Would-Be Gentleman*.

A few weeks after his campus stage debut, Paul received devastating news from home. The Army notified the Lyndes that Cordy had been missing in action in Germany since November 9. His parents hadn't even known their son was in that country; he had last sent word from Belgium. Paul went home for a short visit. Though he wasn't the only one in his social circle to lose a family member in the war, he refused to discuss his loss with anyone when he came back to school, including Hagen, whose brother had also gone missing.

At the end of his first year of college, Paul stuck around campus, as he would do every summer until graduation, to take part in the theater department's summer stage productions. While his friends fit in a course or two between rehearsals, Paul opted to spend his free time on the beach of Lake Michigan or at a local restaurant called Cooley's Cupboard, where he ordered curly fries and ice cream with abandon and let his checking account sort itself out. (Hoy constantly warned Paul about his spending, but Paul continued to live recklessly until he left college.) Paul and Cross found jobs in town at the Toddle House, a small chain restaurant that never closed. Paul took orders at the counter, and his roommate washed dishes. They worked the shift beginning at 7 A.M. and ending at 3 P.M., often heading straight to the restaurant after a night of partying.

The Toddle House drew a sizable line for its handful of stools, and Paul kept the waiting crowds entertained by serving generous helpings of cheek along with the food. "Excuse me, but I wanted a cheeseburger," a patron once demanded. Paul snatched up the burger bun in a tight grip. Seeing no cheese, he took the plate to the kitchen and brought it back. The customer still couldn't find the cheese, and when he asked a second time, Paul grabbed the bun again, stabbed the patty with a fork, and lifted it to reveal the cheese hidden underneath. "There's your cheese!" he shouted, slapping the burger back together.

Paul frequently gave free food to friends who stopped by. He also swiped generous portions for himself. Every day Paul slipped a pecan pie from the restaurant's supply to split with Cross, giving himself the larger share each time. Neither of them cared much when these liberalities got them fired by the summer's end.

One afternoon that August, Paul whiled away the day as he often did, lounging in his room doing nothing. Cross burst in and told him to turn on the radio. President Truman announced the unconditional surrender of Japan, marking the end of the war. Within minutes, the streets filled with screaming celebrants, and Paul and Cross soon ended up seated in the open trunk of a friend's convertible in search of a victory party.

They made their way to Grant Park on Chicago's lakefront, which teemed with thousands of revelers. Freshly pried from his makeshift seat, Paul grabbed a beer and a bottle of Southern Comfort and set out to incite a little bedlam. He lumbered over the small fence around Buckingham Fountain and took a huge belly flop into the water. Police blew their whistles, but that didn't stop a horde of people from joining the fat guy in the fountain. After he had his fill of splashing around, Paul climbed out and ran through the crowd shouting, "I just swam over to tell you they know it's over in Michigan too!"

That fall the Greek system on campus came out of its wartime hibernation. Being in a fraternity topped Paul's ideal of college life, and he rushed with zeal. He set his sights on Phi Kappa Sigma, a brotherhood prominent at Northwestern and at his beloved Kenyon College. The Phi Kaps owned a large house at the north end of campus that survived numerous formals, beer busts, and pool parties every year.

The military still occupied most of the fraternity buildings, so the brothers had to throw their rush parties at private residences. One night that week, Paul came home and practically shouted to Cross that he was going to sleep. He took off his pants but kept his boxers and suit coat on as he sat at the edge of his bed for a smoke. After a while, Paul turned a gooseneck lamp near the bed on his chest and continued sitting there. Finally, Cross asked, "Paul, is there something you're trying to tell me?" Paul shrugged in a way that flashed the Phi Kappa Sigma pledge pin on his lapel. Cross got up and unveiled the same pin on his own jacket. By coincidence, they had attended different Phi Kap parties, and both had pledged the fraternity. Paul reacted with the typical fury he reserved for Cross: "I'm never gonna get rid of you!"

Paul loved being a Phi Kap. He quickly made his mark in the organization by winning the float competition every homecoming with simple concepts and over-the-top performances as obese vampires and hillbilly coaches of enemy teams. As a senior, Paul staged a satire of *Gone with the Wind* in the Phi Kap living room, reorganizing the dialogue and casting himself as a hefty Scarlett O'Hara in a gown made from burgundy and white bed sheets. In the opening tableau, Paul scarfed down food offered to him by a ring of male suitors, telling the audience between bites, "With God as my witness, I'll never be hungry again."

In the spring of 1946, Paul won a spot in Waa-Mu, a variety show named after its sponsors, the Women's Athletic Association and the Men's Union. In these annual productions, Paul would make his biggest mark at Northwestern and discover his talent for sketch comedy. Paul and Rae teamed up to write and perform skits, and the two wrangled over pacing and delivery of jokes (a battle Paul usually won, by most accounts), but they delivered better material as a result. In successive shows, the competitive friends became Waa-Mu's star attraction. "They still talk about Lubotsky and Lynde," Rae says.

Performing and writing sketch comedy came naturally to Paul. He spent hours creating and discarding characters and scenarios when he could have been improving his grades. He eschewed "the Method" technique of acting as too "artsy-fartsy"—"I'd rather get paid," he bristled—yet he inhabited his creations with a Brando-like zeal. Cross found it hard to keep a straight face as Paul regularly flexed his creative muscles: "I would be studying really hard...and he would sit across the room and twirl his hair and start talking to himself in different characters. 'So I would say to myself, Margie, are you gonna put up with all of that shit from that man?' And I can't read. I'm looking at the book, trying not to laugh. And he would go on and on with these characters."

Paul rarely ever stopped performing, especially when it came to playing the smart mouth. His fellow Phi Kaps flocked to Paul's table during meals to hear him mock others. "He had a really razor-sharp malice," Rae says. "I was always a little embarrassed to laugh but I couldn't help myself." Once, after an acquaintance made a feeble attempt at a clever joke, Paul turned to him and said, "It's a pity your mother never had any children." On the physical appearance of a female friend, Paul privately noted, "All I can think of is a baked potato." When he was asked to join Deru, the oldest and most venerable society on campus, Paul used the honor as an excuse to belittle a brother who happened to be the student body president, reminding him every chance he got that "I'm in Deru, and you're not!"

Paul usually spared strangers his lash, saving his best strokes for those closest to him. He particularly laid into Cross, who says Paul expected people to bear his pummeling as a test of friendship. "If you were hurt and turned away from it, then you weren't worth the trouble anyway," Cross says. Paul treated everyone else in a pleasant and approachable way, though he always remained somewhat aloof, rarely lowering the shield of sarcasm he raised around himself.

Liquor, which Paul relished when he wasn't skipping classes to play bridge and eat hot dogs at the frat house, only magnified his nasty side and led to several chemically inconvenienced antics. Hanging out with some brothers at the house one evening after partying in nearby Skokie, Paul started grousing about the stupidity of ballroom dancing. A drunk Cross defended his favored hobby by convincing a drunker Paul to take a spin. Somehow hoisting his overweight friend onto his shoulder, Cross twirled Paul around the room...and inadvertently into a sofa and two lamps that toppled under his massive frame. Paul emerged unscathed, but Cross ended up having to get a hernia operation.

Eventually, Paul came out of the closet—to an extent. A handful of fraternity brothers met in private to joke, gossip, and set free their inner nellies without fear of discovery. In the safety of this secret circle, Paul made loud pronouncements like "I'm the biggest queen on campus!" and doled out female nicknames for all the boys. He christened himself "Wilhelmina," which to his annoyance his friends shortened to "Wilma."

Comfortable as he seemed with being gay, Paul never mentioned dating boyfriends or visiting the gay bars of nearby Chicago, though some friends suspect he carried on at least one secret fling with a fellow theater student. Unaware of any relationship Paul had with other men, Cross assumes his friend pursued no one for fear of rejection. Paul's feelings may have been more complicated than that; he still wrote love letters to Marilyn.

Marilyn only discovered after Paul's death that her former beau spent most of his life in relationships with men. That revelation still confounds her. "Was I such an idiot that I didn't realize that he might at some time be interested in a man?" she says. "Either I had to be awfully dense or something, but I know he liked females and he certainly liked me, because he wanted to marry me." She wonders if Paul's association with theater people may have influenced his lifestyle. "Since he was in showbiz, and around a lot of people who were [gay], maybe that's what caused it.... He was fine before he got mixed up with some of these people."

Paul's collegiate taste of stage success made him hungry for more in the real world, and he let others know it. Forbes recalls her friend periodically turning to her in class and hissing with mock menace, "Someday I'm gonna be rich and famous!" Three weeks before graduation, the big man on campus mused about his future career in a student newspaper profile. "Really, I guess that it is a matter of luck," Paul said. "You just have to hope that you can make the right contacts." Paul had, in fact, made a promising connection. In the spring of 1947, he caught *Three to Get Ready*, a stage revue starring Ray Bolger that played briefly in Chicago. Backstage, he fawned over young cast member Kaye Ballard. "She was just the greatest thing I'd ever seen," Paul said later. "I became a real stage-door Johnny." The young comedienne accepted Paul's invitation to see him in a Waa-Mu show. After the performance, she asked him, "When are you moving to New York?"

Before Paul could move anywhere, he had to graduate, a tricky proposition for the self-described "socializing goof-off always conning professors." Paul had never placed a high priority on academics or scholarly ethics. (He once joked to Forbes about having his hands dipped in hot oil for cheating on an exam.) Now his habit of last-minute studying caught up with him. Days before graduation, Paul learned he had flunked a snap course.

"It was a B-level English course," Paul said. "No one was in it but the football team and me. And the professor, who I never thought had any sense of humor, gave me a V for my grade. It stood for 'visitor.' Well, the card went home, and my father, who was footing the bills, called me up and asked, 'What the hell is V?' When you're desperate you are apt to say anything, so I blurted out, 'Oh, that stands for valedictorian.'"

Hoy wasn't fooled, but his son kept him in the dark about the consequence of the grade. "On the day of the commencement I was not scheduled to graduate," Paul said. "I was all over town the night before and that morning, seeing everybody from the course professor to the dean to the president. Everybody was passing the buck…. The only one who could let me graduate was the student senate. While the orchestra was rehearsing the processional, they held a special session, and I got a cap and gown. The ink was still wet on my diploma when they handed it to me. And my dad never knew."

CHAPTER 2

BIG TOWN, BAD TOWN, DAMN GOOD TOWN

"New York is a terrible place to be broke."

The Algonquin Hotel in Manhattan was no Cooley's Cupboard, but Paul, Charlotte Rae, Cloris Leachman, and Jan Forbes joked around in its storied dining room as if they were freshmen back at their old college hangout. Northwestern felt like an age ago, though none of them had been out of school long. Like Paul, Rae had moved to the city after graduation. Leachman left school after her sophomore year, competed unsuccessfully for the title of Miss America but made enough prize money to fund a move to New York. Forbes, a Pennsylvania housewife for three years, had left her home to visit them for a few days.

Talk that afternoon turned from gossip and movies to the future. No one questioned that Leachman and Rae would become stars, but when speculation turned to Paul, a consensus emerged. Paul wouldn't be famous, they decided, but he'd make a lot of money. Though Paul laughed along with them, everyone at the table knew he desperately wanted both fortune and fame, especially after his taste of college celebrity. Paul's ego led him to believe New York would receive him as Northwestern had, that he would set the town on fire. He gave himself five years to prove his friends wrong, and if nothing panned out—perish the thought—he'd take up teaching.

Paul didn't arrive in New York in the summer of 1948 empty-handed. He had a contact in Kaye Ballard, a support system in his relocated college chums, and mooch money in his father's checking account. His parents, still concerned about Cordy and living on the faint hope of his return, let their son move to the big city without a fuss.

The transplanted Ohioan settled into the cheapest digs he could find, the Park Savoy on West 58th Street. The dump had hosted many struggling performers over the years, including Leonard Bernstein and Judy Holliday a decade earlier and, more recently, Marlon Brando, Steve Cochran, and Wally Cox. Brando biographer Peter Manso described the establishment as "a seedy place, filled with alcoholic pensioners, transient homosexuals, and Broadway hookers." Paul fit right in.

Paul spent most days sleeping and most nights prowling from one communal refrigerator to the next, though not as slyly as he would have liked. Opening a fridge one night, he found a note: "Paul Lynde, for your information, one of these bowls contains poison. Take your choice."

With just a few friends in town, Paul stayed in touch with the distant ones during his first months in New York. Though Marilyn never took him up on his invitations to visit, Paul still held out hope they would someday be together. He also begged Basil Cross to quit school and move east, but his former roommate and whipping boy, recovering that summer from his hernia operation, planned to complete his education. "He wanted something familiar around him, like a security blanket," Cross says. Feeling out of his depth didn't dampen Paul's nasty wit. When Cross inquired about the fiancé of one of their friends, Paul paused for a moment and said, "Pray to God they never have children."

Paul had more to mope about than an inattentive high school sweetheart, loneliness, and poverty. His auditions went nowhere, and he couldn't get an agent. His fraternity received word that fall that their funny brother had won a supporting role in *Tales of the South Pacific,* but Paul's name was not included in the *Playbill* when the Broadway musical opened as *South Pacific* in April. Paul never explained the error. He could have simply been keeping up appearances for the sake of his campus reputation.

In those first months Paul fashioned himself a "playboy of New York," less concerned with casting calls than cast parties. Whether as a consequence of foresight or happy accident, partying turned out to be a wise career move. Playwrights Howard Lindsay and Russel Crouse, the Broadway bigwigs behind the long-running comedy *Life with Father,* spotted Paul doing one of his monologues at a party for the cast of *Inside U.S.A.,* which included Beatrice Lillie and Jack Haley and unknowns Jack Cassidy and Carl Reiner. They invited Paul to perform at the Players Club in Gramercy Park.

Founded by actor Edwin Booth in 1888, the club had held occasional Pipe Night gatherings since 1905, and Paul made his New York debut at one of them on December 19, 1948. The young comic, mistakenly credited as "Paul Lynn," shared the bill with Max Showalter—an actor from the Broadway revue *Make Mine Manhattan*—and Robert Weede, Jerome Hines, and Brian Sullivan, all of the Metropolitan Opera Company. The club set up Paul with free cocktails and dinner before the show, his first decent meal in months.

The onetime gig could have opened doors, but disaster in Mount Vernon interrupted Paul's job search. In early February 1949, the Army sent official word that Cordy had in fact died the day he joined the list of missing in action in 1944. His recently identified remains would be sent back to the family for burial and his name added to the public memorial in the town square as one of 123 residents of Knox County who died in the war.

On February 23, Paul's mother, age 50, died of heart failure. Sylvia had suffered from an illness for six months, but Paul believed she died of a broken heart for the child she loved most. "My mother literally stopped living," Paul said. "She just disintegrated, first needing a wheelchair, then being confined to bed." Paul traveled home for his mother's funeral and again in late May for Cordy's military burial. Cordy's remains arrived in town on May 24, with the burial scheduled the next day. On the morning of May 26, less than 24 hours after his son's service, Hoy Lynde died of a heart attack during an inspection at the A. C. Taylor Packing Company in Mount Vernon. The former butcher, now county sealer of weights and measures, was only 54.

The deaths of Paul's parents and brother worsened his already shaky temperament. "No one knew whether I'd be able to handle it," Paul said. "But I tell you, shock is a wonderful thing. It keeps you from feeling anything until you're better able to handle it. Shock saved me." Phyllis Diller, who befriended the comedian in the mid 1950s, says Paul never seemed to recover from the tragedy. "Three deaths that were just...so close," she says. "It leaves you just so alone...with kind of a death cloud. I don't think he really ever got over that."

With freeloading no longer an option after the deaths of his parents, Paul was forced to turn to stand-up that summer. "I think my father's death had more to do with my doing something with my career than anything else," he said. At the time, small clubs in the city opened their doors to fledgling comics like Kaye Ballard, Wally Cox, and Alan King, but Paul, starting at the bottom, had to settle for the amateur-night circuit and rely on his own writing talents. "I literally created myself—the kind of character I usually play—out of sheer desperation," he said, "since I couldn't hire anyone else to do it."

Bob Downey, the manager of Greenwich Village's One Fifth Avenue, tapped Paul to do his routine about Africa for his regular Monday night amateur contest. This popular college dating spot, which set aside Sunday nights for screenings of old Rudolph Valentino films, wasn't the Ritz, but it gave Paul a much-needed start.

Immediately after his victory at One Fifth Avenue, Paul moved to an apartment on East 82nd Street, and Downey had trouble tracking him down to schedule a legitimate club date. The first night Paul performed as a professional, he shared a stage with Peggy Marshall and the Holidays, a vocal group from *Arthur Godfrey's Talent Scouts*. Decked out in a tux, Paul stepped into the spotlight and sang a few bars of "Civilization (Bongo, Bongo, Bongo)," a tune popularized by the Andrews Sisters and Danny Kaye. The young comic explained the premise of his first sketch, "The Trip of the Month," ducked offstage briefly, then reappeared with crutch and bandaged head as Carl Canker, the surprisingly upbeat survivor of an African safari gone wrong:

We had only been tramping on the trail about four or five hours, and my wife began to complain of her feet. The only shoes she had with her were those high-heeled sling pumps. She just couldn't take it...so we had to leave her there out on the trail. A couple of days later on the way back, I found this piece of her dress, along with her purse and gloves, and to this day, I don't know what happened to her. But what I really remember about that day was, it was the only day it didn't rain, and I got to take some dandy snapshots...

He followed with a few poems, including "New York," in which he described his new hometown: "Rock, steel, sand, and glass / A mass of belching sewer gas / Big town, bad town, damn good town."

Paul drew inspiration for his material from the macabre cartoons of Charles Addams, the G-rated master of the emerging school of "sick humor." Described by *Time* as being so "close to real horror and brutality that audiences wince even as they laugh," this postwar brand of black comedy suited Paul's mood in the wake of his family's decimation. A few months earlier, Lenny Bruce tied for first place in a competition on Godfrey's popular radio contest with standard Bogie impressions and the like. He eventually found his own voice, and by the end of the 1950s emerged as the most popular/reviled "sicknik" in the business. Paul's bit about his high-heeled wife's death in the jungle, which he wrote in a burst of insomniac energy, certainly fit the sicknik mold, but he only did stand-up comedy by necessity and never warmed to the work.

After Paul finally claimed his prize the week of Thanksgiving, Downey extended his run through January. A critic for *Variety* wrote that Paul's self-written act displayed "satiric bite and some good yucks," but the jokes felt "somewhat weak in that it's difficult to satirize mediocrity. Delivery, however, is poised, self-assured, and sincere." *The New Yorker* summed up the work of the "fledgling monologuist" as "rather funny."

The comic found no other gigs and suffered through 1950 in an endless stream of wage slavery. He padded his résumé, if not his pockets, working as a waiter, a sales clerk at Altman's, and a desk clerk at a decrepit hotel. In a scam called "The Laundry Man," Paul and other hotel staffers pocketed money from guests seeking afternoon quickies. They didn't report it in the books and took turns cleaning the rooms.

For a short time, Paul drove an ambulance for a company that provided him with an apartment. The only catch: He had to stay on call, making him a virtual prisoner of his free pad. He typically shuttled elderly patients around, but when he entered the apartment of one of his passengers and found him dead, Paul promptly went back downstairs, put his cap on the seat of the ambulance, and walked away. Because he owned nothing of value, he didn't even bother to return to his apartment.

Forced to collect soda bottles for the return deposit and sell his own blood for five dollars a shot, Paul didn't think his life could get bleaker. Then Marilyn mailed him a wedding invitation. Paul sent her frantic telegrams and letters and made desperate phone calls trying to talk her out of marrying her college boyfriend. He countered with a wedding proposal of his own, but she remained unmoved.

Paul blamed Marilyn's mother for keeping them apart. "Her boyfriend was from a very wealthy Chicago family, and her mother was very interested in that," he said. "I was scared to death of her mother and knew that she didn't want me to marry her daughter." Organ recalls no such tension and claims her mother found Paul charming. She says she simply lost interest in Paul when he left town: "Well, you know, out of sight, out of mind."

At the wedding reception a few months later, Paul asked the maid of honor how the private ceremony had gone.

"Oh, it went very well," she said.

"Just how the divorce'll go," Paul shrugged.

Paul returned to New York and the comfort of his friends. "I was in a group, a Northwestern gang, and we were all in the same boat," Paul said. "So we could laugh together about the rough times. And the kids were great. When they got a job, they shared, inviting me to dinner knowing I didn't have anything to eat. That's how you survived week after week after week…. You have work on your side, which gives you a lot of strength and energy…. Why, 4 A.M. was too early to close the bars in those days. We always found an after-hours place."

Paul's luck finally changed in the winter of 1951. Spivy Le Voe, known in café society by her first name only, hired the comic as her supporting act at Spivy's Roof. The oversized lesbian had managed the ninth-floor penthouse cabaret on 57th Street at Lexington since 1940. "In a supper club all is atmosphere," she once explained. "Without atmosphere, you're a couple of chairs and tables in a bare room. You've got to make the trade feel like guests in a parlor of gaiety. The customer is more usually tight than right." Spivy turned to unknown talent, including Thelma Carpenter, Carol Channing, Ferrante and Teicher, Liberace, and Mabel Mercer, to provide that atmosphere.

If the mood struck her, Spivy performed a number or two from a repertoire of risqué songs that included "Alley Cat" and "I Married an Acrobat." She rarely missed an opportunity to sing for stars like Judy Garland, Judy Holliday, and Martha Raye, who sometimes stopped by after the club closed on weekends. The penthouse hideaway also attracted a small audience of gays and lesbians, which didn't bother Spivy. She just made sure the staff kept an eye on them to avoid any antics that might earn the club a lavender reputation.

Business in the penthouse slowed down considerably on weeknights, and Paul and his boss often sat alone at a table waiting for customers to arrive. When she felt pissy, Spivy used the comic as a verbal punching bag, telling him he had no talent. If the elevator approached, she would yell, "Get your props! You're on!" Paul would scramble to the stage, only to learn the passenger was either the elevator operator in search of conversation or the landlord in search of rent.

During the course of the eight-week run, Charlotte Rae and pianist Murray Grand joined the bill. Though Grand considered his boss a "horror," he and Paul became lifelong friends. "Paul in those days did nothing but eat," he says. "We'd go out, and we'd go to one diner, and he'd eat a whole meal. We'd go across the street to another diner. He'd start from the top and eat all over again. You can't believe what he weighed in those days."

Realizing he needed to shed his flab, Paul went on a starvation diet. He emerged from the ordeal a handsome man, much to the surprise of his friends. "When I met him he was quite heavy, and it was just jolly Paul," Forbes says. "Then, when I saw him a few years later, here was this gorgeous, thin, tan [man], with a beautiful white sport coat on, and these big green eyes, and he just looked marvelous." His weight fluctuated from thin to chunky for years to come, but he never got called lard-ass again.

Spivy found it hard to make ends meet, and the Roof collapsed in late spring. She didn't tell Paul; he learned he was out of a job the night he discovered the club's piano on the sidewalk. As severance, Spivy offered Paul some career advice: Rather than wait years for a job in New York, swallow your pride and look for more accessible out-of-town assignments. With only three gigs in three years to his credit, Paul followed his boss's counsel and joined a summer-stock theater company in Corning, New York, some 250 miles from the Big Apple.

The Corning Summer Theatre, operating out of the newly opened Corning Glass Center, launched as a stock venue that summer. Judy Garland may have made the sticks look glamorous the previous year in *Summer Stock*, her last musical for MGM, but Paul suffered no illusions about the work. He approached his first experience in summer barns—six productions in as many weeks—fully aware, as one reporter explained, that stock actors could be "a bit this week, a hit next week." He also knew he would have to put in long hours, with rehearsals in the morning and late evenings and no stops between productions.

Paul debuted as a professional actor in a small role in *Happy Birthday,* a play by Anita Loos that Helen Hayes had performed on Broadway five years earlier. The comedy starred Joan Blondell, long past her days as a B-film staple at Warner Brothers. Two years earlier, as the star of the same play, Blondell had made headlines for brawling with a producer after he asked her not to spout profanities at his cast. On opening night of this production, she behaved herself and graciously shared five curtain calls with the others.

Paul spent his remaining weeks in rural New York doing minor roles supporting Judy Holliday in *Dream Girl,* Eve Arden and her fiancé Brooks West in *Here Today,* and the starless casts of *Show Boat* and *A Streetcar Named Desire.* He also took the lead as Billy in *Anything Goes,* the Cole Porter musical, playing opposite Betty Reilly, the "Irish Senorita" who usually performed a multilingual nightclub act. Anti-Communist protesters who disagreed with Holliday's leftist politics picketed the theater during her residency, but otherwise Paul's first professional job went off without a hitch. Theater became his "first love," at least when he talked to the press.

Paul returned to his Upper East Side apartment in New York at the end of summer, but his first taste of career momentum pushed him right back out the door to tour in a revue called *What's New.* Wilson Stone, who had worked with Paul in Waa-Mu, organized the show at the request of his girlfriend's agent, who was in charge of bookings for the Statler Hotel chain. Stone and choreographer Gene Bayliss, another Waa-Mu alum, concocted an evening of entertainment and hired a young cast of six: two comics, Paul and Billie Hayes; two singers, Bill Conlon and Elise Rhodes; and two dancers, Richard Goltra and Doris Schmitt. Everyone but Paul had to audition. Stone and Bayliss asked Paul to contribute two sketches, his obligatory African travelogue and a public safety warning about the menace of squirrels from his Waa-Mu days, which he set in well-known parks in the towns on the tour.

The cast rehearsed in New York before trying out the show that November at Baybrook, a seedy nightclub in West Haven, Connecticut. "A very strange thing happened with Paul," Bayliss says. "I don't know whether it was because of his lack of experience working in nightclubs, [but] he would go out and if he did not get his first one or two laughs, he would deliver the rest of his monologue as fast as he could so he could get offstage." Stone and Bayliss discussed the problem with the comic, but Paul could never completely overcome his nerves.

What's New started its road tour that month at the Statler Hotel in Cleveland. "The action falls into the hands of six talented youngsters who all but beat their brains out," reported Winsor French of *The Cleveland Press*. "Each of them gets a chance to do a specialty, some better than others of course, and on that score Lynde was given the very short end of the stick with a tasteless monologue having to do with squirrels in Wade Park." Stone had told everyone to treat the show as a workshop; if an audience didn't respond well to something, the bit could be withdrawn for retooling. Paul's rodent warning didn't make it into the second show that night.

Variety didn't care for the squirrel routine either when it evaluated the Cleveland show, but it appreciated Paul's lampoon of wrestler Gorgeous George in a group sketch called "Giddy Over Video." Still, Billie Hayes—whom French believed had "all the authority of Imogene Coca"—stole the 40-minute show every night when she and Conlon performed "Back in the Old Routine," a song by Stone that Bing Crosby and Donald O'Connor would record as a duet in 1953.

Just before Christmas, the Defiance Automatic Screw Company in Defiance, Ohio, hired the cast to perform for an employee holiday party. Nice work if you can get it—then as now, company gigs paid good money. Vagabond lover—and notorious tightwad—Rudy Vallee headlined the evening, backed by George Gobel, still perfecting an offbeat act that would earn him TV fame, and the talented Professor Backwards, who took words offered by the audience and immediately said and spelled them in reverse. The Tommy Tucker Band, the Dancing Sherwoods, and Gus Hall, as the master of ceremonies, completed the bill.

Nothing about the oddball booking went as planned. Vallee celebrated the season of Christ with a batch of dirty jokes, and the lights shorted out just as Paul geared up to go onstage. Vallee and Gobel lit matches so he could find his props for the Africa sketch. Some audience members followed suit, and those acts of kindness, Paul remembered, set the perfect Christmas mood.

The cast performed at The Boulevard in Queens over the New Year and then in Detroit, but Paul's heart remained set on Broadway. (Despite advertising that suggested otherwise, the producers never meant to bring *What's New* to the Great White Way. Three of the show's cast members recorded a number called "Swell, Wasn't It?" for TV syndication. Paul appeared as a bartender.) After months of trying, he got a call through to Leonard Sillman in New York. The famed producer had a knack for finding fresh talent and showcasing it in a periodic revue called *New Faces*. He had hired Henry Fonda and Imogene Coca for the first version in 1934, and Van Johnson for the version produced two years later. Alice Pearce, Irwin Corey, and John Lund got their start in the 1943 edition. Nine years after that go-around, Sillman sought the cast for *New Faces of 1952*.

Paul told Sillman he planned to fly back to New York to audition. The producer told him to save his money. Undaunted, Paul performed a monologue over the phone, and Sillman—impressed but promising nothing—told the comic to see him when he got back into town. With Wilson Stone's blessing and the cast's encouragement, Paul dropped out of *What's New* and headed back to Manhattan.

CHAPTER 3

YOU'VE NEVER SEEN US BEFORE

"We were paid nothing."

Theater producer Leonard Sillman usually developed his shows around performers. "Some producers collect songs and sketches and then look around for their cast," he said. "I like it the other way round: first the actors, then the material." He got both when Paul appeared at his doorstep and recited Carl Canker's crazy African adventure. "It had me on the floor, doubled up with laughter," Sillman said later. "I signed him fast."

Sillman found inspiration for *New Faces of 1952* when he'd seen a young Eartha Kitt perform in Paris and thought she'd be great in a revue. He found his next cast member and writer back home when his friend Imogene Coca took him to see a nightclub comic named Ronny Graham. Robert Clary, the revue's designated male singer, caught the producer's attention at La Vie en Rose in New York. The peppy Frenchman, who would go on to play plucky LeBeau on the 1960s sitcom *Hogan's Heroes,* had just returned to his performance slot at the nightclub after failing to catch a break in Hollywood, where his only offers of work had been bit parts as Arabs in B movies.

Paul's pal Charlotte Rae landed a spot in the show as the girl comic. Sillman decided she needed more experience, and he helped her land nightclub gigs around the city. She begged Sheldon Harnick, another Waa-Mu performer, to come to New York to write material for her act. Harnick stayed and later won Tony Awards for providing the lyrics to *Fiorello!* and *Fiddler on the Roof*. Sillman also wanted his sister June Carroll in the cast, but she preferred songwriting over performing and repeatedly declined. Friends eventually talked her into it.

After hauling Rae and Graham around town for months of informal performances for rich people and theater folk, Sillman found an investor in automotive heir Walter P. Chrysler Jr. Filling the director's chair took longer. Big names like Abe Burrows, José Ferrer, Moss Hart, Robert Lewis, and Otto Preminger turned Sillman down. John Murray Anderson, a Broadway producer since 1918, did not. "I only aided and abetted in its production," he said. "But I saw that there were no spangles, no chiffon, and I avoided the color pink and all slushy sentiment." (Never able to remember names, the director made it a habit to nickname company members; he called Paul "Suntan.")

Adding to Sillman's headaches, Burrows not only passed on the offer to direct, he hired Rae for his upcoming Broadway musical, *Three Wishes for Jamie*. "We weren't making any money with Leonard. He never paid anybody a penny," said Murray Grand, also lured away. Sillman felt "ready to kill" when Rae accepted, but he forged on, unsuccessfully offering her slot to Nancy Andrews, Kaye Ballard, and other funny ladies. At Grand's suggestion, Sillman found a "pearl of great price" in comedian Alice Ghostley, who did a nightclub act with G. Wood at the Bon Soir.

Ghostley bore such an uncanny resemblance to Paul—mostly in the way she talked—that Sillman reportedly mistook the two of them for siblings. Ghostley has been dismissed as a female Paul Lynde for decades, but a few people who knew both performers insist Paul committed the identity theft. "He was doing Alice Ghostley all the time," Paul's friend Allison McKay says. "In fact, he told her, 'I've become famous doing you!' I really think that she was there first, but he loved the way she did things." Charles Nelson Reilly's recent admission of guilt regarding his own swipe from the Lynde/Ghostley repertoire suggests McKay may be right. When asked how he came up with his trademark "huh-hull" noise, Reilly said, "I stole it from Paul Lynde, who stole it from Alice Ghostley."

"A successful revue must be like a bouillabaisse," Sillman once said. "It's a matter of ingredients. You must have a little salt, a little pepper, a little sugar—and you must have sufficient variety to appeal to everybody in the audience." The *New Faces* bouillabaisse had the right ingredients when it opened on May 2, 1952, at the Forrest Theatre in Philadelphia, but it came out undercooked. Though *Variety* opined that the production fell "decidedly on the credit side of the ledger," Clary says audience members responded to the show by "sitting on their hands."

The first rule of theatrical revues states that every number can't be a hit. Each of the cast members believed his or her material would be the night's showstopper: Paul with his safari survivor sketch, Graham with the Truman Capote send-up "Oedipus Goes South," Clary with the Graham-penned tune "I'm in Love with Miss Logan," and Ghostley with "Boston Beguine," a number Harnick originally wrote for Rae. The tepid applause for Kitt's "Monotonous," which Carroll cowrote with Arthur Siegel, particularly confounded Sillman. "If one, just one, skit slips for one night Leonard reacts as though his grandmother had died," leaked one of the cast members. "No one should take show business that much

CENTER

to heart." Anderson rescued the number—and Sillman's mood—by ordering Kitt to sing it with an intentionally bored delivery.

The cast fine-tuned the show over the next two weeks, during which time critic Arthur B. Waters reported, "attendance was inexplicably light." When the show finally opened on Broadway at the Royale Theatre on May 16, everything clicked. "You've never seen us before," the cast sang. "We've never seen you before, but before this evening ends, *New Faces* and you will be good friends!"

The company gathered at the Sherry Room of the Metropolitan Opera for an opening-night bash on Chrysler's dime and basked in the afterglow of good reviews. Brooks Atkinson of *The New York Times* praised the show for "being uninfected with the sour tone of most of the defamation of character that passes for humor on the radio and stage in this mechanical era." The superlatives didn't stop there: "intelligent, witty, and delightfully varied" (*Newsweek*); "bright, brisk, and generally original" (*Variety*); "crisp [and] cheerfully intimate" (*Time*). Only Walter Winchell seemed to disagree. "It seemed to us that the parched critics were so happy to meet a show *that good* they lost their heads and overwrote the notices."

"The next day the lines were just unbelievable," Clary says. Tickets in those first weeks became a hot item scored only by the likes of the Duke and Duchess of Windsor, Marlene Dietrich, Rex Harrison, and Lili Palmer. Greta Garbo attended a performance and led the audience in a standing ovation. Over the course of the run, such luminaries as Eleanor Roosevelt, Cole Porter, and Mary Pickford would also see the show.

Practically everyone in the cast earned special praise from one critic or another. Kerr gave the comic notice for providing "the funniest bit of the evening" with the Africa sketch. Paul also impressed reviewers for his work in "Of Fathers and

Sons," a send-up of Arthur Miller's *Death of a Salesman*. Mel Brooks, still unknown, originally wrote the sketch for a Broadway-bound revue called *Curtain Going Up* that had come and gone in Philadelphia that February.

Soon after the show opened, Paul shared some faux humility with the editor of his hometown newspaper: "I am not the principal in the show and far from it, but the critics were certainly all wonderful to me. I am especially pleased that my number about Africa was singled out as the best in the show, since I wrote it myself. I needed reviews like this to bolster my morale and confidence, both as a performer and a writer."

Paul had evidently gained self-assurance in his sexuality as well. After the show one evening, a fellow comedian stopped by his dressing room to introduce himself and praise his performance. Mistaking the man for a trick he had hired, Paul waved away the praise and demanded they get down to business.

On meeting Jimmy Russell, the leader of the *New Faces* dance troupe, Paul didn't have to hire his love any longer. Tall and handsome, the Pittsburgh-born hoofer nicknamed "the Monster" by Anderson, had given up acting for dance and soft-shoed on Broadway in *Bloomer Girl, Sweethearts,* and *Sally,* and on the *Garroway at Large* television show in Chicago. Paul's dark side made him a high-maintenance boyfriend, and his relationship with Russell hit several rough patches. Gossip columnist Dorothy Kilgallen may not have been far off the mark when she told readers that Russell "had his eye on" Virginia De Luce, one of his *New Faces* costars. His charming ways could drive Paul crazy. "Jimmy was as cheerful and even-tempered as Paul was manic-depressive," says *New Faces* cast member Faith Burwell. "And they fought a lot, mainly over Paul's jealousy of what he imagined to be Jimmy's wandering eye. Jimmy was flirtatious with everyone, but I believe he was faithful to Paul."

Emboldened by being part of a box office and critical smash, the cast of *New Faces* saw their stars rise with favorable press mentions and invitations to appear on television, make recordings, or perform in nightclubs. Sillman immediately began planning the movie version of *New Faces* and bragged to reporters that 15 of the 17 cast members had already received offers from Hollywood. An Al Hirschfeld caricature of seven of them, including a toothy, bandaged Paul, appeared in *The New York Times.*

The RCA Corporation quickly recorded a cast album with some of the show's songs but none of its sketches. Paul only contributed a few lines in a humorous hoedown called "Lizzie Borden"—also salvaged from *Curtain Going Up*—that reminded listeners how "you can't chop your poppa up in Massachusetts." Princess Margaret begged Sillman for a copy of the recording, while Noël Coward praised the one he owned. When Sillman warned Ghostley not to perform "Boston Beguine" in her nightclub act, she considered using her copy to mime the number instead.

In November, Paul recited his signature monologue on Ed Sullivan's *Toast of the Town,* his first big television appearance after small roles on anthology programs like *Campbell Playhouse* and *The Philco Television Playhouse.* Sullivan's talent coordinators scheduled Paul to share the stage with an Irish tenor, a ventriloquist, bagpipers, and Les Paul and Mary Ford. Even before his run-through fell flat, Paul feared a CBS staffer would knock on his dressing room door and boot him off the show. *Variety* would have supported the decision: "Paul Lynd [sic], a comic now featured in the Broadway legit click, *New Faces,* impressed not at all with some stand-up patter on a trip through Africa. Sullivan credited the comic with scripting his own material—maybe he should hire some writers."

New Faces of 1952 did so well—closing on March 28, 1953, after 365 performances—that Paul had to wait to do more television. Sillman had decided to take the show on a national tour. Friends tried to dissuade him, warning that the uncultured masses outside New York only went to the theater to see "nude girls in feathers and burlesque comics." (The same friends had told Sillman not to do a revue in the first place, insisting audiences wanted more literate entertainment.) Sillman sent the show out anyway.

Enthusiastic audiences in six cities kept the tour going into 1954, but Sillman continued to promote the show as *New Faces of 1952*. He wanted ticket buyers to know that they were paying to see the original stars and not replacements, at least among the featured performers—including Carroll, Clary, Ghostley, Graham, Kitt, and Lynde—who all agreed to take part in the tour.

After downtime to mark Holy Week, the cast reconvened in Boston for a three-week stay. On opening night, Eartha Kitt earned the only curtain call. When her singing career took off with popular chart hits like "C'est Si Bon" and "Santa Baby," Sillman made sure advertisements for the show promoted the "Queen of Song, Rage of the Nation." Some people in and outside of the cast felt the attention went to Kitt's head. "Backstage at *New Faces*," comic Jim Kirkwood said, "I found a bored, languid girl in leopard-skin slacks, black satin waistcoat, foot-long cigarette holder and an affected 'Oh, hello', said with a vague 'Now, I wonder who you are' manner. People haven't got time for that kind of nonsense."

Still, most of the ensemble didn't seem to mind the sudden stardom of the diva in their midst. "People came to see her because she was already a big star and we weren't," Clary says. "I wouldn't say she would steal [the show]. I would say she was moody, and I adored her, but you get used to it if she doesn't feel like saying hello to you one day. You say, 'OK, go on, Eartha.' But she could be absolutely wonderful." Paul shared a different view of Eartha when he told a friend, "She should go back to pickin' cotton."

By and large, the cast of *New Faces* got along on tour, thanks in part to Sillman's fatherly philosophy of holding a company together: "A traveling company is very much like a family on the move. It has its fights and its squabbles but it has to keep moving en masse." Though they would never be great friends, Paul and Clary amicably shared a dressing room. Clary laughed every time Paul turned the removal of his greasepaint into mock torture, yelling a strangled "Aahhhh!" with each swipe of his cotton swab.

A critic in Boston complained that some of the more topical sketches might go over the heads of average folk. "They are clever, sometimes extremely witty," she said, "but for the fullest appreciation, the spectator must be 'in the know.'" Confusing the audience worried the cast when the show opened in Chicago for an open-ended run. "It was a very New York kind of show," Paul said. "And we expected to close in one fast week. Instead, Chicago treated us like we were the royal family."

The extracurricular work some of the performers accepted caused casting headaches. Clary continued with the show, but commuted twice weekly to New York for a month of appearances on Garry Moore's daytime TV series. Ghostley left the company at the end of May to return to the cast of the daytime CBS game show *Freedom Rings*. Jenny Lou Law of the Broadway revue *Lend an Ear* replaced her. Sillman scoured Chicago for other replacements and added Norman Edwards, Joan Ehemann, and Faith Burwell.

Just before a Tuesday performance in mid-August, Ronny Graham caused a crisis when he walked off the job. Pleading "recurring symptoms of exhaustion," he took off for Florida to recuperate. Some reporters in town sympathized with him, but an angry Sillman filed charges of insubordination against him. His defection not only threatened plans to turn the show into a movie but also Sillman's hope to take the original cast back to Broadway. In Graham's absence, five cast members stepped up to perform his material. Paul introduced the cast at the beginning of both acts until Sillman and Graham ironed out their differences. Graham returned to work on October 15.

New Faces of 1952 stayed put in Chicago for much of 1953. Sillman finally announced that the show would close on November 8. "Actually," he said, "we could have stayed on and on. But we signed a contract long ago to do the movie of *New Faces* and that's why we're leaving. Chicago liked us and we liked Chicago." The show's 28-week run set a local record for a stage revue, but the movie deal prevented it from surpassing the 35-week run set that season by Eddie Bracken in *The Seven-Year Itch.*

Sillman's company spent most of November making the film in Los Angeles, then traveled north to San Francisco to continue the tour. On opening night, the cast earned eight curtain calls, but a troublemaker brought them back to reality a few nights later. A woman in the audience who had overrefreshed herself ruined the punch line of a sketch by yelling, "I don't get it!" (Paul recalled her having better timing than anyone onstage.) The audience snickered, which encouraged her to shriek the line again and again. When the police arrived at intermission to take her away, the weary audience stood up and applauded. As the officers escorted the troublemaker to their patrol car, Paul leaned his head out a backstage window and yelled, "*Now* you're gonna get it!"

At the end of January, Eartha Kitt needed time off to honor a nightclub commitment in Buffalo. Paul and Ghostley recommended a substitute. A calypso singer and future poet named Maya Angelou had impressed them on a night out to see her show at the Purple Onion. Ghostley returned a few nights later with Sillman, who liked what he saw and offered Angelou the job. Angelou's management refused to let her out of their contract, and Ann Henry, whom Sillman had discovered in Chicago, ended up filling Kitt's spot. (After another night on the town in search of talent, Sillman passed on the chance to hire a young singer named Johnny Mathis; he hated Mathis's voice.)

The film version appeared in theaters that February. Sillman promoted four of the cast members—Clary, Ghostley, Graham, and Kitt—to star status. Writing about the move, columnist Billy Rose asked, "Is Eartha Kitt being starred because the boss men of 20th Century-Fox have suddenly discovered the Bill of Rights—have suddenly concluded that the Southern moviegoer won't resent a Negro performer playing a major part in an otherwise all-white film? In a pig's eye! The sorry fact is that once the studio decided to make a movie of *New Faces,* it had no choice but to build it around Eartha—the only personality in the cast who had definitely proved she was star material."

Although Sillman removed some of the original sketches to showcase Kitt's chart hits and added a "behind-the-scenes" storyline involving a romance between Robert Clary and Virginia De Luce, Paul's best bits survived the reapportionment. Horner shot the flick with new CinemaScope technology, the wrong choice for the show's simple staging, and one that confounded critics when the film hit theaters. (At least someone wisely nixed plans to employ 3-D technology.) Bosley Crowther of *The New York Times* criticized both the CinemaScope and the comedy by suggesting "the almost incredible surrender of the wide panel to a fellow named Paul Lynde for the painfully labored delivery of a five-minute monologue…exposes the actual disadvantage of such plainly superfluous size." Even the diminutive Clary came across on the wide screen like "King Kong with a French accent," as another critic put it.

Paul later confessed that he hated the film, even though he believed he emerged from it unscathed. The *Newsweek* reviewer respectfully dubbed him a "past master of his art," and Toronto film critics gave him an award for "the best solo performance in a movie shown in Canada in '54." He even received a promising telegram from Louis Shurr, the manager of a fellow comedian: "Please advise when you will be available as Bob Hope would like to use you on his TV show. Bob and I saw your performance last night in the motion picture version of *New Faces,* and we feel we can do some important comedy scenes with you."

After a year on Broadway, a year on the road, and a wide-screen keepsake for their troubles, the most recent cast members of *New Faces* parted ways in Detroit after their final performance on April 3, 1954. The cast promised to reunite in ten years to see where their careers had taken them. For Paul, that journey wouldn't take him nearly as far as he desired.

CHAPTER 4

BENIGN APOSTLE OF DOOM

"It would be nice to have people know who I am."

Returning to New York that spring, Paul now found his place in the East Sixties too small for a conquering young star on the move. He gave Robert Clary dibs on his lease and rented a larger apartment in the area to showcase his new acquisitions: the art he began collecting, two beloved basset hounds named Orville and Wilbur, and boyfriend Jimmy Russell, who moved in.

The "fancier of paintings (contemporary)," as his publicity bio identified him, placed top priority on the dogs, taking them on frequent walks along Fifth Avenue and buying them trinkets like beaded collars. He liked to tell friends, "Orville and Wilbur love their pearls." Russell, the lovesick runner-up, stuck it out as long as he could.

"Paul was impossible," says Murray Grand. "You'd go out with him to a bar. He'd get into a fight and the police were called. It was just a mess. Every time he went out it was another hassle." TV host Robert Osborne, who befriended Paul a few years later in Hollywood, agrees. "Everybody said that Jimmy Russell was crazy about Paul. Finally, he just gave up because Paul was so complicated and all that." As Paul himself later said, "I worked 24 hours a day to make sure the loves of my life wouldn't work."

Paul hoped to exploit his *New Faces* fame on TV. That spring, he joined the cast of *Settlement House,* a pilot put together by CBS as a showcase for comedian Jack Carter, who had been a popular star for NBC at the beginning of the decade. Reginald Rose devised the storyline for the show, which was directed by former radio star Ezra Stone. The cast produced a pilot film to entice advertisers, though the show would be broadcast live from New York if it was picked up. CBS had also corralled Phil Silvers, Celeste Holm, and Paul's friend Charlotte Rae (in a sitcom pilot aptly titled *A Girl From Milwaukee*) as "sponsor bait." Only *Honestly, Celeste!* earned a prime-time spot that fall. *Settlement House* became the first of many failed pilots Paul later called "the troubles I've left unseen."

Hoping to discover another George Gobel, who earned a prime-time berth of his own that year after countless appearances on NBC, scouts from the network scoured New York nightclubs for unknown talent. Kaye Ballard affixed her name to one of NBC's five-year contracts, and when his work with Jack Carter led nowhere, Paul did too. To showcase its new pool of talent, NBC persuaded the Colgate company to sponsor a summer version of its popular *Comedy Hour,* a 60-minute programming block that usually featured Dean Martin and Jerry Lewis or Martha Raye.

Paul passed on the offer to work with Bob Hope on one of the slope-nosed comedian's monthly specials. He also missed an opportunity to guest on Wally Cox's hit comedy *Mr. Peepers.* Instead, he traveled west to Los Angeles for the Colgate show, which alternated its live broadcasts on Sunday nights between both coasts.

Variety caught the first of Paul's four appearances, all of which called for more comic shtick in a *New Faces* vein, and decided he "belongs to the lighter school of comedy, getting laughs reading poetry and otherwise disporting in a breezy manner. He has the markings of a comic going places." In a violent monologue called "You Dance or Else," which he performed on the June 27 show, Paul told the tale of a man who signs up for dance lessons after his fiancée of nine years tells him he's no Fred Astaire:

The registrar asked me three questions:
1) If I were married.
2) If I planned on getting married.
3) Would I marry her?

Another instructor attempted to seduce Paul. "I took her hand out of my pocket and said I'd better go. She switched on a samba, locked the door and took off her jacket. That made me mad, and I hit her with something. I don't remember, but I think it was the phonograph. Anyway, she died right away." Appraising the show a second time after watching this particular episode, *Variety* opined, "Lynde is a good monologuist but he needs better material."

That fall, Paul continued honing his comic skills as a frequent guest on *The Martha Raye Show,* which appeared every fourth Tuesday in a time slot shared with Milton Berle and Bob Hope. Chaos reigned both on the screen and off as Raye fought with her director, who quit just before the first show of the season. NBC had other variety shows on its schedule, including *The Red Buttons Show,* which the network picked up that season after two years on CBS. "I got songs, I got dances, I got beautiful girls," Buttons bragged. "I got Kupke Kids, dizzy bellhops, punch-drunk pugs." What he didn't have was ratings, so his bosses forced him to drop the variety for situation comedy.

The revamped project, still named after its star, debuted at the end of January under the direction of Catskills comic Julie Oshins. Buttons now played a fictional version of himself, with a wife, played by Phyllis Kirk; a best friend, played by comedian Bobby Sherwood, who served as the director of the fictional show within a show; and a meddlesome network vice president, played by Paul. Bill Davenport and Johnny Greene, just the latest in a string of writers hired and fired by Buttons during his TV career, concocted the wacky situations meant to showcase the star and his new supporting cast.

Buttons said he hoped the new format might stave off cancellation. "I think I am on my way now," he said, "or will be shortly with the kind of show I can live with from season to season." Though *Variety* claimed that "nothing [was] wrong with [the show] that a half-dozen good guffaws won't automatically cure," the new approach only lasted 13 weeks before Pontiac pulled out as advertiser and a real NBC executive pulled the plug.

Advertising insiders chalked up the cancellation to the Pontiac curse: none of the shows the carmaker agreed to sponsor pulled in good ratings. Buttons blamed a format that fit him "like a left-handed pool table." He added, "I was playing a sophisticate, a man of means. That's not me. I should play a frustrated, downtrodden guy. But I got into this, and I had to be graceful enough to see it through."

Critics noticed Paul's work on Buttons's show. The editors of *TV Star Parade* touted him as an up-and-comer when they asked their readers to decide "Who Will Be 1955's Top TV Finds?" They also hinted at a brighter future for him: "[A]s this is going to press, there is a rumor bird flying around Radio City saying that *The Paul Lynde Show* is just about set as a half-hour situation comedy television show this summer."

Winning neither the readers' poll nor landing a prime-time gig of his own, Paul turned again to theater. "I would rather perform on the stage than any other medium," he once told a reporter from Mount Vernon. "Some day I hope to direct or produce Broadway shows." At the end of 1954, producers Joe Moon and Paul Vroom had announced plans to bring a revue called *Top Drawer* to Broadway the following spring. Murray Grand provided the songs, Ira Wallach the sketches. Paul agreed to perform and direct. He and Beatrice Arthur, the future star of *Maude*, showcased the material for Park Avenue backers, but the production never got off the ground. "Joe Moon worked for Rodgers and Hammerstein," Grand says. "He didn't have a pot to piss in."

Leonard Sillman possessed more cache, and even before *New Faces of 1952* closed on Broadway, he had laid plans for a follow-up. Various events, mostly financial, scuttled *New Faces of 1953…1954…and 1955.* Instead, that spring, the producer concocted *Come As You Are,* a supper club revue he staged at the Versailles in New York. He made room in this "miniature *New Faces*" for his sister and Paul, both of whom provided material. Connie Sawyer and Dick Smart shared top billing with them. Former cast members of *New Faces of 1952*—Johnny Laverty, Betty Logue, Bill Mullikin, and Jimmy Russell—joined Franca Baldwin and Inga Swenson as supporting players.

Variety decided that the show, which was staged by dancer David Tihmar, had "novelty, talent, and originality," but felt it was "a little too generous in length." *Billboard's* Bob Francis conceded that there was a "dull spot here and there. But who expects more of a revue?" *The New Yorker* applauded the "pleasing fact that you can put an entertaining show together without a single joke about Marilyn Monroe" and praised Paul as a "benign apostle of doom."

The demands of two floor shows a night—for the dinner and after-theater crowds—soon wore Paul down. "I don't know how you do it! I don't know why you do it!" he told Robert Clary, a nightclub natural performing then at the

Blue Angel. One night, as Paul lectured on his safari, a couple rose from their table and started dancing without the aid of music. "They didn't even bother to turn around to see if I had clothes on," he carped.

Fed up playing to the indifferent and inebriated, Paul retired his crutch and other props at the end of June. "All you can talk about is the bathroom, sex, or golf," he lamented. "Those are the only subjects an audience can understand." George DeWitt took his place in the show, which made way for Edith Piaf that September. Paul never stepped on a nightclub stage again.

Canadian columnist Clyde Gilmour offered this wish for 1956: "A chance, at last, for TV humorist Paul Lynde to prove in Hollywood what a lot of us have long suspected: that he is one of the funniest and most original 'character comedians' in his profession." That chance didn't come, but Paul kept busy, with occasional appearances on Martha Raye's show and an assignment in a Hallmark Hall of Fame production of *The Good Fairy* (Paul did not play the title role).

Once again, Leonard Sillman helped bolster Paul's career, this time by offering him an opportunity to work behind the scenes on his latest production. With backing finally secured for another shot at Broadway, the producer planned to showcase *New Faces of 1956*. He hired Paul to direct the sketches and Tihmar to oversee the musical numbers. Tihmar accepted the job after he failed to reach Broadway as director of *Pleasure Dome,* a revue that would have starred Kaye Ballard, Virginia De Luce, and Jimmy Komack. Sillman took Tihmar and some of the material meant for that production.

Sillman's new revue showcased 19 performers, some with talents that suspiciously mirrored the class of 1952. "They were trying to match the previous hit," says Jane Connell, one of two girl comics asked to join the cast. "So they got me to be Alice Ghostley." Connell had won raves for a version of

"Boston Beguine" that she performed onstage at the Purple Onion in San Francisco, and she caught the attention of Sillman when the previous *New Faces* played there. In the current edition, she offered "April in Fairbanks," a song by Murray Grand that Ghostley had planned to perform in the ill-fated *Top Drawer*. Paul persuaded Sillman to hire Billie Hayes, his *What's New* costar, to serve as the other girl comic. Over the past half-decade, she had done little of note beyond a couple of tours in Shubert productions of *Blossom Time* and *Merry Widow*.

Bill McCutcheon, one of the two lead male comics in the cast, worked in nightclubs, but his first taste of fame came after an appearance on Edward R. Murrow's *Person to Person*. The newscaster contrasted the young comedian's fledgling career and one-room apartment in Greenwich Village with those of Arthur Godfrey, who spoke to Murrow from his Virginia estate.

Sillman discovered his other funnyman, T.C. Jones, at the same San Francisco club where he had sat unimpressed by Johnny Mathis years before. Jones did a send-up of Tallulah Bankhead, who was supposed to return to Broadway that season in her own revue, the *Ziegfeld Follies*. People warned the producer that adding a drag act to the cast was suicidal. "I would be hooted out of the theater once and for all," he recalled. "I had persisted because I never think of T.C. as a female impersonator, as a man imitating woman. T.C. on a stage is simply an extraordinarily talented woman." Though viewers of Ed Sullivan's television variety show had learned the truth about T.C. a week before *New Faces* opened on Broadway, a few thickheaded theatergoers sometimes gasped whenever Jones doffed his wig to reveal his true sex at the end of the show. Little wonder that he drew the lion's share of attention (mostly positive) from critics—and even from Paul, who knew a good drag act when he saw it. Other *New*

Faces included Johnny Haymer, Tiger Haynes, Ann Henry, John Reardon, Inga Swenson, and Maggie Smith, a young comedienne and future screen and stage legend who Sillman brought over from England after seeing her perform in a revue at Oxford.

As a first-time director, Paul could be perfectly agreeable during rehearsals, "except when he drank," Connell says. "And he drank a lot." He sometimes came to work loaded, and if he arrived sober, he'd often end up drunk if the opportunity presented itself. Drunk one night in Boston, where the show was tried out, he paid a cab driver $100 for a short trip and entered the theater clueless that he'd paid so much until he checked his wallet.

Paul considered his assignment a "dubious honor, since the other comedians in the show regarded me more as a competitor than a director." The fact that Paul wrote four sketches for the show in his idiosyncratic comic style only made things worse. "Most of my material I have written with myself in mind," he said, "and this makes it difficult to direct other people in it, especially when they assume that, if I offer suggestions or make any criticisms, I don't like them because they are not acting as I would, were I in their place. Sound confusing? Well, truthfully, it is."

Paul frustrated his actors, giving them little guidance beyond criticism that teetered on contempt. "He would let us do a sketch," Connell says, "and then he'd just say, 'Oh that was terrible. Do it again.'…We would do it again—in a different way—until he laughed." Paul's skit about a woman who poisons pigeons bombed when Connell performed it during tryouts in Boston. "I learned it and did the monologue, and I've never had such chills [from an audience]," she says. "I thought it was kind of funny. He could have probably done it. He probably could have gotten away with it. He had the kind of sardonic humor—the irate human

being. But 'Little Miss Milquetoast' up there couldn't cut it, and it was cut."

Boston critics complained about the length and pace of the show, and Sillman trimmed it accordingly. A piece called "Darts" that Paul cowrote with Phil Green survived the try-out. In this "very British triangle comedy," in the words of critic John Chapman, Maggie Smith skewered the upper class of the country of her birth by playing Harriet, a bored woman whose lover (Reardon) hides in the house while she and her husband (McCutcheon) play a game of darts. After the husband is called away to detonate an H-bomb, Smith and Reardon continue the game and ponder their relationship:

> HARRIET: What are we to do?
> MAN: Come with me to Sussex.
> HARRIET: That wouldn't be cricket.
> MAN: To heck with cricket!

In what some critics considered the funniest line of the night, Harriet responds to her lover's tepid profanity with "Any man who would say that would strike the Queen!"

New Faces of 1956 opened on Broadway the day after Paul's 30th birthday. Peter Larkin's sets impressed the critics more than the cast or sketches. "My guess is that you won't see many of them again," predicted Frances Herridge of the *New York Post*. *Variety* pinpointed the problem: "The failure of humor is, by and large, the failure of this *New Faces*. True, there are moments of effective slapstick, mostly burlesques of stage plays, television programs, or moving pictures. The spectator is diverted and titillated, but not captivated."

The show received a mid-run plug by Walter Winchell, while another columnist suggested in August that the producer was "taking orders for New Year's Eve, it's that big of a hit." Sillman made news that October when he decided to cut "Madame Interpreter," a United Nations sketch by the brothers Neil and Danny Simon that he considered in "poor taste" because of the Suez Crisis.

Never matching the success of its immediate predecessor, *New Faces of 1956* closed nine days before the New Year. Despite announcements to the contrary, no tour or movie followed its respectable if unprofitable run of 222 performances. *Variety* placed the show on its list of flops for the season. Even Sillman found fault with it, admitting that it lacked a "complete point of view, and it had too many sentimental songs." With no end in sight to the cooking metaphors, he added, "I should have brewed it for at least another six months or so before serving it." Fully aware that he wasn't cut out for the job, Paul gave up the director's chair permanently after this version of *New Faces*. "[Directing] wasn't his strongest point," Connell says.

Maggie Smith did not enjoy her first taste of Broadway stardom. "I hated it all," she said later, "not the actual experience of being in New York and Boston, just the show." Paul and she remained friends—and to the press they appeared to be something more. A reporter who caught them dining together that year hinted that the two were dating. Smith told another reporter that she had "left behind a boy in London, and I am much too faithful to have noticed American young men. Also, I have been much too busy." Everyone in the cast—including Smith—knew Paul was gay. Still, Paul seemed smitten with the Englishwoman in a way that some of his friends perceived as romantic. "[My husband and I] went out several times with Maggie and Paul," Jan Forbes says. "He was very enamored by her, but [after Smith] that was kind of the end of the ladies." (Murray Grand finds the pairing laughable.)

Paul would eventually invoke the names of Maggie and his high school flame, Marilyn, as a way of deflecting questions about his single status. To the plaintive sound of an imagined violin, he offered dueling sob stories: one about the girl who broke his teenage heart, the other about chances not taken. Smith was "much younger than I and very homesick," he once explained. "I took it for granted it was a father-thing with her, because she just latched on to me, and we were inseparable. Many years later...she'd level with me and say, 'You'll never know how much I cared about you.' But at the time I just never took it that seriously, maybe because I was frightened—scared I'd be hurt again."

Paul may have laid stories of his romantic travails on a bit thick, but America in the age of Eisenhower wasn't ready to hear about his attraction to men. With no interest in following Rock Hudson's lead and marrying for show, Paul had to dish out rote excuses about lost loves if he expected his star to ascend higher.

Still under contract to NBC, Paul returned to prime time that fall in a supporting role on a new comedy called *Stanley*. Max Liebman, late of Sid Caesar's *Your Show of Shows* and two seasons of big-budget, all-star "spectaculars," oversaw production duties, assembling a writing team that included Woody Allen and pioneering female comedy writer Lucille Kallen. Buddy Hackett, an up-and-coming comic who had recently earned notice in the Broadway production of *Lunatics and Lovers,* provided the sitcom shtick as the operator of a New York hotel's newspaper stand who interacts with such characters as opera-loving gangsters, folk-singing children, old army buddies, and his mother.

Paul's college disdain of artsy-fartsiness placed him in good standing with Hackett. "Nobody will be getting his dramatic training on this show," Hackett said. "The first actor that does an interpretation of Stanislavsky or the Actors Studio or the New School is finished." Not that Paul had to extend his talents anyway. He served as an omnipo-

tent narrator who guided Stanley's comic capers by ordering him around in a voice that only Stanley could hear. Paul
never actually appeared on screen, nor was his name in the
credits.

Paul considered this easy TV money an agreeable means
to an end. "I don't know how it is with other actors," he
said, "but I find that TV gets me into the habit of living better than I can in any other entertainment medium and makes
me afraid to leave it lest I should have to give up my creature
comforts."

Liebman insisted the new show be broadcast live from
New York in its Monday time slot, the only sitcom that season to air sans net. That decision allowed the producer to
immediately tweak the show, which was saddled with poor
reviews and ratings. "Hackneyed Hackett," critic Milton K.
Bass complained, "is no better than brackish Berle or mar-
tyred Raye." On seeing the second episode, one wag sniped,
"By comparison, his first show was an Academy
Award–winner."

Star and producer argued about their options. The comic
favored a variety revamp under the title *The Buddy Hackett
Show*; the producer did not. In the end, Liebman decided to
fix the floundering format by importing a new head writer,
Bill Manoff, from the West Coast.

Liebman ordered his writers to add more gags to the mix
and a love interest for Stanley. Carol Burnett, having just
played girlfriend to another dummy—on ventriloquist Paul
Winchell's TV show—played Stanley's sweetheart, Celia. Her
addition to the cast did little to salvage the show's anemic
ratings, though the gig opened doors the following year for
her to perform her breakout novelty song, "I Made a Fool of
Myself Over John Foster Dulles."

The emergency retooling, which included new plots that
took Stanley and Celia out of the hotel, cost Paul what little

airtime he received. Jane Connell, who joined the cast as Celia's best friend, doesn't remember Paul working on the show at all. Despite the changes, NBC canceled the series at the end of December, a move *TV Guide* described as "television's gain." The final episode aired in March. "I thought it was a damn good show," Hackett said. "Out of 17, 14 were excellent, two were very bad, and one was really good. But the critics, they want to pick everything apart, find the motivation, find the significance. But there's no time for that nonsense. All you can do is make 'em laugh, sell the smokes, get some fun out of it, and get off."

NBC never found a prominent place between its test patterns for Paul before the boom time for TV comics came crashing down. Other comedians under contract to the networks also languished in prime time as viewers turned to cathode-ray cowboys. "The inexorable law of overexposure has caught up with the majority of clowns," wrote television critic Jack Gould, to explain the failure in prime time of Johnny Carson, Wally Cox, Jack Paar, and Jonathan Winters, among others. The best Paul could manage was occasional appearances on the sinking ships of comics Ray Bolger, Imogene Coca, and Martha Raye.

Bob Hope tried to ease the worries of those attempting to follow his lead. "There's a lot of money waiting for young comedians," he suggested, "and I don't think people have to worry about there being a lack of places where they can gain experience. Of course, it's not like the old days, but there are still club dates and local stations." Paul's aversion to nightclubs left him only one option: the stage.

The ever-industrious Sillman extended yet another invitation for Paul to work for him, this time in a summer-stock tour with the best material from his past two *New Faces*. The underemployed actor followed the lead of Tallulah Bankhead, who once said she did summer theater "because

I'm prodded by economic necessity...because I'm usually only two jumps ahead of the sheriff."

Sillman made do with less star power than usual: no Clary, Ghostley, Graham, or Kitt. But he did boast some familiar faces, including Virginia De Luce, Johnny Haymer, and (naturally) June Carroll. The newest New Face, Dody Goodman filled Ghostley's comic shoes when the best-of opened at the Coconut Grove Playhouse in Miami at the end of April 1957. As usual, Paul—probably the biggest name in the show—presented himself front and center with his crutch and bandage at the ready. He also performed some of the sketches he wrote for *New Faces of 1956,* including "Darts." Fellow alum Robert Clary, in town for a nightclub gig at the Fontainebleau, sat in the audience on opening night as John Laverty performed the numbers he had introduced five years earlier. Critics weren't impressed with any of the carbon copying. A tour never materialized, nor did an announced return to Broadway that September.

During the short run, someone in the cast organized a quick trip to nearby Cuba. Everyone but Paul and Goodman bailed when they saw the shabby state of the plane hired to fly them there. On the flight, Paul downed daiquiris and Goodman read Christian Science literature. She decided that if and when they landed in Havana, they would dye Paul's hair blond to make him stand out among the locals. "I thought that it would make him very attractive to the ladies," Goodman later told Merv Griffin when she and Paul appeared on his show. "The ladies...yeah," Paul chuckled. "I looked like Vivian Blaine. They followed us...with guns!"

After returning from Cuba, Paul settled for more out-of-town gigs. He played a woman-hating dressmaker named Madame Lucy in a St. Louis production of James Montgomery's musical *Irene* and complained to a local reporter, "Madame Lucy is a man, but all through the script they refer to him as her. What a shock." Two weeks later, Paul appeared at the Starlight Theatre in Kansas City in a production of Cole Porter's *Panama Hattie*. This time he played a butler with the femme name of Vivien Budd. "As usual," he moaned, "your agents louse you up."

Fifty-five hundred people, including former President Harry Truman and his wife, Bess, attended the opening-night performance. The show's publicists promoted veteran Paul as a "comic find," even though Pepper Davis and Tony Reese, a comedy team then known for frequent appearances on Ed Sullivan's TV show—not to mention a stage-frightened dog— earned most of the attention. Still, the show's director considered Paul a big enough draw to shoe-horn his Africa monologue into the production.

With no other prospects in sight, Paul hit the summer-stock circuit again the following summer. For most of May and June 1958, he relocated to New Hope, Pennsylvania, to work at the Bucks County Playhouse, then launching its 20th season. "At the time Paul was a well-known name among theater people but had not reached the point where he could star above the show if there were other stars in it," says Michael Ellis, the playhouse manager. "But he was a first-rate featured player.... His work was always well-received by audiences. They loved him. There were very few other physical comics in the theater and that helped him. Bert Lahr comes to mind as another who was still active. No one could ever play 'agony' and make it funny the way Paul could."

As a featured player, Paul joined headliners Reginald Gardiner in Gore Vidal's *Visit to a Small Planet,* Ilka Chase in William Marchant's *Desk Set,* and Russell Hardie in Wolcott Gibbs's *Season in the Sun.* A batch of *New Faces* alumni swept into town between these shows in a return engagement of *Mask and Gown.* The Sillman revue, which starred T.C. Jones in numbers written by Ronny Graham and June Carroll, among others, had broken local box-office records during its pre-Broadway tryout the previous summer. Although Bucks County audiences couldn't get enough of Jones, Broadway audiences could, and the production ended up lasting only 39 performances in New York. During his second stand at the converted grist mill, Jones again won all the critics' raves and much of the box office take as well as unwanted attention when he and his wife (and hairdresser) separated during the run.

Paul's fortunes that summer paled in comparison. The productions in which he appeared proved disappointing at the box office. Ellis publicly apologized for the choice of one of the season's comedies. "I want to state publicly that I did not perpetrate *Seasons in the Sun* on you as deliberate punishment," Ellis said. "I really planned it as a first-rate summer entertainment. Obviously, something went wrong."

Things only got worse for Paul when he caught a whopping case of stage fright during the first act of the Gore Vidal comedy. As backstage prompters tried in vain to feed him his lines and Gardiner ran out of ways to cover for him, Paul just stood there, saying nothing. After several tense minutes, the stage crew dropped the curtain. "It was the worst moment of my life," he said later. He retreated to his dressing room, but Ellis talked him into going back onstage. He completed the performance without a hitch and received an ovation at the curtain call. Years later when Paul starred in stock at another theater managed by Ellis, the headliner called the cast together and praised the producer as the man responsible for stopping him from ditching his acting career altogether.

Paul had always been a nervous actor. Even after performing his Africa sketch eight times a week for months in *New Faces,* he never went on without reviewing his lines. Sometimes his coworkers made fun of his backstage jitters. Before a TV special, he sat in his dressing room nervously mumbling his part. He thought he was alone until he heard

Jerry Lewis and Phil Silvers giggling at the door. "What's so funny?" he asked. "You!" said the comics. Paul told them he wasn't trying to be funny. "You don't have to try," they said.

Beyond the occasional monologue on Jack Paar's *Tonight Show,* Paul found little work on TV, so that winter it was back to Miami for another production of *Visit to a Small Planet,* again with Reginald Gardiner in the lead. Paul then resigned himself to off-the-radar gigs in two productions of the Harry Kurnitz comedy *Once More, With Feeling,* one of them at a dinner theater in Washington D.C. that gave the "canapés, cocktails, chicken, and comedy" better billing.

Projects that promised relief from what Bankhead called "the citronella circuit" never panned out for Paul. "I want people to recognize me," Paul said. "I can come out a stage door where autograph collectors are waiting, and they just ask me when the cast is coming out." Of the many what-ifs that dot his career and keep camp enthusiasts aquiver with delight, Paul's promised role in *Jack in the Box*—a musical version of Oscar Wilde's *The Importance of Being Earnest* set to open in New York in the fall of 1957—ranks near the top of the list. Turning *Pygmalion* into *My Fair Lady* had paid off in spades the previous year, and Oscar Wilde's comedy seemed ripe for similar popularity. Even better, the copyright had expired.

Paul expected a career boost from the part of Algernon in a cast that included Julia Meade, who was then known as Ed Sullivan's girl Friday. Instead, *Jack in the Box* broke down soon after rehearsals began that August. Anna Russell toured that same summer in a version called *Half in Earnest.* A third version called *Who's Earnest* aired that fall as an episode of the *U.S. Steel Hour.* As *Ernest in Love,* the show finally opened in New York in 1960, though off Broadway.

Paul reunited with Alice Ghostley on a Long Island stage two years later as the stars of *Dig We Must,* another play intended for Broadway. Ira Wallach and David Baker concocted songs and skits that *Variety* described "as slices of 20th century Manhattan life as reconstructed by archaeologists of a future age." Producer Ronald Rawson intended to bring this "better than average sampling of scripting, acting, and composing talent" (*Variety* again) to Broadway. He then announced scaled-down plans to open the show off-Broadway, with Ghostley the only cast holdover. Even that never gelled.

CBS had planned to employ Paul that fall in *The Laugh-Makers,* an "all-out comedy show" written and produced by Nat Hiken, creator of *The Phil Silvers Show.* Robert Dhéry, then in a popular Broadway revue called *La Plume de Ma Tante,* would star, with support from Monique van Vooren, Dick Haviland, and Paul. Less than a week before the pilot's taping date, the network scuttled the project when it turned out that Dhéry's Broadway contract wouldn't allow him to do American TV.

For years, Paul had kept his weight down—and had even accepted diet advice from Walter Chrysler—but he returned to the "trash food" of his childhood when his career didn't live up to his expectations. By the late 1950s, he again tipped the scales at well over 200 pounds. "I was 'on' all the time, using it to get laughs," he said. "I had no personal life, not really, and I was always performing anyplace I went, especially people's living rooms."

Phyllis Diller remembers Paul's act: "He used to pick up a book, and the book was all faked up, and he did material for us. We had a fun time and sat around and giggled." Paul cracked open the large book when he cohosted *The Mike Douglas Show* in the 1960s. The talk show host wondered if it was the Bible. "No," Paul replied, "These are my fears."

The stage fright, his weight problem, the deaths in his family, and now the trajectory of his career took their toll. At a dinner party one night, Paul rose from the table and announced, "I haven't heard one word you've said to me all evening, and I love you all too much to inflict this on you." He later admitted he had planned this as his "farewell address." He had been contemplating killing himself. This would come as no surprise to some who knew him. "He was the kind of person you would be afraid might be a suicide victim in terms of self-hatred and how he dealt with it," Connell says.

Paul's friend Alice Pearce, who had been in *New Faces of 1943* and would later gain acclaim as the first Gladys Kravitz in *Bewitched,* suggested therapy at the Reich Clinic, where she had gone for counseling after her first husband's death in 1957. Steve Allen pulled some strings to get Paul bumped to the top of the long waiting list. At first Paul felt awkward because the psychiatrist assigned to him had the same name as his mother: Sylvia. She soon won him over, though, and he saw her three times a week for months.

"My shrink told me there was nothing wrong with me that a job wouldn't cure," Paul said. He shared anxieties about his career with Diller, who relates, "I remember that he was talking about what his therapist told him: 'Paul, you're going to have to stop trying to live by magic.' Because he would sit by the phone and wait for it to ring."

Finally, it did.

CHAPTER 5

ED, I LOVE YOU!

*"Everybody has a girl for me to meet—
object: matrimony."*

His *New Faces* cachet nearly exhausted, his network deals a bust, Paul knew he had to start taking chances. Few of his prospects sounded iffier than *Bye Bye Birdie,* a Broadway-bound musical finally coming together in late 1959. Against his better judgment, Paul listened to a spiel by the show's creators, all fans of his Africa sketch, and agreed to read the script.

Producer Edward Padula dreamed up the lighthearted look at teenage hysteria and parental panic over rock and roll as a happier alternative to *West Side Story.* Merging the Elvis mystique with decidedly non-Elvis show tunes, the production follows the eruption of a small Ohio town after a rock idol named Conrad Birdie gets drafted and, as a farewell publicity stunt, agrees to kiss a local member of his fan club on *The Ed Sullivan Show.* "I wanted to do a contemporary show on a contemporary subject—going steady among the teenagers—and take one of their heroes and bring him right into the milieu," he explained soon after the show opened. "I wanted to explore that area, without dragging in dope addicts and stuff like that, which is superficial. I had a new subject and went searching for new people to work on it."

Most of the "new people" hired for the show lacked substantial Broadway experience. Padula had directed a show and stage-managed others, but never produced any. He hired lyricist Lee Adams and composer Charles Strouse, who had only worked on revues in New York clubs and at a summer resort in the Adirondacks. They recommended librettist Michael Stewart, whose only claim to fame came from his toil in Sid Caesar's writers room. (He replaced Warren Miller and Raphael Millian, fired after they submitted the first script.) Director and choreographer Gower Champion, best known for dancing with his wife, Marge, in a string of MGM musicals, had directed *Lend an Ear* and *Three for Tonight* on Broadway, but neither of those revues approached *Birdie* in scale.

Padula also offered the Champions the lead roles as songwriter Albert Peterson and his girlfriend, Rose Grant. Gower considered the idea of simultaneously directing and starring in a show "sheer egocentric madness" and turned him down. Marge declined as well; she wanted to spend time with their young son. Gower did agree to choreograph the show, with assistance from Gene Bayliss, with whom he (and Paul) had previously worked.

Dick Van Dyke and Chita Rivera picked up the lead parts instead. Both actors had already appeared on Broadway: he in *The Girls Against the Boys,* a flop revue from earlier that season starring Bert Lahr and Nancy Walker, and she, most recently, as Anita in *West Side Story.* Others in the cast included Johnny Borden, Dick Gautier, Marijane Maricle, Kay Medford, Michael J. Pollard, Charles Nelson Reilly, and Susan Watson.

At Champion's suggestion, Stewart came up with the ultimate put-upon father to balance out a large cast of teenagers and give adult ticket-buyers someone with whom they could identify. Stewart suggested they offer the role to Paul, a friend of a friend, but Adams never thought he would accept. "Paul Lynde was a minor star," Adams recalled, "and we were unknowns."

Champion apologized to Paul that the role in its present form was "minute." Paul reviewed the script, saw only a few lines for himself, and went down to the Anderson Theatre on Third Avenue to decline the role. "Gower stopped [rehearsals] and almost ran to the back of the theater to intercept him," Bayliss says. Paul told the director he'd hunted through the dictionary for a word that meant smaller than "minute" but couldn't find one. "Gower, I would say, literally begged him to do it and promised him that there would be a part built for him," Bayliss says.

Champion's plea swayed the reluctant but desperate actor. "I took it, knowing it was totally on spec," Paul said. "Friends told me not to do it, that [my role] would be the first thing to go if there was any book trouble. But I had great faith in Gower."

As promised, Champion made Stewart expand Paul's role. "The part of Mr. MacAfee was built on Paul Lynde," Bayliss says, "and it has every bit of Paul's snide, wonderful style. They used every bit of his talent." In addition to more lines, Paul also gained two numbers: "Hymn for a Sunday Evening," a paean to Ed Sullivan, and "Kids," an extended gripe about the generation gap set to the beat of a Charleston.

Paul contributed more material when he ad-libbed his way through rehearsals. "He would say things that would make us all laugh," says Watson, who played his daughter. "Whatever he did worked, so everyone just said, 'Leave it in.' He was really a master at that kind of thing." One of Paul's ad-libs ticked off Champion, and he called a meeting to harangue the creative team about it. "Gower stood up and dressed everybody down," Bayliss says. "He said, 'I do not like surprises. I won't stand for it.' He dressed down...everybody on the staff.... The surprise that kicked this off was, if you remember, in the song 'Ed Sullivan,' Paul steps forward and says in his inimitable way, 'Ed, I love you.' That was the surprise. That was not in the script that Gower had read...and Gower blew his top. But it was good, and it stayed, of course."

Reporters would soon want to know how a confirmed bachelor like Paul could capture the turmoil of a parent so well. The actor told them he was just mimicking his father, but that greatly oversimplified matters. Paul had developed the pieces of this character—a devilish leer, a too-tight grin, a chuckle like a dry heave, an air of indignant arrogance thick as smog—throughout the 1950s; MacAfee simply gave him the excuse to bring them all together.

"[Paul's] great quality was he was able to translate his anger at the world, his hostilities, into humor," says Adams. "He had lots of hostilities and lots of boiled-up rage, and he translated that on the stage into humor. In *Birdie,* he played the father of the young girl. He was always upset by having this Elvis Presley–type in his house, so he was able to play that smoldering anger that occasionally burst out, and it was very, very funny."

His position as king of the castle already usurped when Birdie takes up residence in his home, MacAfee loses it when his wife offers him a warm soda for breakfast:

> Last night I gave up my room to a guest who repeatedly referred to me as "Fats." Telephone calls were made on my phone to New York; Chicago; Fairbanks, Alaska; and Hong Kong. I slept in a camp cot with my feet in the fireplace and my head in an ashtray. Outside my window three harpies shrieked, "We love you, Conrad," 4,723 times!... I have just lost two fried eggs.... Gentlemen, the democracy is over! Parliament has been

dissolved; the Magna Carta is revoked, and Nero is back in town! And you don't offer an emperor a warm 7UP!

"It's a brilliant speech," Adams says, "and Paul got the most out of it. He started slow, started quietly, and gradually built it until by the end he was clutching the edge of a table and shaking and saying that last line. The audience went crazy."

Though Paul would later let loose as a stylish swisher on *Hollywood Squares,* the tamer mores of the early 1960s confined him to a stuffier closet. He didn't play MacAfee gay, but he didn't play him straight either. Bayliss says Paul injected an "edge of homosexuality" to his portrayal, and that the role wouldn't have worked any other way. (George Wendt certainly lacked this or any other mystique when he played the character in the panned 1995 made-for-TV version of *Birdie.*) Paul created a sexless ball of rage more effete than effeminate, more fussy than flamboyant. The persona stuck, and variations of Harry MacAfee became Paul's stock in trade, eventually helping him secure a lucrative career as an in-demand character actor.

Before heading to Philadelphia for the show's out-of-town tryout, the company performed a run-through for Broadway gypsies. Reaction was decidedly mixed. The actors themselves felt ambivalent about the material. "When I first read the script, I went, 'This is so hokey. They're doing a thing on Elvis Presley. Are they kidding?'" Watson says. "Here I was, a 19-year-old, thinking this was not very theatrical."

Champion guided efforts to tweak the show into shape, including the decision to have Gautier portray Birdie as a bum. "I wanted social commentary," he explained, "with the emphasis not on the singer but on how and why masses of people reacted to him." The show fared better when it opened on Broadway at the Martin Beck Theatre on April 14, 1960.

L. Slade Brown, a Texas millionaire who backed the production, flipped the bill for the first-night fete at the Astor. Some of the cast stopped at Sardi's to await the reviews. Critics from six of the seven major New York papers loved it. The lone holdout, Brooks Atkinson of *The New York Times,* dismissed the show as "neither fish, nor fowl, nor good musical comedy," but praised Paul for contributing "to the merriment of the nation by simulating indignation and provincial fatuity." One of Paul's lines—"Who's the head of the FBI? Is it Pat Nixon yet?"—particularly amused Kenneth Tynan, the theater critic for *The New Yorker,* and he deemed it the funniest of the show. (After President Kennedy moved into the White House, his brother-in-law Peter Lawford replaced Mrs. Nixon in the punch line.)

Paul grabbed credit for himself when he discussed his role in the show's success. "Parents who had misgivings about *Birdie*—they thought it was an Elvis Presley rock-and-roll thing—brought their kids and ended up enjoying it just as much," he told the press. "I think my role had a lot to do with that." He added that playing MacAfee gave him "new dimension" as an actor. Thirteen New York critics didn't seem to agree with him when they cast their choices for the best work of the 1959–1960 season in a *Variety* poll. They gave Paul exactly one vote—cast by Henry Hewes of the *Saturday Review*—in the category of best performance by an actor in a supporting role in a play or musical. The award, which offered bragging rights but no actual adornment, went to Robert Morse for his work in *Take Me Along.*

The committee that selected nominations for the more prestigious Tony Awards ignored Paul's contributions entirely, but showered the production with eight nods, including ones for Van Dyke, Rivera, and Gautier. Gautier's recognition particularly irked Paul. "Everyone offered congratulations except Paul, who dismissed me as a 'cheap sex symbol' and didn't talk to me for six months," Gautier says. "Me? A sex symbol? I don't think so."

When Gautier told the company he would be opening for Barbra Streisand with a comedy act at the Bon Soir, Paul broke his silence to tell him that he and his friends would be in the audience to watch him fall on his face. "The night was a smashing success," Gautier says. "To Paul's credit he hugged me, a rare thing for him to do, and said he'd been wrong about me, that I did have talent. Of course, he hated stand-up so he was impressed. I thought that was very big of him."

At the Tony Awards ceremony in April 1961, *Birdie* earned six trophies: one each for Padula, Stewart, and Van Dyke, two for Champion (for direction and choreography), and the "best musical" accolade over *Do Re Mi* and *Irma La Douce*. Rivera lost to Tammy Grimes in *The Unsinkable Molly Brown*, and Gautier to his costar Van Dyke. Paul would only make it to the awards ceremony as a performer. He appeared on the Tony telecast a decade later in his pajamas and bathrobe to perform "Kids" in honor of Tony-winning musicals of the past.

Columbia Pictures shelled out $850,000 for the film rights to the Broadway hit, but the studio had to wait until the show closed before filming could begin. The musical has gone on to become a staple of high school drama clubs and professional and amateur stock companies throughout America. Diane Keaton, John Travolta, and Hillary Clinton appeared in local productions, while a teenage Alice Cooper played alongside Jan Murray in a professional production in Phoenix in 1966. The show even won the heart of acting legend John Gielgud, who thought it should have been sent to impress the Soviets instead of a well-publicized tour of *My Fair Lady*.

In spite of his triumph with another Broadway hit, Paul had continued seeing his psychiatrist. "I can hardly wait for your session," Sylvia confessed to him. "All the others are bores! bores! bores!" But she soon took Paul's gainful employment as a sign that her work was done and sent him on his way. Paul swore off therapy from then on, claiming he didn't want to learn more about himself for fear of losing whatever it was that made him funny.

Some of the cast felt Paul could have benefited from more headwork. "I assumed he had a drinking problem even then," Watson says. "But what did I know? He could be kind of gloomy and dark, and I knew to avoid him. He was always very dear to me. I just knew that he needed space every now and then, before the show or if I heard him shouting at someone." Watson wasn't the only company member avoiding Paul. "He was a moody guy," Gautier says. "I think we all learned when to keep our distance or when to be chummy. Of course, if he was drinking, 'stay away' was the rule."

"Drunk, [Paul] was ten times more bitchy, cutting, and unforgivably rude," musician Jack Holmes once said. "Bartenders, waiters, pianists, customers would all gently move right, left, go upstairs, into the kitchen, the bathroom—anywhere to avoid him. Every word out of his mouth was venomous, with a sting that really hurt, into every unexpected vulnerability a human being might have. He could rouse a sane, normal person to instant fury."

Noting his bad behavior, Walter Winchell instructed his readers not to extend Paul any party invites. "Someone did and the words atomic'd," he wrote. Nobody had shared this advice with Lana Turner when she met Paul in Chita Rivera's dressing room after an opening night in Las Vegas. Before the screen legend could speak a word, Paul's drunken brain recalled the brouhaha over the murder of her mobster boyfriend, and he snarled, "You killed him, didn't you?"

Performing the "Ed Sullivan" number on one night, Paul fumbled the line "Me, Harry MacAfee...on *The Ed Sullivan Show*?" with the spoonerism "Me...Mary HacAfee." The actors onstage, well aware Paul was gay, could hardly contain their laughter. Paul fumed. Unscripted moments often set him off. "One time I was backstage standing behind a curtain chatting," Gautier recalls. "The next cue coming up was 'Go 28,' and we'd go into the icehouse scene following Paul's Ed Sullivan song. Well, Mike Thoma, the stage manager, couldn't see me, so he called out on the PA system, 'Dick *Gautier.*' The crew thought he said 'Go 28' and changed the scenery while Paul was still singing. He went berserk as though everyone did it on purpose to screw him up. He took everything personally."

Even the audience could catch hell. Barry Pearl, who played young Randolph MacAfee during the show's last weeks, witnessed one of Paul's outbursts at a Wednesday matinee attended by a listless crowd of blue-haired tourists. Paul and his stage son had just finished doing the "Ed Sullivan" number. "I guess there was a smattering of applause," Pearl says. "As we were being pulled off, Paul yells out into the audience in his inimitable way, 'Why don't you all go home!' I was just this young kid, and I thought, *My God, how could you say something like that?*"

Rivera and Van Dyke both left the production just before its first anniversary. She headed east, across the ocean, to reprise her role as Rose in the London version of *Birdie,* with Peter Marshall as her costar. Van Dyke headed west to Hollywood to start work on *The Dick Van Dyke Show,* a sitcom for CBS. Gretchen Wyler and Gene Rayburn, future host of *Match Game,* replaced them. Paul stayed with the show until it closed on October 7, 1961, after 607 performances.

Paul may have missed out on offers from London and Hollywood, but he kept busy. Columbia Records, which had released the *Bye Bye Birdie* cast album in May 1960, asked him to wax a comedy platter. Loathe to record his pieces at an actual club, Paul invited friends and costars to a studio on a Sunday evening in early June to watch him perform. Frank De Vol, an executive at the company perhaps best remembered for cowriting the theme to *The Brady Bunch,* oversaw the project.

The album opened with Paul's Africa sketch, followed by one of two bits in which he portrayed a woman. He introduced "The Family Just Across the Moat," a Charles Addams send-up that he had first performed at the Versailles.

Paul threw in two bits from his days at Northwestern: "The Monster Stalks," his squirrel warning, this time set in Central Park; and "Let's Be Frank," his sex-ed lecture, along with "Phlegm Falls Drama Club," in which "Laura Bolton" lectures her girlfriends in Iowa about her recent trip to that "island of sin," New York City.

Record buyers couldn't get enough of comedy albums in 1960. Shelley Berman, Jonathan Winters, and Woody Woodbury were just a few of the funnymen who had recently preserved their acts on vinyl. Bob Newhart led the pack to the top of the *Billboard* charts that year with his album *The Button-Down Mind of Bob Newhart* for Warner Brothers. Paul may have been "a rare comedian who can make a perfectly ordinary statement gleam with hilarity," as Columbia touted him, but that didn't mean he could push records. The album tanked. Paul made light of the platter's fate when he joked to Jan Forbes about not being able to find it for sale anywhere in New York.

Paul had better luck on TV. He sang his ode to Ed Sullivan on the emcee's 12th anniversary show in June. That November he teamed up again with former costars Robert Clary, Alice Ghostley, Ronny Graham, Inga Swenson, and his ex, now billed as Jim Russell, for *Highlights of New Faces.* This *Play of the Week* episode showcased sketches from the past two editions of Sillman's revue, with most of the material taken from the more successful and superior 1952 offering. None of the sketches Paul contributed to the 1956 show was reproduced.

Introduced as "a young man bursting with talent...and teeth," Paul continued to get mileage out of his Africa sketch as well as "The Family Just Across the Moat," which had not been used in either production. He joined Ghostley and Graham in a reprise of Mel Brooks's "Of Fathers and Sons" sketch and again played a judge with just a few lines of dialogue in the "Lizzie Borden" production number. *The New York Times* considered the special "witty, alive, and well worth watching," and *Variety* praised Paul's Addams homage as "funny in a grisly way."

Paul's professional relationship with Sillman continued (and concluded) two years later when he wrote two sketches for the *New Faces of 1962*. (Streisand failed the auditions.) He added a Cold War twist to an idea he had used in a Waa-Mu show and suffered unusually critical barbs. "A sketch called 'The Reds Visit Mount Vernon' intends to ridicule the Russians ridiculing the story of Washington and the cherry tree," stated Howard Taubman in *The New York Times*, "but anything so flat would get a Soviet writer thrown out of his union." Another critic deemed the sketch "witless."

Nothing about *New Faces of 1962* pleased critics or theatergoers—including Noël Coward, who called it an "absolute disaster." The show opened and closed during the shortest month of the year. Sillman returned to Broadway six years later with a group of fresh talent that included Madeline Kahn and Robert Klein, with little success. He refused to introduce new editions from then on because, he complained, "the young writers since then have all had messages to give. Or it was rock and roll." Instead, he spent the remaining years of his life trying to put together another highlights version of the franchise for New York audiences.

Paul continually rejected Sillman's requests to join the cast, though he did eventually sign up as a financial backer. The show was never produced except as an hour-long nightclub offering in 1977.

Perry Como, onetime "King of the Jukes," hosted a popular Wednesday night variety show that had been on the NBC schedule since 1955. After catching a performance of *Bye Bye Birdie*, Como's producers asked Paul to recreate his star-crazed sycophant in the presence of the calm, collected Mr. C. Signed to a one-shot appearance for the end of April 1961, Paul played a man on a family vacation in Paris who goes bonkers at the sight of Como and asks the crooner to autograph his son's forehead. The sketch got big laughs, and Paul accepted an invitation to play "Perry's pal" for the rest of the season, which ran until the first week of June. The "nut next door," as Como called his TV neighbor, even dropped out of two performances of *Birdie* at the end of May to join the Como company at McCormick Place in Chicago for two shows in front of 10,000 people.

Hoping to counteract the rising costs of big-name guest stars, Como and his producers formed a stock company over the summer and invited Paul to join it. The Kraft Music Hall Players, named in honor of the company that sponsored the show, included "good, versatile troupers, just under the star level; up-and-comers, yet seasoned," according to *TV Guide*. Stand-up comedian Don Adams, better known now for *Get Smart*, was a nightclub fixture who had appeared on Arthur Godfrey's *Talent Scouts* in 1954. At the time of the Como gig, Kaye Ballard was also appearing on Broadway in *Carnival!*— another smash musical directed by Gower Champion. Jack Duffy and Sandy Stewart earned spots in the troupe as boy and girl singer.

"Como's show is much superior to other variety shows, and I've been on them all," Adams said. "Como's writers make the difference." Goodman Ace, former scribe for Tallulah Bankhead and Milton Berle, led a team of five that included Selma Diamond, who was considered the "number 1 femme jokesmith in the business." On her status as the sole female among Como's comedy contributors, she cracked, "It's like being Red China. I'm there. They just don't recognize me."

The team came up with what *TV Guide* called "snappy lyrics and fancy patter" for the show. In Paul's case, that patter often played out along the lines of this exchange from the second show of the 1961 season:

> PAUL: I'm sorry I missed your show last week, Perry, but I couldn't make it. I was behind bars.
> PERRY: You were arrested?
> PAUL: No, I was drunk. That night I went to a lot of bars to try to get 'em to put your show on television but they were watching the World Series between the Yankees and those wonderful Cincinnati Reds.
> PERRY: You know, I think you're drinking too much.
> PAUL: I've been drinking for 20 years. I'm not full yet.

The "Greenwich Village bachelor," as Kraft described him in publicity, charmed TV viewers across America every week in breezy routines in which he might greet famous guest talent with a line like "Are you anybody?" or suggest that Como order the West Point Glee Club to sing "Anchors Aweigh" just to see "if we might start a little something."

"He got away with murder on *Perry Como* because at the table reading, if something wasn't funny, he'd go 'yuck' and they would scream with laughter," Kaye Ballard has said. "If I said it wasn't funny, I'd be out. He got away with murder. They adored him. Perry Como adored him." Though he came to loathe the character he played, Paul never failed to praise Como for helping to make him a star. "I loved doing the Como show," he said later. "That was show business in the most pleasant way. Perry proved it could be done without a lot of shouting and temperament."

With newfound prominence to market, Paul fielded a wide range of offers: portraying a murderer on *The New Breed*, a detective show starring Leslie Nielsen, and appearing in *Subways Are for Sleeping*, a new Broadway musical, and *The Errand Boy*, a Jerry Lewis comedy. Kowtowing to Como every Wednesday meant Paul could rarely accept extra-curricular assignments, though he did find time that winter to fly to Los Angeles to appear on *Henry Fonda and the Family*, a CBS special from producers Norman Lear and Bud Yorkin. He joined his *Birdie* costars Van Dyke and Pollard as well as Cara Williams and Dan Blocker in sketches that skewered American domesticity.

The idea of starring in his own series appealed to Paul, but most of the offers he received were variations on his *Birdie* persona. He didn't want to play an uptight father again and passed on the roles. He also nixed a deal to star in *The Hathaways*, a short-lived sitcom featuring Jack Weston, Peggy Cass…and three chimpanzees. He finally accepted the starring role on *Howie*, a comedy with no monkeys, just a crazy son-in-law.

Chrislaw, a company owned by Peter Lawford and funded in part by his in-laws, produced the sitcom. (Patriarch Joseph Kennedy was kept abreast of every project.) Lawford had hired Bill Asher as director on the strength of his extensive work in television, most notably *I Love Lucy*. Asher had directed the iconic episode in which Lucy and Ethel can't keep up with a speedy conveyer belt in a candy factory as well as many of the show's mayhem-in-Hollywood adventures. He had also helmed episodes of *Our Miss Brooks*, *Make Room for Daddy*, *December Bride*, and *The Thin Man*.

Asher first met Paul backstage after a performance of

New Faces of 1952. They had worked together on *The Colgate Comedy Hour* but didn't talk seriously about doing another TV show until Paul's exposure on Como's show. "Some people are just made to do television," Asher says. "[Paul] was one of those people."

Sidney Sheldon based his *Howie* script on a play of the same name by Phoebe Ephron that had lasted less than a week on Broadway in 1958. Paul starred as Walter Simms, a New York attorney at odds with the mildly beatnik ways of Howie, his unemployable live-in son-in-law. Had this particular frazzled father met Harry MacAfee, the two would have found they had a lot in common.

Will Hutchins, the former star of *Sugarfoot,* a TV Western, portrayed the title character. Paul knew which one of them would be a hit with female viewers. "I don't have Will's appeal," he said. "Mothers don't want to pinch me or put me in their purse." Peggy Knudsen, who had appeared frequently as "the other woman" in a number of 1950s TV shows, took the role of Mrs. Simms. Mary Mitchel played older daughter Barbara, and Sherry Alberoni, a former Mouseketeer, played younger daughter Sally. Alberoni says she enjoyed working with Paul, whom she describes as "nice and kind," but she was more thrilled by meeting Lawford and his wife, Patricia, sister of the president, at the wrap party.

The end product laid on the kind of wisecracks for which Paul had become known. Believing his daughter has married into money, Mr. Simms is crushed to learn otherwise:

"What happened?" a friend asks. "From your description, I expected a combination of J. Paul Getty and Jack Lemmon."

"He turned out to be all lemon...no Jack, just lemon."

The "nervous Nellie of the networks," according to *TV Guide,* spent much of the spring anxiously awaiting an announcement about the fall TV schedule. CBS scrutinized his pilot, while Como considered another season of work for

NBC. "Television has been very good to me," Paul said. "The exposure has been great, but it scares me to realize how fickle those audiences can be." He definitely wanted a show of his own, but he worried that his career would mirror those of Red Buttons, George Gobel, and Martha Raye. "One season they're on top," he said, "and the next—nothing."

CBS briefly considered Paul's pilot for the 1962 fall schedule after Proctor and Gamble pulled its full sponsorship of Dick Van Dyke's floundering sitcom. The Lorillard Tobacco Company agreed to share the time slot, but they preferred *Howie*...until an impassioned plea by Sheldon Leonard, the producer of Van Dyke's program, changed their minds. Paul's former costar kept his job, and Como agreed to keep his Wednesday night time slot opposite Van Dyke. Asher, Lawford, and Sidney Sheldon would have better luck the next season with *The Patty Duke Show*. Asher would also direct *Johnny Cool*, Chrislaw's first feature film, and marry one of its stars, Elizabeth Montgomery.

Paul waited for Como's decision while on a sabbatical from the show. Ignoring the warnings of friends and agents, he accepted a low-pay, no-billing offer to reprise the role of Harry MacAfee in the screen version of *Bye Bye Birdie,* which began production that May. "I decided to take it because I love movies and I always wanted to do them," he said. The studio made the deal after considering other actors, including comedian Mike Nichols, for the role.

Sitcom star Van Dyke joined Paul as the only other holdover from Broadway in the cast. Champion passed on the offer to direct the film when Columbia Pictures and he failed to agree on the conditions of a long-term contract. Columbia also offered Rivera her original part, but Janet Leigh ended up with the job. Gautier declined his offer out of worries about typecasting and the absence of the original director and librettist. Jesse Pearson, who portrayed Birdie in the national touring company, accepted the gig instead. Watson met with producers about reprising her role, but they told her they wanted someone younger to play Kim MacAfee. "They got Ann-Margret," she says. "Compared to how I looked, she seemed much older."

At 21, Ann-Margret may not have passed as a teenager, but she brought other assets to the role. The former Northwestern student and Waa-Mu performer won the role after catching the attention of director George Sidney at a New Year's Eve party in Las Vegas. (The director and his fetching protégé would also work together on *Viva Las Vegas* in 1964 and *The Swinger* in 1966.) Not so mysteriously, the movie's focus shifted to the Swedish-born sexpot—who, Paul groused, played the lucky teenager as if she were remaking *Gilda,* the scorching Rita Hayworth classic. Paul, at 36, had to dye his hair gray to pass as her on-screen father.

Screenwriter Irving Brecher, whose previous work included screenplays for the Marx Brothers' *At the Circus* and *Go West,* threw biochemistry and Russian ballerinas on speed into the script and changed Paul's lines considerably. The big-screen MacAfee, as his name now read, acted even more uptight, becoming unhinged at the mere thought of his child's lost innocence. "My daughter is not going to be kissed by...that wiggler," he tells his wife. "I know that show-business crowd, probably living in sin.... I never told you, but one summer I worked for the circus. Oh, those midgets—wild!"

Paul's ode to Ed Sullivan survived in its original form. The host even appeared in the film as himself. (Will Jordan had aped his voice in the stage production.) Paul's show-stopper, "Kids," changed considerably, with new lyrics for Van Dyke and Maureen Stapleton, who played the overbearing Mama Peterson. Paul had fewer words to sing and less to be angry about, forgoing the question "What's wrong with

Sammy Kaye?" and realizing by the song's end that "nothing's the matter with kids today."

Whether or not Paul and Van Dyke really feuded on the set, as Dorothy Kilgallen suggested, Paul made no secret of his disdain for the new script. He forever trashed the project as "Hello, Ann-Margret." Still, he earned his share of good reviews when the musical hit theaters in 1963. "Mr. Lynde alone is worth the price of admission for his hard-core dual portrait of the parent at bay and the male ego rampant," *The New York Herald Tribune* decided, while *Variety* deigned Paul a "comedian powerhouse...deserving of star billing."

The process of moviemaking impressed Paul more than the end product. "For the first time in my career, I am enjoying work," he said. "Doing this picture is the first time I have performed with any degree of calm. I guess it's because there is no audience, because you can do it over again if it wasn't right the first time."

With assignments in Hollywood keeping him too busy for the therapist's couch, Paul played hardball with the producers of Como's show. "I have set my price so high that I'll be a little surprised if they ask me back," he said. They didn't, and Pierre Olaf took his spot as a Kraft Music Hall Player that fall. Paul appeared one final time—on Como's Christmas episode—because the cast recorded their season's greeting that June. Ratings for Como's show dwindled that year as viewers flocked to *The Beverly Hillbillies,* a new sitcom on CBS that bolstered Van Dyke's ratings so much that the former candidate for cancellation finished its second season in the top ten.

Promotional duties during the summer of 1963 led Paul back to Ohio. He joined Rock Hudson, Arthur Godfrey, Paul Anka, and John Russell as the star attractions at the All-American Soap Box Derby in Akron. Thousands of people crowded the street to catch a glimpse of the five men, three of whom took part in a mock race while Paul and Hudson handled the finish-line flags. Hudson received the lion's share of attention, especially from a smitten reporter who wanted to know about his love life. Her report appeared under the headline, "Hudson Prefers Blondes, Brunettes, and Redheads: But No Marriage Plans."

Though no one in Akron questioned Paul about his romantic entanglements, his growing popularity inspired more press coverage, some of it intrusive. Gossip rags on both coasts took note of this peculiar new star with typically innocuous items. Before Paul left for Los Angeles, a professional busybody had reported: "Pat Neal and Paul Lynde threw a loud party for Maureen Stapleton, who's testing for the loudmouth mother in *Birdie*."

A West Coast clack also chimed in: "Newcomer Paul Lynde is a hit in *Bye Bye Birdie*. And he has the right idea— be eccentric and you get noticed in Hollywood. Paul, who lives in a hotel, has bought himself an eight-foot statue, which he calls Ondine, for company." (Ondine is a mythological sea-nymph whose unfaithful lover is cursed to stay awake so he can breathe.)

Other items reflected attempts by Paul's handlers to cast him as a ladies' man:

> What were comedy star Paul Lynde and beautiful singer-
>   actress Dawn Nickerson whispering about at Chez Vito?
> Paul Lynde has to hire a shapely secretary to handle his
>   fan mail.
> Funny girl Jorie Remus at the Bon Soir gets roses daily
>   from Paul Lynde.

Paul exploited Marilyn, Maggie, and other members of the female sex as his beards whenever possible, but sometimes

words failed him. During an appearance on *The Celebrity Game* in May 1964, the bachelor found himself at the mercy of Eartha Kitt after they exchanged a few pointed jokes about how they hadn't talked since *New Faces*. "Not a word," Paul deadpanned.

When host Carl Reiner asked the panelists, "Do you object to the Hollywood custom of calling everyone 'darling,' 'sweetheart,' or 'baby'?" Kitt replied, "Yes. Well, there's a yes and no. I object to someone like, maybe say, Paul calling Joseph Cotten 'darling.' It makes me feel kind of squeamish, but anyway, since we don't have to worry about that problem." Paul forced a chuckle and played along. "When I came out here, I wanted to be part of the gang," he explained. "I said, 'Hi, baby, hi darling,' to Burt Lancaster, and he gave me an Ivy League kiss and a belt in the mouth." A noticeable chill settled between Paul and Kitt for the rest of the show.

The scrutiny over his love life followed Paul everywhere. When Mount Vernon celebrated Paul Lynde Day in mid 1963, a guest at a Chamber of Commerce luncheon asked the star, then 37, why he hadn't married. Since he couldn't easily blame his high school sweetheart with her friends and family in attendance, Paul whimpered about the failure rate of Hollywood marriages. "Besides," he said, "I'm very selfish."

CHAPTER 6

TITAN OF TRICKS

"Just once I'd like to play a villain in a movie. I'm always on his side, because the hero is such a bore. That's why you like Scarlett O'Hara and think Melanie is such a drip."

When Robert Morse saw Paul stumble toward him at a party, he may have regretted beating the comic on the *Variety* ballot in 1960. Morse was Paul's favorite kind of prey: an actor in the middle of a brief career slump. "Oh, yes. I remember when you used to be so *fam-ous!*" Paul cackled in his face. "Well, where are you now?" Morse laughed along with everyone else, but Paul didn't stop. Finding it harder and harder to play along, Morse tried to sneak away. Paul tailed him from room to room like a coyote, never stopping the barrage.

After he moved to Southern California in July 1963 to pursue more film and TV work, Paul could be counted on to make the Hollywood scene and—the further he got in his cups—cause one as well. He didn't discriminate, laying into friend or foe alike, no matter what their social status. Celebrities such as actor Steve McQueen experienced his wrath, though Paul usually picked on stars whose luster had waned or never waxed. He unerringly homed in on their primary weaknesses, and his blows devastated their targets because they rang with truth (and perhaps because actors can be a sensitive lot). At a reunion of some cast members of *New Faces of 1952,* Paul asked Carol Lawrence if she had read Shirley MacLaine's recent autobiography. Lawrence said she had read part of it and nearly burst into tears when Paul exclaimed, "Part of it? You're that busy?"

At George Sidney's wrap party for *Bye Bye Birdie,* a fuddled Maureen Stapleton infamously cut short the endless kudos for Ann-Margret when she sputtered, "I'm the only one on this picture who didn't try to fuck Ann-Margret." She had overlooked pansy Paul, who got in a good one of his own that night. When dinner came around, Paul polished off his restorative, took a bite of the meal, and brayed for all (including the hostess) to hear, "What is this shit?"

To no one's surprise, Paul fell off one guest list after another. "In Hollywood, you're judged by the company you keep, and you get described like one line in *TV Guide* very quickly," Robert Osborne says. "If you're Angie Dickinson, you're a good gal and you don't talk; if you're Roddy McDowall, you're loyal and friendly and you don't tell stories; and if you're Shelley Winters, you talk and you're loud. Paul had a reputation for being funny and difficult and dangerous. People of a certain social strata would not include him in their thing because it's too dangerous, it's too difficult, and you don't have to. There are plenty of people who can fill a seat."

Paul rented an $85-a-month duplex apartment on the first floor of a remodeled Spanish bungalow on Phyllis Avenue in West Hollywood. The house came with a formal garden and room for his Ondine statue, which he had purchased at a Beverly Hills gallery. His art collection took up so much space that he hung some of his paintings in his kitchen.

Paul's brother Johnny lived in nearby Glendale but died of a heart attack in August 1965. Sister Helen lived in Santa

Monica, and while he kept in touch (and, some friends say, even supported her), Paul didn't seem to care for her much. "She had not a whip stitch of humor...none," Jan Forbes says. "She wore horn-rimmed glasses, and she would talk to you right there [in your face]...[He] thought she was so dull. Oh, brother." In 2001, Helen fired off an angry letter to the producers of an *A&E Biography* about Paul in which she chastised them for acknowledging Paul's homosexuality.

If he wasn't working, shopping, or dieting, Paul haunted The Gallery, a nearby watering hole on Santa Monica Boulevard. "A lot of young actors, would-be actors went there," says friend Jim McLernan, one of Paul's neighbors. "It just sort of had a uniqueness of its own...I remember John Wayne's son Pat Wayne used to be there. Oh, you never knew whom you'd see there. But Paul, when he went there, he'd sort of light up the whole room."

Sometimes Paul hung out at the bar with chums from the neighborhood, if the Jekyll-and-Hyde effects of his drinking hadn't driven them away. "He never seemed to have a lot of friends around," Osborne says. "We would always include him whenever we'd have a gathering or party. Unfortunately, one learned after a while that you had to be very careful whom you had him around."

Paul showed no such caution when choosing his own company. He pursued a promiscuous sex life with an assortment of seedy and sinister men, some of them fresh from prison. "He wanted a companion," says Rose Marie, his friend and fellow game show panelist. "He'd always pick the wrong kind." Dick Sargent, the gay actor who worked with Paul on *Bewitched* and stayed with the same partner for two decades, described Paul as "a sad character, always with some tired hustler, or some new 'lover' who'd be gone in a few weeks. He was so flamboyant in that way."

Invariably, Paul's behavior with these temporary love

interests turned violent. Neighbors called the police during one of Paul's loud fights with a lover du jour, and the bickering couple cooled down in jail. Osborne and a friend came over the next day to clean up the broken dishes and furniture and found a bowl's worth of macaroni and cheese caked to the wall. The pasta had been used as a weapon the night before, and they needed knives to scrape it off.

Though Paul doubtless liked the drama surrounding his amours, he didn't care to deal with the extra hassles that went with them. A friend offered to call the cops after one of Paul's tricks absconded with his gold jewelry, but Paul declined. "Nah, he deserves it," he said. After dozens of hand-wrapped Christmas presents disappeared from his home, Paul waited two days to call the police, a sign that the thief may have been more than just a burglar. A late-night mugging near his home could just have easily been a bungled pickup for all the cruising Paul did there.

Osborne saw a streak of masochism in Paul's attraction to unsavory men, a bad habit brought on in part by a sense of self-loathing that affected many gay men in those less liberated times, particularly actors living a double life in Hollywood. "Those were the kind of people he liked to hang out with, and if you do that, you're putting yourself in harm's way right there," Osborne says. "You're trying to be in trouble or get beaten up or something like that. You're obviously not looking for somebody that you're going to want to go to a concert with."

Paul may have avoided the opera when dating rough trade, but he showed no qualms mixing them into other areas of his life every now and then. Meeting up with Basil Cross and another college friend one night in Chicago, Paul emerged from his limo with a handsome but hard-edged man. Though Paul introduced his pickup to Cross as one of his writers, the man carried on more like a spoiled date than an employee, periodically butting into the conversation to pester Paul about their dinner plans.

"So, how long has he been your writer?" Cross asked as he and Paul prepared drinks in the kitchen.

"Since about noon yesterday," Paul said.

"Oh. Where'd you sign the contract?"

"In the airport."

Cross maintained a straight face. "Do you change writers very often?"

"I have a whole staff of writers."

Not being choosy, Paul never wanted for dates, but he also didn't want them around for long. Jan Forbes saw several of these beaus come and go over the years, many of whom Paul cast aside because he couldn't tolerate hangers-on. Others beat him to the punch and left when they couldn't tolerate him anymore. "At that time, he was drinking too," Forbes says. "It would just make it too miserable."

Paul's only reliable companionship came from a new dog he bought to replace his basset hounds. He had given away Orville and Wilbur in New York after his psychiatrist told him they were interfering with his private and professional life. With his career back on track, Paul bought a Dandie Dinmont he named Harry MacAfee. The pup would have his own career appearing in dog shows across the country, though only when his owner/handler found time in his increasingly busy work schedule.

For his first project after moving permanently to California, Paul took another stab at prime-time glory. He spent the summer working on a sitcom pilot, this one titled *The Paul Lynde Show*. Screen Gems produced the show in conjunction with Paul's newly formed Hoysyl Productions, named in tribute to his parents.

Paul tossed ideas around with *Birdie* scribe Michael

Stewart. "I wanted to find a character that would let me exploit Paul's unique talents without having to make him a Mr. MacAfee once again," Stewart said. "I also wanted a basic situation that would be readily identifiable yet exotic enough to allow me to be extravagant, larger-than-life, and deal with less ordinary problems than are usually dealt with on most series. And so we have Stanley Werpel....the brother-in-law." Paul would play the cantankerous brother of a famous Hollywood actress, one who sleeps on her living room couch, takes her kids' allowances in poker games, tries to sell the family mutt, and ignores the romantic advances of his sister's secretary.

Bill Asher wanted nothing to do with the scenario, which Stewart then offered to Milton Berle, who also passed. Paul spent time working on ideas with Bob Weiskopf and Bob Schiller, writers for Lucille Ball, but Asher eventually turned again to Sidney Sheldon, who, with producer Bob Finkel, dreamed up another version of Harry MacAfee for Paul to play: Paul Lang, president of the Happy Toy Company. His profession embarrasses his teenage children—surfer son Arthur and boy-crazy Barbara. In turn, their beach lingo and romantic entanglements confound him. "Teenagers are like icebergs," Lang tells his housekeeper, played by Bibi Osterwald. "The only part that's showing are the curlers and telephone wires and rock and roll records. It's what's going on underneath that you have to watch out for."

The show even borrowed Paul's signature rant from *Birdie* about teenagers as its theme song. "I want to make this show so good, it'll be irresistible to anyone who sees it," Paul said. Even though test audiences—which included a group of Brownies—left screenings unimpressed, NBC penciled the show into a Sunday time slot. The network eventually passed on the pilot, but debated whether or not to put Imogene Coca's *Grindl* or *The Bill Dana Show* in the spot. Sheldon Leonard, producer of the Dana vehicle, took another trip to Cincinnati to plead his case in front of the bigwigs at Procter and Gamble. Despite last minute indecision by NBC, Leonard kept his show on the air, though it was the first casualty of the fall ratings war. Rejected again, Paul turned his attention to other shows.

By the mid 1960s the sitcom had become an American religion, and its formulas and clichés required a steady sacrifice of character actors to appease worshippers. Paul's familiar Midwestern wiseacre provided the perfect offering for this prime-time ritual. He did guest stints on popular gems like *The Patty Duke Show, The Jack Benny Show,* and *The Beverly Hillbillies* as well as forgotten trifles such as *Grindl, The Cara Williams Show,* and *Hey, Landlord* (on which he played an egotistical men's hairstylist). Producers of *The Munsters, I Dream of Jeannie,* and *The Farmer's Daughter* asked him back for return engagements.

In these appearances, Paul essentially played variations of the same manic, ineffectual character he perfected in *Bye Bye Birdie*—"a stumbling, bumbling, blustering boob of a guy," in his own words—with an added dimension: overweening smugness. Paul's self-satisfied routine could even brighten the hokey proceedings of "The Singing Mountie," *F Troop's* second season opener. On the trail of fur thief Lucky Pierre, Sgt. Ramsden, the title character played by Paul (never has the Mounties' motto, "We always get our man," rung more true), tries to impress Captain Parmenter, played by Ken Berry:

> RAMSDEN: With my new techniques in criminology, do you realize that I can sift the ashes of a campfire and know exactly how long the fire has been burning, what food the man was eating, and how tall he is?
> PARMENTER: You can tell all that from sifting ashes?
> RAMSDEN: On a good day I can even tell the color of his eyes.

PARMENTER: If you can do all that, how come you've never found Lucky Pierre?
RAMSDEN: I've never found his campfire.
PARMENTER: How do you know he's in the area?
RAMSDEN: I've been following him by the broken-twig method.

"He was playing the same character all the time," humorist Frank DeCaro says, "but you wouldn't want it any other way." Paul thought differently. "They won't let me change the shark grin, the maniacal laugh or the sound of my voice— a flat Midwest twang, a Rotarian right out of Chicago!" he descriptively whined in an interview. Still, character acting put money in the bank, even on shows that went nowhere. Paul earned more money for his guest stint on *Two's Company* than the star of the doomed sitcom pilot, Marlo Thomas, a year away from fame on *That Girl*. (Paul would pop up as a guest star on that show too.)

In 1964, the year NBC passed on *The Paul Lynde Show,* Screen Gems and Bill Asher had better luck at ABC with a pilot titled *Bewitched*. The show became a milestone of TV's high-concept era, which saw an explosion of sitcoms designed "to get audiences laughing at the very idea of a show before they heard the first joke," as Craig Tomasoff put it in *The New York Times*. For a short time, flying nuns, favorite Martians, reincarnated mothers, and mixed-monster families joined other crazy characters in prime time. *Bewitched* was built on a typically paranormal concept: A beautiful witch lives as a suburban housewife with an uptight mortal husband who tries to keep her from performing magic.

Asher's new wife, Elizabeth Montgomery, starred as Samantha Stephens. Dick York played her husband, Darrin, for the first five seasons, Dick Sargent for the final three. Costars included Agnes Moorehead as Samantha's mother,

Endora, and David White as Darrin's slightly amoral boss.

Committed to using Paul any way he could, Asher invited his friend for an appearance on *Bewitched* in the spring of its highly rated first season. (Only *Bonanza* had more viewers that year.) Paul played Harold Harold, Samantha's high-strung driving instructor, in "Driving Is the Only Way to Fly," and his work impressed the entire company. "They were blocking traffic, and a guy repeatedly is honking his horn, and Paul Lynde calls out the window at him, 'Selfish!' " says scriptwriter Richard Baer. "He said it with such disgust and such disdain that it was hysterical. I wouldn't have written it for anybody else, and nobody else would have done it the same, but it was probably my favorite line, and it wasn't even a joke."

The star and her guest hit it off immediately. "I truly enjoyed every minute of it," she told Herbie J Pilato, author of *Bewitched Forever*. "When you're working with someone who is as totally off-the-wall as Paul was, it gives you a lot of freedom creatively. His instincts were fascinating." The actress insisted Paul return. "She wanted to bring him on the show for good," Asher recalls. "And I said, 'Well, let's create a practical-joking uncle.' "

Asher turned to writer Ron Friedman to flesh out Uncle Arthur, a perennial bachelor who meant well but couldn't resist using his magic powers to stir up a little harmless chaos. "The Joker Is a Card," which first aired on October 14, 1965, marked the warlock's first visit to the Stephens household. To the consternation of Endora, Arthur pops in under the lid of a serving dish. "Sorry, I can't get up," he says. "I'm up to my neck in work!" He would make similarly wacky entrances via a television, a painting, a mirror, the toaster, and an ice bucket, armed with similar puns that amused his niece and possibly the viewing audience.

Like the man who played him, Uncle Arthur hated being upstaged. When Darrin lobs a clever jab his way, the warlock comes back with, "Watch it, buster. In a war of wits, you're unarmed." Hearing that Endora is hosting a Halloween shindig, Arthur asks, "When do you want the life of the party to appear?"

> ENDORA: You mean you?
> ARTHUR: Who else?
> ENDORA: How about half past never?
> ARTHUR [*to SAM*]: She's joking. She's not very good at it, but that's what she's doing.

When young Tabitha's friends lukewarmly react to his birthday-party magic tricks, Arthur says, "There's nothing tougher than a matinee audience." Even Samantha takes some heat when she tries to one-up her uncle. After Arthur appears out of nowhere with an adorable poodle for Tabitha, Samantha asks where he got the pet.

> ARTHUR: In a thunderstorm. It was raining cats and dogs!
> SAMANTHA: And you stepped in a poodle!
> ARTHUR: Not bad, Sammy. Been funnier if I'd said it.

On other occasions when Samantha beats her favorite relative to a punch line, Arthur moans, "I wish I'd said that." In a nod to a famous conversation between competitive wits James Whistler and Oscar Wilde, Samantha replies, "You will, Uncle Arthur, you will."

The unmarried, well-tailored Arthur wasn't specifically gay, but, as with so many Paul Lynde roles, he may as well have been. In an episode from season seven called "The House That Uncle Arthur Built"—Paul's last appearance on the show—Arthur can't suppress his practical-joking ways and botches his engagement to the future "Mrs. Uncle Arthur," a beautiful but snobbish witch played by Barbara

Rhodes. "If she knew I were the titan of tricks, the highness of high jinks, the prince of pranks, why, she'd drop me like a hot potato." And drop him she does.

Though Uncle Arthur only appeared ten times over six seasons, the role gave Paul his most lasting sitcom fame. "He made a mark bigger than the number of shows he did," says Richard Michaels, director of over 50 *Bewitched* episodes. Many viewers assume Paul did the show more often because his appearances were such stand-outs, especially as the show grew increasingly stale. The criminally lazy use of the sped-up conveyor-belt gag—this time with chocolate-dipped bananas—in season five's "Sam's Power Failure," would have been interminable without Paul's frenzied deliveries of lines like "Just throw them to me here, honey!" And Paul was probably one of the few actors who could deliver genuine laughs by telling Napoleon Bonaparte, "OK, Emperor, stand up...all the way."

Paul told the press, more than likely just to make good copy, that he didn't want to become a regular cast member because of the show's "curse." Paul's friend Alice Pearce appeared for the first two seasons as nosy neighbor Gladys Kravitz. She passed away in 1966, months before winning an Emmy Award for the role. Marion Lorne, who played the befuddled Aunt Clara, passed away in 1968, ten days before she won an Emmy as well.

Dick Sargent once described Paul as "difficult at times." That was an understatement. On a Screen Gems press junket to Mexico in the spring of 1968, Sandra Gould—the second actress to portray Gladys Kravitz—watched as Paul grew agitated by an unsupervised horror of a little girl making a racket in the aisles. Decks awash on the airline's poison, Paul got up, grabbed the girl by the arm, dragged her over to her mother and said, "You keep this little girl quiet, or I'm gonna fuck her!" Gould never tired of telling the story.

The Ashers—Bill in particular—learned to tolerate Paul's nasty side. "Elizabeth would get mad at him, not very often, but she would," Asher says. "She would get mad when he'd get smart with people in restaurants and things. When we were out to dinner or at parties, he'd get drunk and he'd knock the people that were sitting closest to him. He'd hit them with insulting remarks, and I would have to step in. There were two people that used to do that to me, Desi [Arnaz] and Paul. They'd insult somebody and I'd keep them down for a while, and then finally some jerk would get up and say, 'All right now, let's have it out,' and first thing you know I'm in a fight, and it was awful....He'd pick on the women—you know, what they looked like, and he would just destroy them. It would be done in a good-humored way, but after a while that kind of stuff doesn't go too far."

The Ashers invited Paul to their home for dinner in part to avoid public scenes. Paul joked that he usually let the Ashers talk him into another *Bewitched* guest spot during those blurry nights. They also often convinced him to stay overnight so he wouldn't go home under the influence, knowing all too well that cars and a drunken Paul didn't mix. One night, a police officer pulled Paul over for driving erratically down an L.A. street...and sidewalk. When the officer approached the car with his ticket pad, Paul rolled down the window and bellowed, "I'll have a cheeseburger and fries!" On being told to step out of the car to walk a line, Paul said, "I get out of the car to walk the line, there'd better be a net under it."

This story, without question the most famous of the many anecdotes about Paul, varies with each retelling. Sometimes Paul wants a cheeseburger and a milk shake, sometimes a burger with everything. The endings change too. In their respective autobiographies, Peter Marshall and Rose Marie both report that the amused cop recognized the star and took him home. However, Asher insists he sprang Paul from the tank.

For all he enjoyed himself after-hours, Paul kept his drinking under control when he worked. He didn't want to bungle his fledgling movie career. Lacking movie star looks, Paul could never expect a run like Rock Hudson's. And though Paul blamed Peter Sellers for cornering the market on multiple-role comedies, he probably lacked the necessary acting skills to pull off that brand of shtick. Instead, Paul pursued the fussy sort of roles often played by Tony Randall.

Momentum of a sort seemed to be on Paul's side even before *Birdie* hit theaters in 1963. He joined a bevy of character actors—including William Demarest and Edward Andrews—in cameos for Walt Disney's *Son of Flubber,* the sequel to Fred MacMurray's recent hit *The Absent-minded Professor.* Paul played a smarmy sportscaster who calls the football game in which a player's uniform is inflated with "flubber gas" to gain a competitive edge.

Paul's TV-ready shtick translated perfectly for those sitcoms of the silver screen, the fluffy sex comedies of the 1960s with stars like Doris Day, Jack Lemmon, and Debbie Reynolds. Writer-director David Swift had Paul in mind when he added the role of a henpecked handyman to *Under the Yum Yum Tree,* an adaptation of Lawrence Roman's Broadway comedy. Imogene Coca did the pecking. Jack Lemmon starred as Paul's boss, a Lothario landlord who uses his apartment building as a dating service for himself. Paul loved the laid-back conditions on the set. "I was around the pool constantly—it seemed I never worked," he told Earl Wilson. "In fact, when Imogene and I worked, we had to be introduced to each other over [again]!" Bosley Crowther of *The New York Times* praised Paul and Coca as "killing" in their supporting roles, but Judith Crist of *The New York Herald Tribune* booed the sex comedy as an "offensive blob of smut and suggestiveness on a 110-minute leer." Lemmon himself considered the dud a "real crock."

A year later, in what he considered his favorite film role, Paul displayed a merrier variation on his persona as a chipper cemetery-plot salesman in *Send Me No Flowers,* a Norman Jewison film that marked the last teaming of Rock Hudson and Doris Day. "There's always plenty of sex in their comedies," the director explained, "but it's the cleanest sex invented." Hypochondriac husband Hudson secretly buys a plot for three—himself, his wife, and her future husband. "You want to surprise her?" salesman Paul asks. "Well, this'll give her a real thrill! It makes a very thoughtful gift." Critics gave Paul good notice—praising, among other qualities, his "excellent trouping"—but Crist considered the comedy "another Technicolored puddle of slick." Hudson hated the movie and called his scene with Paul "completely distasteful."

Movie money didn't come much easier for Paul than his quickie parts in the teen beach romps that gained popularity after Hawaii's statehood in 1959 helped spur a surfing craze. Bill Asher directed five of the most successful films of this genre, all for American International Pictures, a "major minor" studio best known for its Vincent Price fright shows and Roger Corman cheapies.

Like Edward Padula, Asher wanted to show teenagers in a good light—with as much of their bodies exposed as possible. "The key to these pictures is lots of flesh but no sex," he explained. "It's all good clean fun. No hearts are broken, and virginity prevails." Asher used a bevy of scantily clad young people: Annette Funicello and Frankie Avalon whenever possible; Harvey Lembeck as the not-so-wild one, Eric von Zipper; and any well-established actor or icon willing to endure the slipshod proceedings.

Asher's formula spawned many imitations, and, in 1964, Paul appeared in one of the few that did well at the box office. Taking its title from Pepsi's ad slogan, *For Those Who Think Young* essentially functioned as a feature-length product placement directed by Leslie Martinson. (Martinson followed this opus with the first big-screen *Batman*.) Paul teamed with comedian Woody Woodbury as the nightclub act "Woodbury and Hoyt." At the time, Woodbury still toured comedy venues, and he did some of his patented shtick for the movie, though he scrubbed it up for younger audiences. Paul offered nothing remotely traceable to his own nightclub career, unless he performed the evergreen "Back to the Farm" somewhere along the way. Bothering to review the picture, *Variety* judged Paul—billed just below romantic leads James Darren and Pamela Tiffin—as the "biggest talent waste."

Asher had higher ambitions for Paul when he coaxed him into doing *Beach Blanket Bingo*, the fourth installment in his beach oeuvre, this one cowritten by Leo Townsend, a screenwriter who had named names during the Communist witch hunts 15 years earlier. Avalon and Funicello starred, backed by youthful Donna Loren, Deborah Walley, and Jody McCrea and seasoned pros Buster Keaton, Don Rickles, and Earl Wilson, who appeared as himself.

Paul portrayed Bullets, the snarky manager of Sugar Kane, a girl singer played by an unknown Linda Evans. The movie wrapped in a matter of weeks in December 1964. Years later, Wilson recalled: "One day when the sun shone to 80 degrees and yet was so shivery that the bikini babes got goose bumps on their other bumps, Paul said, 'I came prepared. I brought both sunglasses and overcoat.'"

Critics hated this sunscreen commercial on a sugar rush. *The New York Times* proclaimed it suitable "for morons," but *Variety* conceded, "What is most pleasant about this frolic is the superb performance of Paul Lynde as the frothy, pushy talent manager whose major ambition is to get 'pearls' for Earl Wilson." Paul called his seventh screen effort his "sea epic" and could only shake his head in bemusement when it achieved cult status in the 1970s.

The closest Paul's film work ever came to presenting him with an acting challenge may have been his drag scene in the 1966 spy spoof *The Glass Bottom Boat.* Doris Day starred in this Frank Tashlin comedy as a tour guide at a rocket research laboratory who gets mistaken for a Soviet agent. Paul played Homer Cripps, a suspicious security guard hell-bent on catching Day in the act. He ends up uncovering Dick Martin and Edward Andrews together in Day's bed, which he acknowledges with a knowing smirk. When he dons an evening gown and bright-red wig to spy on Day in a powder room, Cripps tells his quarry, "I'm very partial to satin. I was married in satin. That is, my first marriage." Soon after, Robert Vaughn, in a walk-on as his Napoleon Solo character from *The Man from U.N.C.L.E.,* gives Paul a once-over.

"My dress cost more than any of Doris Day's," Paul joked to the press. "The day I walked in fully dressed and made up—everybody was just raving—and she came over and looked me up and down and said, 'Oh, I wouldn't wear anything that feminine.'" Privately, Paul told a friend that the director shot Day's close-ups through a Navajo rug.

Paul's career as a film comic petered out by decade's end with a cameo in *How Sweet It Is,* a 1968 comedy from director Jerry Paris starring James Garner and Debbie Reynolds. As a harried cruise-ship purser, Paul tells Europe-bound Reynolds that the C deck, populated by out-of-control teenagers, is anything but romantic:

> On C, there's no "together." C is for cheap, crowded, cramped, crummy. Look, I'm very busy. I have enough trouble trying to keep these boys and girls apart. Why do you want to be together for anyway? You're married.

Though Paul took full advantage of long breaks on the set—an actual cruise ship headed to Acapulco—the film, which one critic called an "aimlessly frisky comedy...[that was] about as sweet as a dill pickle," did nothing for his screen career—or for that of anyone else attached to the production.

Never achieving the level of success he had wanted in movies, Paul decided he should be more selective in accepting cinematic projects. He seemed to sense the changing tides. "The new breed of directors want to be Svengalis," he complained. "They like to create their own stars. They do not want established stars." After nine mediocre movies, Paul wouldn't return to the big screen in anything but animated form for the next ten years. Whenever asked about this dormant part of his career, he had a ready reply: "Why make another bad movie?"

Some of the other roles Paul turned down or lost during the 1960s sound more intriguing than the work he ended up doing. His name cropped up in the industry press as a possible costar on screen with Tony Curtis in *How Now Bow Wow,* Jayne Mansfield in *Playboy,* Jack Lemmon in *Good Neighbor Sam,* and even Rock Hudson in the thriller *Seconds.* He declined a role in Danny Kaye's *The Man From the Diner's Club* and passed on an opportunity to costar in *Myra Breckinridge.* Paul hated Gore Vidal's novel about a Hollywood homosexual who takes revenge on the town's insiders after getting a sex change operation. "It has to be the world's worst," he bitched. "Gore could only have written it for the money." He still considered playing a talent agent in the film, but Mae West accepted the role.

Paul also considered a return to Broadway—this time with better billing—in *Hello, Dolly!,* which was to be directed by Gower Champion, and *Shooting for the Moon,* a musical based on Phil Silvers's Sergeant Bilko character. *Dolly* hit it big; *Moon* never made it into orbit. "I don't see why the part wouldn't work with another comedian if Phil Silvers couldn't do it—say, Sid Caesar, Jackie Gleason, or Ernie Kovacs," insisted producer Ralph Fields when the project was announced. Devoting an entire column to the issue, Brooks Atkinson refused to accept anyone in the role except Silvers. "Even Milton Berle and Jerry Lewis working together could not make one Bilko…. Mr. Silvers, who is Bilko and vice versa, is not to be regarded as an interchangeable buffoon. [The] cheap, scheming, gleaming Bilko is his man. No substitutions allowed." Fortunately, for all involved, plans to bring Bilko to Broadway fizzled.

Of all these might-have-beens, the on-again, off-again life and death of *Sedgewick Hawk-Styles: Prince of Danger* disappointed Paul the most. This "high-concept" pilot, shot in 1965, cast Paul not as a frustrated father or carefree bachelor, but as an egotistical, bumbling criminologist in Victorian England. "If you didn't get Sherlock Holmes, you got me," Paul explained. Asher directed, and Larry Cohen and Bud Freeman drafted a script in which Queen Victoria asks Styles and Dobbs, his Watsonian sidekick, to reclaim the Magna Carta, stolen by Styles's nemesis, Count Bastion.

VICTORIA: Two hours ago, I received this extraordinary note demanding one half million pounds for the return of the Magna Carta.
STYLES: Count Bastion?
VICTORIA: Yes, he says he will destroy that priceless charter unless we meet with his demands.
STYLES: And what do you suggest we do?
VICTORIA: Pay the ransom.
STYLES: Odd he would send you this note, isn't it?
VICTORIA: Well, I am Head of the British Empire.

STYLES: Are you?

DOBBS: Styles! Have you gone daft?

STYLES: Strange you're so eager for Bastion to have that half million.

VICTORIA: I'd give anything to get the Magna Carta back.

STYLES: Would you? [*aside to Dobbs*] Watch this. [*to Victoria*] Would you...Count Bastion! I compliment you on your disguise. [*Victoria screams as Styles tries to rip her hair off.*] My queen! My queen!

DOBBS: That's a good one, Styles.

Paul's supporting cast included Maurice Dallimore as Major Dobbs, Hermione Baddeley as his "medicated" housekeeper, and Tim Stafford as the housekeeper's young nephew. Jane Connell of *New Faces of 1956* ascended to the throne after Alice Ghostley declined the royal role. (Connell would reprise Queen Victoria on an episode of *Bewitched* in March 1967.) The cast felt certain *Sedgewick* would be a hit. "We all thought it was duck soup," Connell says.

ABC made space for the show on the fall schedule announced in early 1966, but replaced it with *The Pruitts of Southampton,* a new series starring Phyllis Diller that several authorities, including *TV Guide,* consider one of the worst shows ever to pollute prime time. Paul popped up on an episode of the show in January, just before it was renamed *The Phyllis Diller Show,* to play Harvey, Diller's ne'er-do-well brother.

Paul blamed the axing of his show on others. "It was killed by the nuts running the network," he said later. The reason: a power struggle between head of programming Edgar Scherick, who liked it, and executive head Tom Moore, who pulled the plug after Scherick quit that March. *Variety,* on the other hand, reported that the sponsor of the time slot preferred Phyllis over Paul. Asher has the simplest explanation for why *Sedgewick* never made it to air: the young man who fell out of Paul's hotel window in San Francisco.

James Binger Davidson, a native of Hastings, Nebraska, had quit college to pursue an acting career in Hollywood. He joined the Screen Actors Guild in May 1963 and, under the name Bing Davidson, snagged small, uncredited parts in a Jimmy Stewart film called *Take Her, She's Mine* and the Doris Day comedy *Move Over, Darling.* Four months before his trip with Paul, he changed his professional name to J.B. Davidson, with no upswing in his career. He supported himself by working for an encyclopedia company and at a bar.

Jim McLernan planned to introduce his friend Davidson to Paul, but the fast operator never gave him the chance. "Jim was a friend of mine that I told Paul about," he says. "Jimmy was working as a bartender down at some bar on Wilshire, and Paul had gotten a glimpse of him coming into my apartment one night. And doesn't Paul go down there and meet him on his own. He told him he was a friend of mine and so forth, and of course Jimmy was very flattered.... He liked Paul."

On July 17, 1965, a day after Paul finished taping his first episode as Uncle Arthur on *Bewitched,* the twosome traveled to the City by the Bay. Their Saturday-night club crawl included a stop at the Gilded Cage to watch Charles Pierce perform his famous drag act. Paul returned to their eighth-floor room at the Sir Francis Drake Hotel around 2:30 A.M. Davidson showed up 15 minutes later, creating "a bit of a scene" in the lobby, according to a hotel security officer who had to escort him upstairs.

When the officer left, Davidson told Paul to watch him perform a trick. He opened the window and climbed out to hang from the ledge by his fingers. Police officer Richard Fenlason, patrolling outside, saw him dangling and radioed the fire department while his partner, Charles Warren, ran to the room. After holding on a few minutes, Davidson began to slip. Paul clutched his wrist and told him to grab hold of his neck, but Davidson fell 80 feet to his death. The deputy coroner listed the cause of death as "attempting a practical joke while drinking."

Paul described the aftermath of the devastating accident as the worst time of his life. "I know it looked strange," he later told a magazine. "He was younger than I was. He was good-looking, and why was he there with me? Why did he jump?—no, he didn't jump—why did he fall?" The officers who witnessed the fall assured Paul he would be all right. "They were up in that room in a matter of seconds after he jumped," Paul explained. "They said, 'Don't worry. Paul, we saw it all. We're not going to let them wipe you out with this.'"

The wire services and a few papers, including *The New York Times* and the *Mount Vernon News*, covered the incident, but Paul's low-grade celebrity prevented a high-grade scandal. He maintained that Davidson's parents absolved him of any responsibility in "the kindest, most beautiful letter." Still, given the funnyman's temper when steeped in liquor, cynics can't resist speculating on what really happened that night. "You could imagine Paul going, 'Watch out for that first step!'" Frank DeCaro says. "You could totally see him doing that."

Davidson's death may or may not have sunk the pilot deal—Sedgewick was announced in *Variety* a month after the accident—but that didn't matter. CBS picked the project up almost as soon as ABC dropped it. Assuming he had a season's worth of shows to produce, Asher started working on new scripts. Then a bigwig at the network called. "We've decided not to go with it," said the executive.

"Why? Any reason?"

"Well, we've decided it's not for us."

"No, don't give me that shit! It's because of the homo-sexuality."

"Well, that too."

CBS compensated everyone handsomely for the rejection. "I got paid more for that show than anything," Asher says. But Paul never stopped brooding about the show's demise. "I cannot tell you how much I loved that show," Paul once said. "People have prints of the pilot in their private collections. They'll say, 'I ran it last night, and everybody just died laugh-ing.' Well, of course, tears come to my eyes and I say, 'I don't want to hear about it....' It's my fondest hope that someday somebody will blow off the dust and get it on the air. I like to think *Sedgewick* is not dead."

Though leery, Paul played the pilot game yet again the following season with *Manley and the Mob,* an "explosive new series" that Fred De Cordova produced and directed for Four Star Television. (De Cordova, an NU alum and Phi Kap, would end his lengthy career, which included directing *Bedtime for Bonzo,* as the executive producer of *The Tonight Show.*) Gerald Gardner and Dee Caruso, writers for *The Monkees* and *Get Smart,* dreamed up the premise: "In the great tradition of Sam Spade, Philip Marlowe, and Harper: Manley Tombs, the coolest private eye in the history of detection."

The supporting cast included Hope Holiday as Tombs's secretary, Nehemiah Persoff as mobster Corbo, and John Barbour as Woodrow, one of Corbo's dumb henchman. The publicity department pretended Manley's "never-ending bat-tle with the city's notorious Mob [was] given bold dimension by the Bogart-like performance of Paul Lynde." Paul himself dismissed it as "an incredible rehash of *Get Smart.* It didn't sell, and I was not unhappy."

Another promising project for Paul fizzled that year as well. In August, he started work on *Silent Treatment,* an independent film billed as the first silent feature since Chaplin's *Modern Times*. Ralph Andrews, a game show producer, came up with the idea and took it to Frank Worth, a well-known celebrity photographer. Worth put up the money for the production from his stock in a camera invention and asked Andrews to direct it.

Paul earned a rare starring credit as an executive at the Bobble, Bangle, and Bead advertising agency who wants to promote the Din-Din Credit Card Club. For publicity, a file clerk, played by Sherry Jackson, suggests they find someone with no money to use a card. Beach bum Marty Ingels fits the bill, but overextends his credit—and taxes Paul's patience—by purchasing items like a $27 million navy destroyer.

Worth and Andrews worked their Hollywood connections to coax countless stars into cameo roles: Nick Adams, Cliff Arquette, Gene Autry, Godfrey Cambridge, Jackie Coogan, Wally Cox, Richard Deacon, Phyllis Diller—as a lady of the evening employed by Never on Sunday, Inc.—Jerry Lewis, Rowan and Martin, George Raft, Barry Sullivan, Rudy Vallee, and Doodles Weaver. "The great thing about the film is the fun all these stars had making it," Worth explained. "They put everything they had into it—things the script didn't even require. It's unbelievably funny."

Andrews shot the movie in 21 days on location in Los Angeles and Las Vegas, then took out a full-page ad in *The Hollywood Reporter* to offer "a loud thank-you to my silent cast—Marty Ingels, Paul Lynde [and] Sherry Jackson." Excited about a project that gave "new life to my career," Ingels told reporters, "I guess I should have been born 30 years earlier."

Presaging Mel Brooks's *Silent Movie* by a decade, *Silent Treatment* was supposed to usher in a wave of silent-screen activity that included similar projects planned by David Swift and Frank Tashlin. Those films never got made. "Good comedy should be seen and not heard," Andrews said at the time, but for reasons that remain unclear—even to Ingels—the movie has never been released. "I don't think I've even seen it," he says.

Despite these setbacks, Paul still enjoyed his slim share of celebrity. At noon on a Friday in late 1967, Forbes picked up her college friend from the Pittsburgh airport. He had arrived for her daughter's wedding the next day. Around 3 o'clock that afternoon, Paul asked, "What time's the rehearsal?"

"Well, at 5 o'clock, but the church is only two blocks away. It only takes me two minutes to get ready."

"But you're not famous," hissed Paul.

CHAPTER 7

ALL IN THE HOLLYWOOD SQUARES

"Those contestants, they don't care if Paul Lynde makes you laugh. They want a refrigerator."

Paul stood on a beach next to Rick Nelson, the pop idol son of Ozzie and Harriet. The time was the summer of 1967, the show was *Malibu U,* and the banter was more suggestive than viewers may have expected.

RICK: Paul, I'm glad you could be our guest lecturer this week.
PAUL: Yes, you should be, Ozzie...This isn't Malibu U, it's Haight Ashbury South!
RICK: We're just a bunch of clean-cut, wholesome young people running around having a good time at the beach.
PAUL [*arms crossed*]: That's what they said about the Red Guard.
RICK: Come on, everybody! Let's show Paul Lynde what fun is, Malibu U style! [*The kids roll up Paul's pants and carry him to the water for a quick frolic. Paul returns.*]
PAUL: You know, I have to admit, that was fun. I think I'll go hang 11.
RICK: No, Paul, I think the correct expression is "hang ten."
PAUL: Look, you got your problems, Ozzie; I got mine.

Whether or not the writers intended this peculiar joke as innuendo, Paul's winking delivery certainly made it sound so. Times were growing more permissive, and television comics like the Smothers Brothers and Rowan and Martin began pushing limits—and the buttons of nervous network censors. Paul played his part in this expansion of America's comedic taste—or lack thereof—on one of the least likely platforms for barrier breaking: a daytime game show.

In creating *Hollywood Squares,* producers Merrill Heatter and Bob Quigley took the format of their *Celebrity Game* to the next level of silliness by arranging nine stars on a vertical tic-tac-toe set. Contestants had to get three squares in a row by guessing whether or not a celebrity answered a question correctly. The rules of the game, which host Peter Marshall announced with tongue-twisting speed at the beginning of each show, hardly mattered to anyone but the contestants. "Most of them would ask Hitler a question if it meant winning a couple of hundred bucks," Marshall once joked. People watched to see laid-back stars crack wise, not to find out who took home a fur by Dicker and Dicker of Beverly Hills.

"It was a comedy show with great names, and you'd get to see people a little bit off-guard," says Jay Redack, a writer for the show who eventually became one of its producers. "You'd get to see somebody who plays a big doctor on television and realize they know nothing about medicine. That was always the fun part about the show…. It was terrific seeing people not plugging a movie or a book, just having fun."

The show had been on NBC's morning schedule only a week in October 1966 when Paul made his first appearance as a guest. *Variety* praised Paul's "quick wit" and gave a nod to regulars Wally Cox, who continued the nebbish role he had created on *Mr. Peepers,* and Cliff Arquette, who appeared as his bumpkin alter ego, Charley Weaver. The trade paper overlooked the other regulars—Morey Amsterdam, Abby Dalton, and Rose Marie—and guests Eartha Kitt, Michael Landon, and Gisele MacKenzie.

Les Roberts, producer of the show for its first three years, offered Paul his initial guest stint after Jackie Mason refused to return for a second day of taping. During a frantic midnight phone call, with taping only hours away, Roberts's talent coordinator gave him a choice of three comics who could fill the empty square on short notice: London Lee, Charlie Callas, or Paul Lynde. "Boy, did I make the right choice," says Roberts.

Paul appeared on *Squares* occasionally over the next two years and a number of times on a short-lived nighttime edition that aired weekly on NBC in 1968. The producers asked Paul to take a permanent seat on the daytime version that fall simply because, as Roberts puts it, "he was just so damned funny."

Game shows, like infomercials and *The Love Boat* of later years, gave underemployed celebrities the chance to make some easy green while keeping their mugs in the public eye. Paul appeared on one of his first game shows, *Freedom Rings,* while still playing in *New Faces of 1952.* Beginning in the 1960s, he trolled the game show circuit seemingly nonstop. "You can get him coming out of your faucet," quipped comic Jack Carter.

The usually unscripted gigs on such shows as *Everybody's Talking, How's Your Mother-in-Law?, You Don't Say,* and *Funny You Should Ask* gave audiences a rare glimpse of the real Paul Lynde, who was much funnier than any of his characters. Rosalind Russell, herself no slouch in the wit department, thought Paul deserved his own show on the strength of his comebacks on *The Celebrity Game.* When he appeared on *The Dating Game,* dressed in a pink jacket and bright-red foulard, a contestant asked him: "I've just given you bachelor number two. What are you going to do with him?" With no hesitation, Paul shouted, "Go dancing!"

The jokes didn't stop off-camera, even when Paul was the punch line. An earthquake hit the L.A. area during a taping of *You Don't Say* and people scrambled out of the studio. Paul struggled to unhook an uncooperative lavaliere microphone. When he made it to safety in the hall, his partner for the day told him she had noticed his plight on her way out the door.

"Well, why didn't you help me?" Paul asked.

"Before the show, we were told not to touch the stars," she explained.

At the peak of its popularity, *Hollywood Squares* attracted celebrities from all walks of fame: NBC prime-time stars Redd Foxx and Freddie Prinze, not-so-desperate actors George C. Scott and Helen Hayes, aged screen legends Ginger Rogers and Gloria Swanson (who looked baffled during a cast photo shoot with a show-sponsored race car), up-and-comers David Letterman and Steve Martin, and even cartoons made flesh, such as Big Bird and Charo. "Although we never got big movie stars like Newman or Redford or Eastwood," Roberts admits, "we had Burt Reynolds, Raymond Burr, Glenn Ford, and virtually every top comic except Red Skelton and Johnny Carson."

With so much talent to showcase, the producers gave a lot of thought to who sat where. Before Paul came along, they considered the corners the hottest real estate on the board, reserving two of them for Arquette and Cox, and treated the middle box as just another seat. "We didn't realize early on that the center square was the star of the show," says Redack. A rotating list of guest talent sat there, including Ernest Borgnine—the first occupant—Glenn Ford, Fred Gwynne, Buddy Hackett, and Vincent Price. Whenever Paul appeared as a guest, he sat wherever the producers placed him, but once he became a regular he made the neglected middle space his chaotic throne.

Frequent guest Nanette Fabray summed up the "natural bents" of the show's regulars in a 1971 interview: "I'm a red-headed Billie Burke; Rose Marie plays the man-hunting bachelor girl; Bill Bixby is hip and knowledgeable." Fabray's interviewer finished off the description of the lineup: "Charley Weaver, Wally Cox, and Paul Lynde are, well, Charley Weaver, Wally Cox, and Paul Lynde."

Paul played the outrageous bachelor who seemed to hate everything except his own snide comebacks:

> In preparing chicken à la king or chicken Kiev, what is the first thing you should do to the chicken?
> *Tiptoe behind it with a hammer.*
>
> According to *New Woman* magazine, are most children happy? *Oh, I hope not.*
>
> True or false? Eating carrots can turn your skin orange.
> *Well, she should take it easy on the coffee.*
>
> Were cigar store "wooden Indians" ever women?
> *Only those made by a nervous whittler.*
>
> Is the Egyptian sphinx male or female?
> *You can't tell—it's buried in the sand.*

Paul's persona clicked with viewers and ratings noticeably dipped when he took a week off. He soon became the star of the show, receiving more mail than any other cast member, including Marshall. He also drew the devotion of some famous fans. Greta Garbo, who hadn't laughed since *Ninotchka*, sent a fan letter to "La Belle," as she called him.

Former First Daughter Margaret Truman told Marshall that her father, the ex-president, planned his famous walks around the show because he liked Paul so much. Acting legends Alfred Lunt and Lynn Fontanne quoted zingers back to Paul when they met him in Maggie Smith's dressing room after a show in London. Even celebrities of a younger generation, like Elton John and Alice Cooper, considered themselves hip to the Square.

Other stars could have done without Paul's comebacks on *Squares*:

> According to *Women's Wear Daily,* Dorothy Lamour was famous for her sarongs, Katherine Hepburn for her trousers, and Lana Turner for skintight sweaters. What was Joan Crawford famous for? *Six weeks.*

> What does Liberace's family call him? *The bad seed.*

> Cher says that when she's 80, hers will be down to her hips. Her what? *Her halter tops.*

> John Wayne has a size-18. A size-18 what? *Pinafore.*

> Liz Taylor refers to it as "the fat one." What is it? *They both look the same to me!* (Taylor drew several cheap shots from comedians in those days, but Paul's jokes may have bugged her more than most. She reportedly threw a party when he died.)

Despite his popularity, some viewers questioned Paul's authenticity. A housewife from Paterson, New Jersey, raised doubts about Paul's wit when she wrote to Steve H. Scheuer's answer column for the TV Key Service:

I watch *Hollywood Squares* each day...in fact, it's the only time I turn on the TV during the day when the hubby is at work and the kids are at school. I can't get over Paul Lynde and his glib answers...he's easily one of the funniest ad-libbers of all time. Now, my neighbor, also a *Hollywood Squares* devotee, tells me that Paul Lynde has writers prepare his ad-libs.

"Your neighbor is wrong," Scheuer responded. "Paul Lynde is a fast wit and his *Hollywood Squares* ad-libs are his own."

Scheuer's reporting skills left something to be desired. Paul rarely uttered a word on the show that wasn't provided to him by a staff of writers who took pains to tailor jokes to his uniquely bitchy delivery. "We would have long meetings several times a week just working on 'stuff for Paul,'" Roberts says. "It was a toss-up as to which of us could best reproduce his marvelous delivery when we were testing a one-liner amongst ourselves."

Lloyd Garver, a *Squares* scribe who fashioned contestant questions from checkout-line literature and considered women's magazines his "bibles," wrote many of Paul's setups. "Obviously, for Paul the area of interest wasn't as important as the way the question/straight line could be worded," he says. "We found a fact, then we worded the question in a way that would lead to an answer that we knew was right up Paul's alley and that he would deliver for a big laugh. Racy, raunchy, double entendres, silly short answers, snippy put-downs, and outrageous replies were all within his repertoire."

Affectionately described by George Gobel as "flaky as a mud fence," Redack shared Paul's sense of humor and ran lines with him before every show. "Sometimes I'd give him the inflection to help him sell the joke, and he'd write that down and finally go out and deliver the thing," he says. "It was the most unusual type of comedy there is, perhaps, because in a movie you have a script, on television you have the punch lines and sit around the table and rehearse it. On *Squares* [Paul responded] blindly, accepting the fact that if I say this, they're going to laugh."

The center square sometimes cracked himself up. "Paul would often laugh at his own answers, never realizing until that moment what it was that made them funny," Roberts says. "He trusted us implicitly. I don't think he ever balked at a joke he was given—and in turn we trusted him to give our work its best delivery." The writers learned that zingers no longer than five or six words usually worked best for him. If a joke bombed, Paul could always get laughs by feigning anger at himself and the audience. "Let's see what you would say," he would sneer. Other times he would yell down from his perch, "Jay...we need to talk!"

The producers trusted some of the Squares to wing it on their own, while they didn't expect any humor out of others. "It was a straight game show," Marshall recently explained. "We would give Paul a couple of jokes. Wally Cox was never briefed.... Mel Brooks was never briefed.... We'd give Cliff Arquette some jokes. We'd give [George] Gobel some jokes, and maybe if Vincent Price came on or Joan Rivers—a couple of jokes...Rose Marie, maybe. But everybody else played it straight."

With the quiz show scandals of the late 1950s still a recent memory, the Federal Communications Commission insisted the show run a disclaimer during the credits, a piece of blink-and-you'll-miss-it small print: "The areas of question designed for the celebrities and possible bluff answers are discussed with some celebrities in advance. In the course of their briefing, actual questions and/or answers may be discerned by the celebrities." Rival game show producer Mark Goodson translated: "Comedian material originates somewhere other than in the celebrities' heads."

The producers provided the stars with bluff answers "so they wouldn't look stupid," says Roberts. "For instance, if the answer was an early president, we wanted to make sure no one said JFK." Beyond these hints, the producers never provided the actual answers—they wanted to manufacture spontaneity by keeping everyone partly in the dark. Worried about looking stupid, Paul kept up on current events by reading *TV Guide, Time,* and the L.A. papers, especially after his sister Grace told him he came across as less than knowledgeable on the show.

Well aware that many of these scripted jokes would have sounded stale in anyone else's mouth but his, Paul claimed them as his own off-the-cuffs. "The writers write those questions, but not my answers," he once asserted. "The wit is mine." To this day, some of Paul's friends still believe he created every side-splitter on the spot.

Perpetuating this myth landed Paul in occasional trouble. An easy gig dedicating the new high school in Mount Vernon in 1970 turned into a nightmare when Paul learned the organizers expected him to be funny for 30 minutes without a script. He talked them into a brief speech and an autograph session instead.

Even on *Hollywood Squares,* Paul wasn't always safe— too many turns could exhaust his material. Phyllis Diller, who had discussed performance anxiety with Paul in the past, knew well the look of fear in her friend's eyes when she sat next to him during a taping one night. "He ran out of answers because they called on him so many times that he used them all up," she says. "He was terrified because he wasn't going to sound like Paul Lynde. Well, the show goes on. He mumbled something."

Decimating a fellow actor at a party was one thing, improvising jokes acceptable to the TV-viewing public and TV-programming executives was another. When Paul did work up the nerve to wing it, his wit rarely let him down. Partnered with the hairy costar of *Me and the Chimp* as an Emmy presenter in 1972, Paul left the audience roaring when he chastised his simian friend, "You forgot to use your Feminique." Afterwards, he humbly proclaimed the gag "the saving grace of the most dreary evening ever on television." Robert Berkvist of *The New York Times* disagreed. "If the hysteria that greeted Lynde's gag was an index to the creative sensibility of the talent assembled at the Hollywood Palladium that night, the nation's viewers are in for bleak times."

On the game show, Marshall once asked, "True or false? Over the recent holidays, our own Rose Marie entertained on a cruise ship." As planned, Paul answered, "Entertainment? Not according to the reviews." He got more howls by adding, "She thought it was a troop ship," then, after signs of indignation from Rose Marie, he topped off the moment with "I should have said 'a tramp steamer.'"

Hollywood Squares taped a week's worth of episodes in one evening. After spirits flowed during the dinner break, things usually got racier both on-camera and off. "[We were always] kidding with one another, especially at dinner," Rose Marie says. "Everybody would have stories to tell and different things that had happened to one another, things like that. It was a big family."

Paul felt genuine affection for some of his coworkers, including good sport Rose Marie, to whom he once sent two dozen roses on her birthday, which was the least he could do after poking fun at her age. (True or false? People tend to start shrinking a little after about age 30. *Did you know that Rose Marie is standing up in her cubicle?*). The death of Wally Cox hit him particularly hard. "Wally was the original flower child, a very enchanted person in this disenchanted business," Paul said the day Cox died in 1973. The two had both stayed at the Park Savoy 25 years earlier and had worked together on other TV shows over the years. According to Jim Backus, they enjoyed other activities together as well. "They would go across the street from the studio to a bar and both would come back loaded," he said. "I don't think viewers ever realized that they were blind drunk, but they'd do the show absolutely loaded."

Some viewers caught on. Columnist Earl Wilson once asked Paul to respond to a reader who wondered, "Weren't some of the Hollywood Squares a little high on a couple of recent programs?" Paul fessed up that "We were a little overtrained on some vin rosé from San Jose." After dipping his beak, Paul joshed around with most of the Squares. He forged an unlikely friendship with the upstanding Lennon Sisters, who were often paired in twos on both sides of Paul's seat when they did the show. Just before the end of a commercial break, Paul would antagonize Peg Lennon with distracting reminders of the foods she most missed on her diet. "Chocolate cake," he would whisper menacingly. Another good friend, Karen Valentine, who appeared as a semiregular, had to be moved to another level on the board because some viewers thought the two chatterboxes gave each other answers.

Paul also harassed contestants during breaks with snipes about their performance ("I got you on that one, didn't I?") and even their appearance. "He just wouldn't like the way someone would dress, or he wouldn't like their demeanor and so he would just get on their case," Marshall says. "I would say, 'Will you leave them alone, Paul? Just ignore him.'"

Sometimes after taping, a group of Squares carried the convivial mood of the set into the early morning. On a lark, Paul joined Marshall, Rose Marie, Nanette Fabray, Lily Tomlin, and Wally Cox on a visit to a trendy topless bar. Paul bristled at the nude dancers and stag films all around him. "Can you believe it?" he shuddered. "That's disgusting!" Boredom set in quickly, and the gang left in search of food. Minutes later, police raided the bar and threw everyone in jail. "I was so upset because we weren't amongst them," Marshall says. "It would have been so much fun: Paul Lynde caught in a topless bar, and Lily and Rose Marie, who's very proper...and we just missed it." (On another nightclub outing, an excited drunk approached Paul. "Are you...are you Paul Lynde?" he said. Paul assured him that he was. "Please don't leave," the man pleaded. "I want to get my wife. She just hates you!")

Though Paul rarely brought beaus to the set, his coworkers caught occasional glimpses of his chaotic dating life. In the spring of 1971, British Columbia tourism officials invited Marshall and some of the regulars on a junket to Vancouver and Victoria as a thank you for promoting the vacation destination on the show. Paul hesitated.

"I don't want to go. Who could I take?" he bleated.

"Take anybody you want to take! We're family, for God's sake," Marshall said.

Paul showed up at the airport in a hat that made him look like Greta Garbo, with a young blond ski instructor in tow. He seemed to enjoy himself, but Marshall eventually found him moping at the hotel bar.

"What's wrong?" Marshall asked.

"Oh, the son of a bitch!" Paul said. "It's not working out at all."

"What's happened?"

"When I met him, I said, 'Would you like to go to British Columbia?' He says, 'I'd love to. I've never been there.' Then I find out he's been up here twice with George Cukor!"

The writers of Paul's comebacks, which grew saucier over time, flirted with his queerness but stayed mindful not to overdo it. "We could get away with a lot with Paul, and we tried to balance it nicely," Redack says. "He was never outwardly gay...but because of what he did, so terrifically, it broadened his appeal. We did butch jokes. We'd do a sports thing: he'd say, 'By day I'm a lumberjack,' which was just great. He could do a gay joke, a straight joke, and he could do something that had nothing to do with preferences at all. It was because his timing was impeccable, with his little winks and expressions, and he was magnificent."

According to Amy Vanderbilt, is a 19-year-old too young to wear mink? *If he's old enough to be drafted, he's old enough to wear mink.*

Is the electricity in your house AC or DC? *In my house it's both.*

In a recent column, Billy Graham said he would like to urge young people to reserve sex for the only place it belongs. Where is that? *A state prison.*

According to author Desmond Morris, do chimpanzees kiss the way humans do? [*With a wink*] *Better.*

According to the old song, what's breaking up the old gang of mine? *Anita Bryant.*

True or false? Bob Hope and Jackie Gleason were recently seen in Central Park dressed as women. [Nervously] *Was anyone else identified?*

Used to the silly styles adopted by character actors, most viewers probably considered Paul's persona nothing more than a sissy act. "You know, he had that Buddy Hackett kind of lisp...He always dressed in these silk shirts, and the nice little jackets and whatnot," Redack says. "A lot of people knew he was gay, of course, and other people just thought it was kind of a put-on." Producer Sandy Gallin, who worked with Paul on many projects, believes most people just considered Paul "quirky" and left it at that.

Paul relished teasing the audience as he purred and preened with an ambiguity he mastered in the much stuffier closet of the 1950s and early 1960s. Even when his coy nudges felt more like elbows in the ribs, straight America grew none the wiser about his sexuality.

Queer kids wise to Paul's winking got a taste of gay culture beyond Judy Garland records and the animated adventures of Johnny Quest's dad. Frank DeCaro counts himself among Paul's disciples. As a teenager, he tried out for a role in his high school production of *Bye Bye Birdie* for one simple reason. "I wanted the part of the father, Harry MacAfee, more than anything, because Paul Lynde, whom I always idolized, played him on Broadway," he writes in his memoir *A Boy Named Phyllis*. "Like a lot of gay boys, I had been doing a drop-dead Paul Lynde impression since I'd first seen him as Uncle Arthur on *Bewitched* and Dr. Dudley on *The Munsters*. 'That's disgusting' was my catchall catchphrase for years."

To suburban housewives and adolescent girls, the center square came off as a sex symbol of sorts. "[I choose] the funniest and one of the best-looking men in the world, Paul Lynde," a contestant once gushed when picking Paul during a game. The star lapped it up. "He was a great big handsome, good-looking guy, terribly bright and very funny," Diller says. "I don't think it ever occurred to [the public that he was gay]." Readers of the *Los Angeles Times* listed Paul as one of a handful of celebrities they wanted to see as a nude centerfold back when Burt Reynolds's assets in *Cosmopolitan* made the issue a hot topic.

Paul's appeal proved that TV audiences could appreciate a gay man as long as they knew didn't have to hear about his private life, says DeCaro. "If you use double entendre and suggestion, the people who get it, get it, and the people who don't get it don't get offended...because they don't get it," he says. "[Paul] was a bitter, jaded queen kind of character. That's really always appealing, as long as you don't say, 'I'm a homosexual.' People love a jaded queen as long as they don't talk about being gay." Paul may not have broken down any barriers of intolerance, but by exposing his viewers to gay humor every day, he at least got them laughing with a homosexual instead of at one—a small step towards greater acceptance but a step nonetheless.

Even given all these reasons, it still remains a mystery why America was taken with a cupcake firing lavender salvos at them every day for years. One answer may be that the program's format limited Paul's actual camera time to a few minutes each episode. Any more of Paul's anticharm might have been overkill. For this reason, much as Paul would have hated to admit it, he and *Hollywood Squares* were made for each other. "*Squares* was the perfect venue for Paul, because you were in and out, in and out," Marshall says. "He could have done a half hour show for me every day and I would have seen it. But the general public, I don't know if they could have taken a half hour every week."

Previous page: Lynde on stage in a Kenley Players production of *Stop, Thief, Stop* (1975). This page, from top: In his Boy Scout uniform ("I looked like Kate Smith's niece!"); the Lynde children (including baby Paul) circa 1927; with Reginald Gardiner in *Visit to a Small Planet* (1957).

Photo courtesy Bucks County Playhouse, New Hope, Pa.

Clockwise from above: Lynde's comedy album, *Recently Released* (1960); one of his last publicity shots (1980); Lynde and Charlotte Rae in a Waa-Mu production at Northwestern (1947); *The Waa-Mu Washingtons*, 1948 (Charlotte Rae and Lynde play parents to John M. Rusch's George Washington).

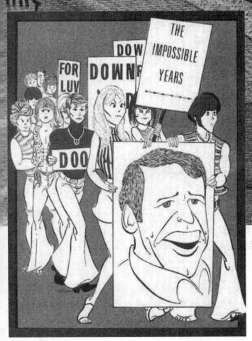

From top: The biggest star of the Waa-Mu Stage (circa 1947); Lynde poolside (1969); flier for the Kenley Players production of *The Impossible Years* (1969).

CHAPTER 8

JUDY GARLAND TIME

"I love to perform. When the telephone rings, I don't say, 'Hello.' I say, 'Yes, I'll do it.'"

On any given summer day throughout much of the 1970s, Paul might wake up from a bender in an Ohio hotel and decide he needed John Kenley's help. The Midwestern theater impresario, who employed Paul for his summer stage productions, had a license to dispense pharmaceuticals. Kenley only administered his star's desired stimulant on one condition, to which Paul reluctantly agreed. When Paul dropped his pants and bent over, he had to recite zingers from *Hollywood Squares*. His amused boss would then inject a reviving shot of vitamin B12 into Paul's bare ass.

Regional theater, hotel hangovers, B12 pick-me-ups, compromising positions with an older man. It sounds like the penultimate act of a VH1 bio-documentary, but the truth was not so tawdry. Despite his hectic schedule, Paul saw the summer stage (or "amateur night in Dixie," as Betty Hutton once described it) as a boon. He didn't need to work in Ohio, but only a fool passed up the pay—and public admiration—offered during a seasonal sojourn on the straw-hat trail. That he received star billing after years as a second banana only sweetened the deal.

For much of the 1960s, Paul kept busy as one of most popular comics-for-hire on TV. After leaving the Como show, he showed up on an occasional *Ed Sullivan* here, an *Andy Williams* there, even an appearance on Jack Paar's program when the host aired the first footage of the Beatles in American prime time. Variety show producers quickly recognized Paul's ability to milk laughs from the most mundane material. Mel Brooks, Carl Reiner, and a critic or two agreed that Paul could get laughs reading a phone book, tornado alert, or seed catalog. In some cases, these sources would have been preferable to the dismal lines Paul sometimes delivered as a prime-time comedy temp.

Paul's well-defined persona and honed delivery made the writer's job that much easier. "We used to go to lunch with him, and it was like the Pied Piper. People would want to follow him down the street," says Sam Bobrick, a writer for the *Kraft Music Hall,* a Como-less weekly series on NBC in the late 1960s. "He had a certain magnetism and a certain attitude, and it was fun to be around him. If a comic has such a definite personality, it always gives you something to write with. It's not like you have to create anything. It's there, so you know what he can do or can't do."

By the decade's end, the in-demand guest star bragged that he clocked upwards of 200 hours of airtime each season. Though the boast may have been nothing more than Hollywood hubris, he appeared frequently on variety shows starring Steve Allen, Bob Hope, Alan King, Jerry Lewis, Dean Martin, and Jonathan Winters, among others.

Paul approached these comedy assignments with his usual trepidation. On an appearance on ABC's *Hollywood Palace* in October 1965, he teamed with actress Carmen

Phillips. "We were friends for years but he never would work with me," Phillips recalled. "The interesting thing was right before we were to go on I was having my usual cigarette and coffee—and he was a nervous wreck, saying, 'How can you be so calm?' That's when I realized he was nervous. The job made him nervous."

A perfectionist, Paul often found his nerves frayed when working with old pros like Hope and Martin who didn't believe in extensive rehearsals. "It doesn't make you feel too secure when Dean walks up to you just before a sketch dressed like Moses and asks, 'What is this for?' And you're not exactly at ease rehearsing with a dancer all week and then thrown into a sketch with Dean at showtime. I need more security than that."

Paul preferred working with Jonathan Winters, who hosted a variety show on CBS for two seasons in the late 1960s. He often named Winters as one of his favorite comedians, and Winters apparently returned the compliment, at least according to a dog-eared newspaper clipping Paul carried in his wallet for years. Today, the celebrated comic declines to speak about Paul, citing an unpleasant "episode" between the two of them.

By and large though, Paul saw variety shows as an often annoying means to an end. "It isn't just a line here or there," Paul said. "It's whole sketches, such as one of those things on the *Dean Martin Show* where you say to yourself, 'If you're going to take the money, you'd better do it.'" On one episode of Glen Campbell's CBS show, Paul starts a scene talking on the telephone: "Ace's Animal Acts...You want a tap dancing hippo? How about three of them?...Well, they're brothers, and I'd hate to break up the act." Campbell enters holding an underrehearsed duck whose antics upstage them both.

Paul still managed to press a few diamonds out of these dreary comedy coal mines, especially in skits that played the limp wrist for laughs. As an interior decorator on an episode of Martin's show in late 1969, Paul sang a frenzied rendition of "Think Pink" from the Fred Astaire film *Funny Face*. On the *Music Hall* a few weeks later, he appeared in drag as a runaway wife who returns home to husband Alan King. For another episode on that show, Paul stood inside a telephone booth, dressed in a tuxedo, with a cape and bolero hat:

> Hello, *Daily Gazette*? This is Boyd Blowhorn, the food editor. Put me through to my secretary, please.... Hello, Ronald? Listen, I'm reviewing that new French restaurant tonight, but I forgot the exact address. Would you look it up for me? Thanks, Ron—Ronald, hold it! I see the sign from her: La Chance—right under my nose. What a goose I am!

Paul's reputation as a popular comic-for-hire, not to mention his willingness to put up with shoddy material, paid off in 1968 when he accepted a regular spot on *Dean Martin Presents the Golddiggers*. Shecky Greene had originally signed up for the comedic duties on this ten-week summer replacement series, and when he bailed days before the first rehearsal, Paul came to the rescue—for his usual fee. "They didn't have to rewrite any of those first shows," he said. "After all, [Greene's] a good comedy-actor too. It just seemed natural and right for me to do the same things."

As a rule, place warmers like the *Golddiggers* not only offered "the same format and same guests" as the shows they replaced, according to Cleveland Amory, "but a good part of the time, the same jokes." But while Dino generally offered contemporary amusements, the Golddiggers focused on the 1930s, exhuming old tunes, period fashions, and cultural references like dance marathons, Bonnie and Clyde, and abdication speeches.

Paul worked well with the hosts, Joey Heatherton and

Frank Sinatra Jr. The son of Ol' Blue Eyes made sure everyone knew he earned the gig on his own and gladly promoted the work of the 12 young women recruited as Golddiggers. "What's really great is that most of these girls are brand-new to television," he said. "It'll give our show a fresh, new look." Paul disagreed: "Imagine putting those untalented girls on nationwide television!"

When the temporary show debuted at the end of June, Paul earned his usual share of good notices. "Somehow the stars, Miss Heatherton and Sinatra, got lost in the shuffle, and when they appeared, it seemed they were guest stars," wrote Cynthia Lowry. "A pair of real pros, both mature performers, dominated the hour: Paul Lynde and Barbara Heller."

Paul's comedy cohort had performed in the past with Ben Blue and Jackie Gleason, among others. "When I was a kid, Barbara Heller was on the Dean Martin and Joey Bishop shows," playwright Charles Busch once said. "She was a long, stringy Kay Thompson type. She'd rip her wig off, and I would scream. She had absolutely no dignity whatsoever." Paul hated playing opposite her because she got more laughs than he did...when she remembered her lines.

Mentally taxed by his refusal to use cue cards, Paul claimed exhaustion and missed the final two shows of the season. Comedian Avery Schreiber took his place. He passed on an offer to join Martin's cast during the regular season, but agreed to front the replacement episodes the following summer. He joked that he and the crew had made a bet that he wouldn't complete all nine episodes. Promoted to costar level, the comic shared hosting duties with singers Lou Rawls and Martin's daughter Gail. Ever the critic, Paul thought the younger Martin had no talent, but, for the sake of a lucrative paycheck, he kept this opinion to himself.

Still milking the nostalgia craze, the new version of the show featured material from the 1920s, 1930s, and 1940s.

Paul joined Rawls in a running bit about a cowboy and Indian. "It was planned to have Paul Lynde and Lou Rawls call each other 'Lone Ranger' and 'Tonto,'" said reporter Joan Crosby. "But they couldn't get clearance. So they have resolved it by having Lynde say to Rawls 'Hey, yoo-hoo, Indian person,' to which Rawls responds, 'Yes, my cowboy friend.' They do nine cowboy-Indian spots in the series. Lou said, as lots of others have said, that Paul really breaks him up. In one skit, Lou put on a majorette's cap that was tall and furry, and Paul ad-libbed, 'Why that looks like a fuzzy ice cream cone.' Rawls laughed so hard he couldn't continue the scene."

Though Paul wanted to get rid of Heller, he didn't want to be doing monologues on the show. "If I'm bombing, I want someone out there bombing with me," he said. After successfully lobbying the producers to chuck Heller, he found more compatible replacements. "[Heller] couldn't put up with him, and he couldn't put up with her," says one of those replacements, Allison McKay, perhaps best remembered for her commercials as wife to the "Liquid Plumber" plumber. "Paul was not easy to work with, but I thought he was a comedic genius. So, for me, anything he asked me to do, you know, 'How high?'"

Martin taped his own show in the same studio, and the summer series had to be shot as quickly as possible in the spring to make room for the star's return. In spite of the rushed atmosphere and poor quality of writing (which included shamelessly recycled material), Paul still demanded perfection and called for numerous rehearsals. "He hated it when you broke character...no *Carol Burnett Show* there," McKay says. "It was really tough. I thoroughly enjoyed him, and he cracked me up [so much that] I just wanted to explode. But he would have been so upset because it destroys your timing. He was really a perfectionist, and I appreciated it."

In one sketch that Nancy Walker had done years earlier,

McKay played a drunk and Paul her husband who danced around the stage singing Rodgers and Hart's "I Married an Angel." McKay took a swig of warm beer, set it down, and watched the foam unexpectedly shoot up in the air. "I just stood up, and Paul was livid," she says. "It really wasn't my fault, and I don't think he was mad at me. He was mad at the idea that we had to do it again. So I just said to the audience, 'We have to do this again on the account of this dumb beer can, so would you please laugh again, because if you don't I'm going to get fired!' They all laughed, and they laughed again when we did it, and it turned out OK. But, boy, was he irritated. I could just hear that under [his breath]…kind of like a growl."

Paul once confessed the source of his performance anxiety to a plumber on a service call. The worker "came to my house for the fourth time to fix the same leak," he said. "His fourth trip, I pulled him aside and told him, 'Do you know how lucky you are? Only you and I know that you're a lousy plumber. I do a bad show and 40 million people know it."

Paul won his bet by finishing all nine outings of the show's second summer, the high point being his rendition of "If I Ruled the World" while dressed as Adolf Hitler. Though he continued to work with Martin throughout the regular season, he passed on a third go-around with the Golddiggers, and Charles Nelson Reilly took over his spot as resident male comic when the show returned the following year.

Paul may not have considered *Hollywood Squares,* variety shows, or his other TV work glamorous gigs, but they made him a household name. That renown would earn Paul tens of thousands of dollars when he appeared with the Kenley Players—"America's most exciting summer theatre"—in 1969.

Kenley, a veteran of the New York theater world, had danced for Martha Graham ("Boy, you had to have 12 o'clock kicks. I don't mean nine o'clock kicks, I mean 12 o'clock," he recalls), stooged for Phil Baker in a Broadway revue that audience member Al Jolson sometimes hijacked, and worked behind the scenes for theater kingpins the Shuberts. In the early 1940s, he applied his experiences to producing his own shows in Pennsylvania. After a stint in the Merchant Marines during World War II, where he learned his pharmaceutical skills, he picked up where he left off, eventually producing shows each summer in Warren, Dayton, and Columbus, Ohio.

Variety dubbed Kenley the "high lama of summer stock" for good reason. He knew what his audience wanted to see. "In summer theater Neil Simon sells, Woody Allen sells," he explained during his heyday. "You don't want to put on Bernard Shaw or Tennessee Williams. The people think they're depressing and that keeps 'em away."

After making a mint in the late 1950s by showcasing cast members of Jack Paar's late-night talk show, Kenley realized that Midwesterners cared more about stars of the tube than stars of the stage or screen. "I used to go to MGM," he once said. "Now I go to NBC and CBS and ABC." He usually headlined his musicals and comedies—either well-known productions or Broadway flops that he reworked and sometimes renamed—with purveyors of prime-time pap who had time on their hands...or moths in their wallets.

Scores of stars appeared on Kenley's stages: Zsa Zsa Gabor in *Blithe Spirit,* Martha Raye in *Wildcat,* Shari Lewis—sans Lamb Chop—in *Funny Girl,* William Shatner in *Arsenic and Old Lace,* and the incomparable Joe Namath in *Picnic.* Andy Williams and Selma Diamond appeared together in a well-received production of *Bye Bye Birdie.* Other Kenley Players during Paul's first season included Bob Crane, Abby Dalton, Jo Anne Worley, Jane Powell, Arte Johnson, and Vikki Carr.

Kenley first met Paul during the Chicago run of *New Faces of 1952.* Thirty years earlier, the show's director, John Murray

Anderson, had given Kenley his break on Broadway and a more theatrical last name than his original, Kremchek. Kenley stopped in town as producer of *Maid in the Ozarks,* a hillbilly revue so bad that one Windy City critic asked his readers to help him burn down the theater.

Kenley never thought to recruit the comic until his sister-in-law raved about Uncle Arthur on *Bewitched.* He realized Paul could exploit his *Birdie* persona in *The Impossible Years,* a Broadway comedy by Bob Fisher and Arthur Marx, son of Groucho. Alan King had originated the role of an expert on child-rearing who can't figure out his own kids; David Niven played it in the 1968 film.

Content with the pace and pay of his career in Hollywood, Paul wasn't keen on returning to the stage. After *Birdie* closed in 1961, he rarely stood in the footlights, save special occasions like three appearances on *That's Life,* a Robert Morse series taped at the George Abbott Theatre in New York. But Paul couldn't refuse the hefty percentage deal Kenley offered.

Kept on an allowance for years by his financial manager, Paul knew just how to spend his summer-stock windfall: on renovations to his home. When he first arrived in California, Paul had immediately wanted to build a mini mansion—a regency house with seven rooms and three bedrooms—next to Beverly Hills. "That's like being able to boast, 'I live next door to the Vanderbilts,'" he said. "First, you build your swimming pool. Next, the gazebo. The house comes last. That's the way they do things in Hollywood." After his manager reminded him of his salary, the actor shelved this fantasy...and only occasionally shelled out money for big-ticket items like a Cadillac.

Five years later in 1968, with plenty of paychecks to cash, Paul purchased a home in West Hollywood, near the Beverly Hills pads of Norma Shearer and Katharine Hepburn and conveniently located near the studios. The new homeowner liked to boast that his mansion on Cordell Drive had been owned by Errol Flynn, with whom he had appeared on a Martha Raye show a decade earlier. He usually failed to add that the screen swashbuckler had merely bought the place for Nora Eddington, his second wife, as part of their divorce decree.

Still, as a lifelong star worshipper, Paul relished his property's Flynn-related provenance, if only so he could make jokes like "I had to spend a fortune alone getting the mirrors off the ceiling." He would spend several more fortunes—some $300,000, he claimed—remodeling a house that he said originally looked like a nightclub. The money he earned in Ohio allowed him to exercise his ever-evolving tastes in home décor. "Let's be realistic," he once said of his Kenley currency. "The price is right and helps me live in the manner I choose—when and how I please."

Paul spent a year in the house before hiring an architect and interior designer to fix it up. After the project dragged for two years, he asked Forbes with some frustration, "What is this castle a substitute for?"

That castle, a multilevel town house, appeared much smaller from the street than it actually was. The architect raised the ceilings by six feet and added windows for a better view of the skyline. The decorator filled the place with antique Chinese accessories, though Paul insisted that space be made for his statue of Ondine and the Steinway piano he had purchased during his New York days. (He claimed he could only play "Silent Night" on it.) He covered his den in memorabilia. "I have my whole career in that room," he said. "I don't want that stuff spread all over the house." He purchased two huge stainless-steel refrigerators for the kitchen, and joked that one object in particular—a Venezuelan fox rug in his living room—would infuriate Doris Day, a well-known supporter of animal rights.

Paul designed his dining room to put guests at ease, choosing for its walls a red paint he had seen in a New York restaurant. He almost didn't sign off on his decorator's plan to use a mirrored tabletop and ceiling, but warmed to this "Mae West" décor when he realized it would reflect the water from his pool. He said his female guests particularly liked the arrangement. "They respond romantically in the reflection of the candlelight in the mirrors on the ceiling and the tabletop," he said. "So they're happy. And when the ladies are happy, the men are happy!"

The pool area had space to entertain over 200 people if necessary, with a gazebo built to house a bar and second kitchen. Paul rarely used the pool for swimming, though he enjoyed sitting beside it to tan and using it as a backdrop for publicity photos. When the contractors finished, Paul gave credit to the man who made the project possible by dubbing the area the "Kenley Pavilion."

In 1971, *House Beautiful* featured a photo spread of this "bachelor's dream house," as one reporter described it . "This house is like therapy," Paul told the magazine. "You can come home tied up in knots and sit down or go out on the balcony and look at the lights and immediately feel better."

For his first production as a Kenley Player, Paul spent a month memorizing his lines, a week rehearsing with the cast, including leading lady Frederica Minte, and another three weeks performing it. The company debuted in Warren, in a theater with 2,500 seats, moved to Dayton, to play to another 2,700 people nightly, and finished in Columbus, with 4,000 ticket buyers for every performance. "Because of the vast capacities of his auditoriums," a Kenley competitor once complained, "he is able to pay television names weekly salaries out of relation to reality."

So many fans clamored for seats to Paul's play that many

turned to scalpers or accepted spots on the stairs and in spaces where they could only hear the star's distinctive voice. Paul begged Kenley to cancel the show in Warren on July 20, the night of the historic moon landing, certain the audience would stay home to watch another Ohioan, Neil Armstrong, take his giant leap. His boss wouldn't hear of it, and Paul ended up playing to a packed house. "I've competed with kid actors and animals in this business, but never anything like that," Paul said. "I've never played to audiences more hip, warm, or responsive."

Paul earned some of the best reviews of his career for a "virtuoso performance [that] piled laugh upon laugh," as Bob McKnight of the *Cleveland Press* raved. Critic Gene Gerrard of the *Columbus Citizen-Journal* fawned even further: "I am convinced that he is a comic genius." Kenley realized his "star theatre" had acquired its biggest star yet, taking out a full-page ad in *Variety* that trumpeted "84,000 Tickets Sold for 24 SRO Performances!" (Four of the eight blurbs in the ad came from Warren papers—all of which promised Kenley never to print a bad review.) Paul knew why he sold out so many shows. "It's *Hollywood Squares,*" he said. "That's what fills those seats. And never, never in a thousand years would I have imagined that reaction from appearing on a daytime game show."

"[Paul] was the funniest man who ever lived," Kenley says. "*The Impossible Years* opened with the line 'chapter six,' and when Paul said it, the whole audience burst into laughs. Who the hell could get a laugh out of 'chapter six'? He was a good actor. He really could have done anything, but my public wanted a roar, and I had to give them roar time.... I had difficulty with a play once. I said, 'This line isn't getting a laugh.' He looked at me and said, 'It will tomorrow, John.' He had a good mind for a gag."

Kenley mandated in contracts that his stars sign autographs at the end of each show. Paul never quibbled, even though hundreds of audience members wanted to meet him every night. "The autograph lines make me feel like Godzilla," he said. Following his final bow, the headliner changed out of his costume, barked to the boss, "John, get me vodka, no ice," and spent an hour or two greeting fans. In Columbus, he almost always met local big shots and old acquaintances like the mayor of Mount Vernon or Ruth Domigan Truxall, his high school drama teacher.

While working for Kenley, Paul kept his backstage boozing and frolics with young men under relative control. Aside from an after-show nip, he didn't get serious about his drinking or his carousing until after the autograph sessions. Wearing one of his tight silk shirts, a golden Gemini sign necklace dangling about his exposed chest, his pinched face handsome in the light of a disco ball or lava lamp, Paul hit the scene with a fishbowl-sized martini glass and attitude. To the patrons of Ohio gay bars, he was a sex god. "He would cruise like mad, a great cruiser," Kenley says. "Oh, he'd cruise the town, and he wouldn't take no for an answer when he got drunk."

Occasionally, the drink got the better of Paul. During a special run of *The Impossible Years* in Miami that winter, Paul fancied a brash young actor in the cast who wasn't interested. Kenley remembers the fellow as "a pimply-faced kid" who "was screwing all my girls. I wondered how he got them, but he'd get them." One night at a party in Paul's dressing room, the actor found himself on the receiving end of one of the host's tirades. "You'll never make it in this business," Paul shouted at him. Against his better judgment, the actor stood face-to-face with Paul and told him, "If Paul Lynde can make it in this business, anybody can!" Kenley had already seen Paul tear into a young actress simply for flirting with some men in the cast who had caught his eye, and he had no desire to see how this turned out. He fled the scene. "I don't know how much blood was shed," he says.

Nervous about a repeat performance of the Miami fracas, Kenley tried to batten down the hatches when Paul returned to Ohio in 1970. He asked Jan Forbes to serve as Paul's caretaker, but she wouldn't leave her family. As it turned out, Paul behaved himself for the most part and impressed critics and more standing-room-only audiences in a production of Woody Allen's *Don't Drink the Water.*

This time Paul played an American caterer (with the requisite wife and kids) mistaken for a spy in a Communist country. Paul asked Charlotte Rae to play the missus, but his college comedy partner had already committed to another stock production in Cincinnati. Instead he toured with Nancy Andrews, the "theatrical godmother" who had picked him as the winner of the amateur contest at One Fifth Avenue 20 years earlier.

Though most audience members left the theater satisfied, a few "stone faces" could send Paul's confidence level plummeting. "Why these people come to shows like this one is beyond me," he told a reporter in Columbus. "I've got to feel that they're simply bored with life and don't really know how to enjoy [themselves]. Really, I feel sorry for them."

Paul called his annual visits to Ohio stages "Judy Garland time…a labor of love and an ego trip any actor would find difficult to resist." Feted as a VIP wherever he went in the Buckeye State, Paul bragged, "In Ohio, I could almost run for governor!" His home state recognized him over the years with a governor's award for his charity work, cast him in "Let's Hear It for Ohio" commercials, and named him an honorary congressman, the closest he came to upholding his family's tradition of public service.

In 1971, Paul returned to the Kenley stage in Neil Simon's *Plaza Suite,* a trio of playlets all set in the same room at the famous New York hotel. He worried that this "dirty play" might be inappropriate for the young people in the audience, but he couldn't find a suitable alternative.

Kenley hired Elizabeth Allen, one of his occasional leading ladies, as the costar, but she injured her leg just before the tour and Renee Orin replaced her for most of the performances. For the third year, Paul garnered good reviews and standing-room-only audiences, even as the film version starring Walter Matthau played in local movie houses. In Columbus, what had become known as "Paul's Wall"—a divider in the local auditorium's balcony used to block off seats that weren't usually needed—came down each night so an additional 675 people could see the show.

That year, Paul extended the tour an additional week for a stop in Atlanta. Recovered from her injury, Allen joined him. Performing outside Ohio worried the star. "I'd never been in the South, and I was very leery about playing Atlanta. The theater—it's an auditorium—seated just under seven thousand. They'd only done musicals. They could do *Aïda* with elephants! This was their first legit play. And *Plaza Suite* is basically a two-character show. When Liz Allen and I walked out on that huge stage—the ovation—it was unbelievable." To accommodate the crowds, producers added two performances to the schedule.

Paul toured more cities to the itinerary every summer after that, soon securing his position among summer-stock royalty, such as it was. Peter Marshall, who also worked for Kenley, told Dinah Shore that for years the two biggest draws in stock were Burt Reynolds and Paul Lynde—or as Paul himself described the two of them, "Sex and Fun!"

According to parakeet experts, can a drop or two of bourbon be good for your bird?
No, after a drop of bourbon, I get mean!

Despite his money and relative fame, Paul's career left him resentful and unhappy. Never content with his own success, he envied the greater achievements of other actors like Oscar-winning friends Cloris Leachman, Patricia Neal, and Maggie Smith. Many friends assumed that Paul would lighten up after making it big. Instead, they watched him grow worse. "It was almost as if he was a kid who thought that once he became famous, then he'd step into nirvana and everything would be wonderful," says Robert Osborne. "It didn't happen that way. But I was confused because he was so bright. He obviously knew that wasn't the way it worked.... I'm not sure that he could have been happy. I'm not sure that was in his makeup."

Paul's home brought him some happiness, and he wanted to share that joy with friends by throwing small but elaborate dinner parties. These get-togethers sometimes became exercises in terror. Though the evenings started pleasantly enough, with Paul preparing the meal or hiring someone else to do it, he would eventually become a drunken dictator, exerting control over who sat where and when they could leave. Kaye Ballard came over one night when Paul confined his guests to the patio so that they wouldn't dirty the house, an act she found even more galling months later when he casually ashed his cigarette on her new white carpet.

Jim McLernan says the pressures of hosting magnified Paul's worst traits—his insecurity and self-centeredness. "He wanted to try to prove to people that he was a great host and a good entertainer," he says. "But because he was so insecure [and] hoping everything was going all right, he would drink too much during the course of an evening."

The host who designed his dining room specifically for the comfort of guests could shatter their sense of well-being when he'd had one too many drinks. At a dinner party one

evening, Paul attacked a friend from college, who left in tears. Fortunately for the others in the room, he found a better sedative than cocktails. "His dog came and put his paw on Paul's knee," Leachman says. "And Paul calmed down immediately."

CHAPTER 9

LIKE HAMLET EVERY WEEK

"It's **The Paul Lynde Show.** *If it fails, it's my fault."*

Each year, a New York-based research company called Marketing Evaluations, Inc. tracks public opinions to compile Q Scores on prime-time performers. In 1971, Paul placed fourth on the company's list of favorite TV comedians, behind Flip Wilson and Carol Burnett, both stars of their own popular shows, and Bob Hope, an American institution. Not bad for a game show panelist and professional guest star.

Paul's popularity made him impervious to the changes that upended his primary income source later that fall. Hoping to spur programming diversity, the FCC enforced a new prime time access rule, which gave local stations the right to program the 7:30 P.M. slot usually controlled by the Big Three. Though angry, the networks took the loss of 21 hours from the weekly prime-time schedule as an opportunity for drastic programming changes. CBS sped up plans to doff such yokel content as *Green Acres, Hee Haw,* and *Mayberry R.F.D.,* and all three networks axed two-thirds of their variety shows.

Johnny Cash, Don Knotts, Jim Nabors, Lawrence Welk, Andy Williams, the rotating hosts of the *Kraft Music Hall,* and other stars got kicked off the air at the end of the 1970-

1971 season. None could match Ed Sullivan for longevity, but that didn't stop CBS from sending him a pink slip after 23 years. The reason for mass layoffs, at least according to singer Tennessee Ernie Ford, was simple economics: "They 'produced' themselves right off the air," he explained. "There's an awful lot of homes between Hollywood and New York who don't care about how fancy the draperies are."

Three of the four survivors—*The Carol Burnett Show, The Glen Campbell Show,* and *The Dean Martin Show*—booked Paul as solidly as he had ever been scheduled and continued paying him the standard $7,500 fee. With an unwritten rule that variety appearances had to be separated by three weeks, Paul didn't even have time to visit *The Flip Wilson Show,* the only other one still standing in prime time. (Had Paul been a popular guest star on drama shows, he would have made much less. Except for a trio of guest spots on *Burke's Law* in the mid 1960s, which was more tongue-in-cheek than other cop shows, Paul stuck to comedy.)

Paul had continued to roam the gay guest-star ghetto for sitcom assignments, though less frequently than in his mid 1960s heyday. He made new contributions to the canon of prime-time sissies in two *Gidget* TV movies and a short-lived animated series. Karen Valentine played the title character in *Gidget Grows Up,* a pilot gussied up as a made-for-TV movie that aired at the very end of 1969. The Screen Gems project borrowed sets from *Bewitched,* including the Stephens' living room and the advertising offices of McMann and Tate. In the recycling spirit, Paul imported a foppish foulard not unlike the one he often wore as Uncle Arthur to play aging child star Louis B. Latimer.

Leaving sunny California to take a job in New York as a guide at the United Nations, Gidget encounters Latimer, described as a "wacky cinephile" but really just a vainglorious landlord. The sign on his building read LOUIS B. LATIMER

PRESENTS THE LATIMER ARMS, STARRING LOUIS B. LATIMER AS 'THE MANAGER.' She plays on Louis B.'s narcissism by reminding him that he was once considered "the logical successor to Jackie Coogan's sneakers." Paul reprised the character a year later for *Gidget Gets Married,* this time with Monie Ellis as the lovable "girl midget."

Having played villainous parts for the Saturday morning cartoons *The Perils of Penelope Pitstop* and *The Cattanooga Cats,* Paul may well have voiced the first gay man in prime-time animation on *Where's Huddles,* which ran as a summer replacement series on CBS for ten weeks in 1970. Not only was the cartoon the first such series on prime time since *The Flintstones,* it borrowed plots from the older Hanna-Barbera series and even the voices behind Fred (Alan Reed), Barney (Mel Blanc) and Wilma (Jean Vander Pyl).

Cliff Norton starred as Ed Huddles, a professional football player whose meager salary left him and his teammate (and neighbor), Bubba McCoy, always on the lookout for a fast buck. (The gang formed a singing group...opened a car wash...made glue in the garage.) Another neighbor—a foulard-wearing, cat-owning single man named Claude Pertwee, played by and drawn to resemble Paul—wants the "savages" kicked out of the neighborhood.

"Determining that the program is funny was not difficult," wrote *The New York Times.* "Fumbles [Huddles's helmet-wearing dog] laughed unceasingly at each of Claude Pertwee's misfortunes, and when he stopped for breath the hilarity was picked up smartly by a canned laugh track." CBS announced plans to reserve a permanent space for *Huddles* on its schedule the following January, and Hanna-Barbera decided to entice viewers back by announcing an impending pregnancy on the final show of the summer. Paul placed little faith in the network's promise, and bad reviews and lackluster ratings scuttled the idea.

Still burned by the failure of *Sedgewick Hawk-Styles,*
Paul usually told people he didn't even want a series of his
own. "They keep throwing pilot scripts at me," he said, "and
I just tell them, 'Why should I look at this? You've got something a hundred times better on the shelf gathering dust.'"
But when good friend Bill Asher waved the pilot carrot in
his face again in 1971, Paul backed off his pledge. "Paul's
an enormous talent," Asher said at the time. "I have always
felt that he has a bigger potential as a television personality
than anyone I know. He's funny, and how many people can
you say that about?"

As the mastermind behind ABC's first unqualified hit,
Asher had shrewdly locked up a spot on the network's schedule for a ninth and tenth season of *Bewitched.* To keep
Elizabeth Montgomery from accepting a lucrative offer at
CBS, the network promised to reserve a spot for another one
of the couple's Ashmont Productions if they decided to end the
long-running show.

When ratings and Montgomery's enthusiasm for
Bewitched sagged, the Ashers decided the show's eighth season would be its last. The last original episode aired at the
end of March 1972. Asher's deal meant a rare full-season
commitment for the replacement, and he presented the network with two choices for that slot: Paul's pilot, aptly titled
The Paul Lynde Show, and *Temperatures Rising,* a comedy
set in a hospital in Washington, D.C.

As he waited nervously for the network to call with its
decision, Paul greeted friends on the telephone with an
unenthused "Oh, it's you" and gained 30 pounds gorging on
comfort food. When ABC placed both series on the fall
schedule, he celebrated the new assignment by starting a
crash diet and confessing self-doubts. "I just wish this had
happened to me 10 years ago," he said. "I would have had
a better chance."

Paul had toyed with the idea of resurrecting *Sedgewick* for his pilot, but Lucille Ball suggested he do a domestic sitcom instead. "She told me that I'd probably win an Emmy for [*Sedgewick*] but wouldn't last more than two years," he said. "She told me that if I went with a family format, I just might be on the air for years to come. And she should certainly know what she's talking about." Paul should have been more dubious; at the time Ball also thought she was perfectly suited to play Auntie Mame in her disastrous film version of the Broadway musical.

Though he must have known Paul's persona had changed greatly since the days when he only played excitable patriarchs, Asher agreed with the grand dame of comedy. "We must have you with young people!" he told Paul, unaware that casting the hip center square as a father would end up seeming more "high concept" than a witch in suburbia. "I must have something going for me with the teenagers because we *do* communicate," Paul said. "What's marvelous is that the kids *laugh*. I'm their idea of the Establishment. Only they think I'm on their side, that I'm laughing with them at this guy. Which I am."

Paul never let go of his hopes for a *Sedgewick* revival. "It's still my favorite," he said, "but I shouldn't say that, now that I am working on this….[Sedgewick] is a man I've never really gotten to play. That's why I like him. He's not so Paul Lynde." Twentieth-Century Fox had shown interest in a *Sedgewick* movie, but the deal never gelled. "We couldn't put it together," Asher says. "I keep thinking it was the homosexual thing. I mean, who knows why a picture doesn't get made?"

Harry Ackerman, who had an impressive track record at Screen Gems with *Dennis the Menace, The Flying Nun,* and the *Gidget* projects, served as executive producer of *The Paul Lynde Show.* This new version of the twice-used title cast Paul as Paul Simms, a put-upon lawyer in sunny California

at odds with a free-spirited son-in-law who can't hold down a job. In other words, a *Howie* for the 1970s, with Howie as a watered-down flower child instead of a watered-down beatnik. He eventually accepted the premise, with minor kvetching. "This particular idea didn't particularly intrigue me," he confessed.

Sam Bobrick and Ron Clark updated the scenario to better reflect the times, which meant groovy clothes and lingo (or as Paul Simms called it, "that mod double-talk"), and a scene that takes place in a porno theater:

> PAUL: You may not believe this, but not too long ago I saw *Snow White* here.
> TICKET LADY: What a coincidence! Just next week we're showing *Snow White Makes Out With the Seven Cycle Freaks*.
> PAUL: Shame on you! To think, you're probably someone's grandmother.

No one jumps on a bandwagon faster than a klatch of television programmers, and ABC probably gave the green light to this show because its concept mirrored an extremely popular sitcom the network had rejected. "I know what you're thinking," Paul told one reporter. "It sounds like an upper-class *All in the Family*. There'll be no ethnic humor whatsoever, just questions of contrasting social values."

When other reporters shared similar thoughts during a preseason publicity session, "Paul the Knife," as one of the writers called him, attacked. "Personally, I don't see any resemblance," he sniffed. "My TV family doesn't live in a hovel, and I certainly don't look like Carroll O'Connor." He bitched that the Bunkers didn't represent the average American family. "The characters are a typical Brooklyn or East Side family—sections of New York I don't like.... Ours is a real family show, and my public is the family." Paul then refused to answer their questions about his history of failed pilots. "Why talk about negative things?" he said. "Let's talk about positive things! Like my new show!" He lightened the mood by reciting a few dramatic lines from *Macbeth*.

Just as the season began, Paul managed to keep his cool when he promoted his show on *I've Got a Secret*. He didn't confess *the* secret, just that he once weighed 260 pounds. He told host Steve Allen that he would be playing a father on his new series, then added, "I know it's hard to believe." Paul shot panelist Pat Carroll a nasty look when she laughed a little too long at the quip.

With his own series finally in production, Paul cut back on his other work. He skipped a fourth visit to Kenley country, but made his network contract provided time off for a play in 1973. He purged his calendar of TV commitments and even considered giving up his lease on the center square. Ultimately, he decided to do both shows—the recognition on *Hollywood Squares* was too valuable. Save Peter Marshall, no one on the show made much money from it; they kept coming back for the valuable face time in front of a huge audience. The producers weren't about to let Paul go anyway, especially now that the show had spent two consecutive years as the most watched game show in the Nielsens, largely thanks to his presence. He had been needed to help launch a weekly version for syndication in the fall of 1971, and now the producers tailored their shooting schedule to accommo- date his. "We film a whole block of *Squares* at a time," Paul said, "weekends, evenings, whenever I'm free to race over to the studio."

Paul's stature on the show occasionally inspired ludicrous rumors. One that would later float around political circles: Ronald Reagan, while governor of California, supposedly

pulled strings to get Paul out of some legal trouble. Because of his help, the grateful producers used contestant questions to keep the presidential hopeful's name in circulation after his second term as governor. However silly this theory may sound, Paul did in fact like Reagan: "He has charisma and glamour," he said. "And I love his wife—she wouldn't marry an idiot."

In casting *The Paul Lynde Show,* June Allyson came up as a possible Harriet to Paul's Ozzie, but the former MGM star had already committed to a national tour of *No, No, Nanette.* Paul then suggested Elizabeth Allen, his most recent leading lady on the summer-stock stage. "ABC thought I was too attractive," Allen later said, "but he told them he didn't want someone who they thought looked like his wife—a funny person. He insisted we test together, and when we did, they saw I was right."

Allen doubled as convenient cover for her TV husband as well. "Paul is one of Hollywood's most eligible bachelors," one wag wrote. "He's only been seen in public with costar Elizabeth Allen, and insiders speculate that that's nothing more than friendship." That's exactly what it was. "He was my best friend. I adored him, and my mother adored him," Allen said after Paul's death. "He used to come to my house for dinner and we'd go out to the movies. I knew him better than anyone else, outside of his sister, Helen. He was very tough on himself. When he had a little too much to drink, his humor could be very cruel. But what he said was the truth."

In the 1950s, Allen had appeared as the Away We Go Girl on Jackie Gleason's TV show. She earned a Tony nomination for her work in the 1962 musical *The Gay Life* and originated the role of spinster Leona Samish in the Richard Rodgers–Stephen Sondheim musical *Do I Hear a Waltz?* three years later. She also starred with John Wayne in *Donovan's*

Reef and in the short-lived TV drama *Bracken's World.*

To quash additional complaints that they had ripped off *All in the Family,* the producers changed the name of Allen's character in the play and 1962 pilot from Edith to Martha. Though Allen insisted she wouldn't play Paul's stay-at-home wife as a "stereotyped spouse with the frilly apron, fussbudget temperament, and long-suffering patience," she rarely seemed to do much beyond serving as Paul's straight man and as the dispenser of his after-work tranquilizers:

> MARTHA: I'll get your martini...straight or on the rocks?
> PAUL: Just fast!

Paul inevitably shot his wife down when she tried to match him quip for quip. "Watch it, Martha," he says after one of her comebacks, "mistresses are very 'in' this year."

John Calvin won the role of Howie Dickerson, the liberal thorn in Paul's conservative side. His TV father-in-law made sure people knew that the young actor wasn't another Meathead in the *All in the Family* mold. "You can see he's totally different from Rob Reiner," he said. "John's an enchanting man, which I do not call Rob Reiner." During publicity sessions, Paul played up Calvin's fresh face by mentioning his recent graduation from UCLA. "He won the Hugh O'Brian Acting Award—what that means I don't know—but he did. It's his first professional work, and he's a great-looking guy."

More than once, the writers found excuses for the buff Calvin to doff his clothing. The actor had no problems with the assignment, telling one reporter, "Maybe we haven't gotten to the point where nudity is accepted, but we sure have come to a time where it can be talked about and referred to for as long as ten minutes on a 30-minute show.... The way things are going, actors will have to practice a little nudity in front of their own in-laws, so they'll be able to take their jobs without being self-conscious."

Jane Actman, an original cast member of *The Prime of Miss Jean Brodie* on Broadway, played the eldest daughter, Barbara. Having only moved west in 1970, the actress had done occasional guest spots on *Room 222* and as David Cassidy's girlfriend on *The Partridge Family*.

Naturally, Barbara's nonconformity bothered Paul, particularly when it involved nudity, which strangely came up often in the Simms household. In an episode titled "The Bare Facts," artist Howie unveils a nude painting of his new bride. Paul flips out:

> PAUL: I'm going to burn this!
> BARBARA: You have no right to do that. It doesn't belong to you.
> PAUL: All right, all right. I'll buy it.
> BARBARA: I don't want to sell it. I want to hang it.
> PAUL: If you do, [Howie] hangs with it.
> BARBARA: Dad, you're being pretty square.
> PAUL: That's because most of you is pretty round.

Pamelyn Ferdin portrayed the younger daughter, Sally. A seasoned acting veteran at only 13 years old, Ferdin had dozens of TV appearances to her credit, including *Star Trek, The Andy Griffith Show,* and *The Brady Bunch*. Because of a network dictate, she had to give up her semiregular role as Felix Unger's daughter on *The Odd Couple* to join Paul's cast. "I'm not sure if Tony Randall ever forgave me," she says.

Smart-mouthed Sally—"too old to spank and too young for a religious sacrifice," in her father's words—gave Paul another set of headaches:

SALLY: Wait till you see what Barbara brought home. Is
he heavy!
PAUL: He's fat?
MARTHA: No, he's groovy.
PAUL: Well, why didn't she say so? It took me a whole
year to learn "groovy."

"Want to end the Vietnam War?" TV insiders used to joke.
"Put it on ABC and it will be canceled in 13 weeks." The
perennial third-place network had high expectations for *The
Paul Lynde Show* and promoted the new sitcom during its
coverage of the Summer Olympics by asking viewers to
"share the joys of family living with Paul Lynde." Some critics
felt uneasy about sportscasters plugging comedies—"that Paul
Lynde sure is a funny fella," one of them said. Meanwhile,
the murders of 11 Israeli athletes at Munich's Olympic Village
hung over the games.

At first, the network planned to pit *The Paul Lynde Show*
in direct competition with *All in the Family* on Saturday
nights. When Paul heard that, he said he "pulled the shades,
got a bottle, and started drinking." Instead, the network
scheduled it as a lead-in to the *Wednesday Movie of the Week*
and the highly touted *Julie Andrews Hour* in an attempt to
rescue the entire evening, its lowest rated of the week. Paul
shared his time slot with Carol Burnett's variety show, a top
25 hit, and the police drama *Adam-12,* which had finished
the previous season in the top ten. The competition, which
one reporter said was "enough to make any pussycat spit,"
did not favor the rookie.

Screen Gems had to turn away hundreds of fans who
wanted to join the live studio audience, the first time the
sitcom factory shot a series that way. Paul asked his sister
Helen not to attend, knowing her presence would make him
nervous. (On tour, Paul usually posted a sign backstage that

stated DO NOT TELL MR. LYNDE WHO IS IN THE AUDIENCE.) Though an emotional wreck, he shared cautious optimism for the show. "I think the first time we'll wipe out anybody in the ratings," he said. "It's the second show that will tell." And tell it did: Though *The Paul Lynde Show* started off strong with Nielsen families that September, ranking in the top 15 its first week, ratings sank with each new episode—and network hopes with them. By its fourth week, the show had plummeted to the Nielsens' bottom echelon, 46th of 62 shows.

Critics weren't any more impressed than the audiences. "While a show like CBS's *Maude* expands the limits of usable domestic subject matter, other new entries like ABC's *Paul Lynde Show* and CBS's *Bob Newhart Show* extend the already overextended tradition of stale sitcoms— symptoms of TV's banal-retention syndrome," wrote a nameless reviewer for *Time*.

Other arbiters of TV taste at least paid their respects to the comic master. "Most of the time [Paul's] so outrageously overboard, he belongs in a swimming pool," insisted *TV Guide*'s Cleveland Amory. "But just when you simply can't bear him any more, darned if he isn't darned funny. The whole show is his, and it's absolutely wild, but because he's so wild to begin with, you're willing to play along." John O'Connor of *The New York Times* dug deeper: "Paul Lynde's peculiar brand of comedy transforms the clichéd proceedings into a malicious parody of the genre. With manic nasality, knees locked from tension, and the conviction that the daily rat race is being won by the rats, the comedian obliterates the theory that father knows best."

Worried that the cast didn't have enough comedy experience, Paul insisted on trotting in guest stars. Charlotte Rae showed up as Paul's sister in two episodes, one in which her eccentricities cause problems when Paul entertains a Japanese businessman played by the most un-Asian of actors, Ray

Walston of *My Favorite Martian*. Tom Bosley, Alan Hale, Gordon Jump, and Dick Van Patten—as the operator of the porno theater—also put in appearances. Paul even played straight man to 9-year-old Jodie Foster, who appeared as the youngest resident of a commune that Howie and Barbara temporarily call home.

Mabel Albertson, who cornered the prime-time comedy market on controlling mothers and mothers-in-law, played the "Merry Widow," Paul's least favorite relative. She had played mother to Darrin Stephens on *Bewitched*, but her tit-for-tat with Paul played out more like the Endora-"Durwood" relationship:

> MABEL: Do you know what I like about your sense of humor, Phil?
> PAUL: The name is Paul, and what do you like about my sense of humor?
> MABEL: Nothing, Phil.

The show's feeble attempts at trendy social commentary only highlighted its similarities to *All in the Family*. Paul's writers tried to tackle hot-button topics of the Nixon era like pornography, ecology, women's lib, race relations, and rock music culture. "I know about those rock festivals," Paul says. "It's 50,000 kids trying to go on a trip without leaving the grass. They're not music lovers. What they really love is playing touch-and-grab in a cow pasture."

Failing that, the writers invariably fell back on easy sitcom silliness with jokes centered on sex and the ever-present martini in Paul's hand, as in the episode "P.S., I Loathe You":

> PAUL: Martha, a refill.
> HOWIE: You know, part of Dad's problem could be his proclivity for the excessive use of alcoholic beverages.

PAUL: Love me or leave me, Howie. You made me a lush! Martha, one more for the road.

BARBARA: Daddy, we learned in physiology that it's very bad for your health.

MARTHA: Yes, they do say it enlarges your liver.

PAUL: That's it! This AA meeting is over! Don't wait up for me.

MARTHA: Where're you going?

PAUL: Down to the corner liver enlarger!

Whereas *Hollywood Squares* demanded little of Paul beyond showing up and staying moderately sober, *The Paul Lynde Show* inspired its star to pick up the pen again and rewrite subpar scripts. "What we start out with each week is a premise which you know will work and 53 pages of dialogue which you know no one is going to say," Paul said. "You can rehearse and block from that. But by the time we film, every line has been thrown out and rewritten." Asher, who directed the first four episodes of the series and continued serving as the story editor, gave his star free reign to alter what he liked. "He was very inventive in the sense of creating comedy as well as negating things, not liking things," Asher says. "He was right. I'd change them."

After he received a script for an episode, Paul took it home to solicit suggestions from an audience of friends outside the business. He also exploited the proven writing skills of Jerry Stiller and Anne Meara, who frequently played Howie's bickering parents. "The four of us would sit around and totally rewrite everything," says Allison McKay, who appeared occasionally as Paul's secretary. "Paul just finally threw up his arms and said, 'Somewhere, someone's getting paid for this, and it ain't us!' That was the bottom line. We wanted to look good, so it was either sink or swim."

The censors weren't so thrilled with Paul's new lines, which unsurprisingly leaned toward the risqué. "I remember he would be complaining about the censors," Ferdin says. "He would say these jokes that would just crack me up, and Bill Asher or Elizabeth Allen would say, 'Oh, that's not gonna get by the censors.' " Paul put some of the blame on a nervous network with a reputation for family-oriented shows like *The Partridge Family* and *The Brady Bunch*.

The ratings, wrangles with censors, and his increasingly futile attempts to salvage scripts wore on Paul. "I've aged ten years doing this show," he said. "I should probably have a face-lift.... I'm carrying the whole load myself. The show depends too much on me. It's like playing *Hamlet* every week."

During the four days of rehearsals that led up to a Friday-night taping, Paul frequently took out his frustrations on the cast and crew. Some guest stars quietly grumbled about the tension on the set. "I apologize to the guests for not having more fun," the star said. "But there's too much to think about in a three-camera show." Though Paul claimed his preshow chats with the audience were the only part of the work week he enjoyed, he willingly sacrificed real laughs when he thought the cast played too much to the crowds and not the cameras. "It's something you constantly have to watch," he said. "I've said to Bill, '*Please*—always keep on top of me. Make sure I'm playing to the home—a little screen—not to a bleacher full of people.... The audience *will* become your director, and you'll play bigger for them.' " He asked Asher to shoot the show sans spectators. The failed experiment only lasted a week before the studio audience returned.

Paul's TV family learned to steer clear of him when he was in a pique, especially after he'd had one too many highballs at lunch. "I felt sorry for him many times because he would come to the set, and you could tell he was anxious and frustrated and unhappy," Ferdin says. "He did drink, and so then when he drank, he would get sarcastic and mean…. I didn't know why he was unhappy, so at those times you just left him alone." McKay says Paul let his nerves get the better of him. "Paul was always like being on the edge of an active volcano," she says. "I remember trying to calm him down one time, and I said, 'Are you a Scorpio?' And he said, 'Hell no, I'm a Gemini. I'm a real sickie.' "

The kidney-shaped pool installed on the set particularly irked Paul. Screen Gems proclaimed the inground addition to the Simms abode a first for a three-camera show and featured it prominently in the opening credits. Reportedly, this aquatic set decoration existed for the sake of a married bigwig at the company who used it for after-hours swims with girlfriends. To justify the expense, the company tried to use the pool as often as possible.

In the episode "Unsteady Going," Martha tries to break up a fight between Paul and the father of Sally's boyfriend and gets knocked into the pool—not once, but twice, and both times to the indifference of her preoccupied husband. Though Calvin's skills as a scuba diver seemed ripe for the pool, Paul spent the most time in the water, usually to salvage soaked props like an alligator briefcase or a lawn mower. "If I have to fall in that damn swimming pool again, I'm gonna kill somebody!" the star would seethe whenever he had to take a comic plunge.

In a familiar sitcom dilemma, played out in the episode "To Wed or Not to Wed," Howie and Barbara discover that a clerical error has voided their marriage. They decide to get rehitched in the backyard pool, despite papa Paul's best efforts to "pull the plug on this Esther Williams remake." Chuck McCann played the spaced-out minister who officiated the New Age nuptials. "Chuck's going in the fucking pool this time," Paul sighed with relief. He spoke too soon. The entire cast, dressed to the nines in wedding attire, had to join McCann in the offending water hole.

In his good moods, Paul boosted the cast's spirits with jokes and party invites to his home, which became a weekend ritual. (Ferdin says she realized her TV dad was gay when she met one of his houseboys there.) Paul's generous invitations extended both ways: He sometimes brought friends on the set, including a few young men Asher remembers as making "a lot of noise. They were not behaving." The boys may have grown overexcited on learning they were sitting in the same dressing room Judy Garland had used when she filmed *A Star Is Born*. "I'll try not to end up like her," Paul told columnist Earl Wilson.

While Paul didn't especially like kids or know how to interact with them, he nevertheless bonded with Ferdin over dogs and her passion for rescuing animals from shelters. The two often swapped dog tales, Pam about her latest rescues, Paul about Harry MacAfee, whom he sometimes brought on the set but rarely let anyone touch. "You could tell that he just loved my stories about animals, because usually if I tried to talk to him about other things, he wasn't interested," Ferdin says. "But over the course of the year that we were filming the show, he would open up to me, and he told me once, 'You know, I love animals because they don't judge you. They just love you.' And I said, 'You're right, Mr. Lynde.' At that point I really didn't know what he meant, but obviously now I do." Paul even gave Ferdin money to support her rescue operations. "He wouldn't be able to show me love. He wasn't a warm individual towards me, but he would in his own way, like, 'Here, kid, here's some money. You go to the shelter and rescue that dog.'"

Though critics yawned and ratings disappointed, the Hollywood Foreign Press nominated Paul for a Golden Globe as best lead actor in a comedy or musical series. He competed for the award with Alan Alda, Bill Cosby, Redd Foxx, Carroll O'Connor, and Flip Wilson. At the awards dinner that January, Paul stole everyone's thunder by making caustically funny comments all night. When Foxx won the comedy award, Paul stood up and yelled, "I was robbed!" and then mocked Bud Yorkin, who accepted the award for the absent star of *Sanford and Son*. Presenter Chad Everett chastised the bad sport from the stage: "Next year, sir, you may make your own speech if you get the award." *The Hollywood Reporter* said Paul at least deserved a trophy for his "ad-lib heckling." Instead the sore loser won a security escort out of the building.

Although Groucho Marx apparently enjoyed *The Paul Lynde Show,* ("My father called after one of the shows and said he liked it," said Arthur Marx, who with his partner Bob Fisher provided nine of the 26 scripts. "That floored me. He usually doesn't like family shows or what I write."), Paul openly disparaged his meal ticket. "I'll be happy if it is picked up [for a second season] but I won't be crushed if it isn't," he told Joyce Haber of the *Los Angeles Times.* "I don't get the return for what I put into it. But I don't want anyone out of work. Bill Asher's promised me continuing writers for next season; we have none now. I have to rewrite every show. I'm exhausted."

In early April, ABC announced its upcoming fall lineup, sans *The Paul Lynde Show.* Five of the nine new sitcoms that debuted on the Big Three the previous September won renewal for a second season: *The Bob Newhart Show, Little People* (or *The Brian Keith Show*), *M*A*S*H, Maude,* and *Temperatures Rising,* Asher's other Screen Gems sitcom. Paul's shot at prime-time glory joined freshman sitcoms *Anna and the King, Bridget Loves Bernie,* and *The Sandy Duncan Show* in the debit column for their networks. ABC planned to fill Paul's time slot that fall with a new sitcom called *Bob & Carol & Ted & Alice*. That show would serve as a lead-in to the Wednesday Movie of the Week, which won renewal, and the long-running *Owen Marshall, Counselor at Law*, which replaced the axed Andrews.

Paul joked that he considered asking consumer advocate Ralph Nader to investigate the Nielsens. Instead, he threw a somber farewell party at his home for the cast and crew, then distanced himself from the debacle. "I hated that series before we ever started production and paced the soundstage just gritting my teeth and counting the days until it was over," he said. "My agent told me recently that during that period he was afraid to walk into my dressing room for fear of what my mood would be at that time. I answered him, '*You* were afraid. Who wasn't?'"

Allen knew it wouldn't work. "We kept telling them we needed to get rid of the kids and the funny neighbors and friends and concentrate on us," she said. "By the time they did, it was too late." Actman also shared her complaints a few months after the cancellation. "There was no real father-daughter relationship between Paul and me. Look at the way Archie Bunker feels about Gloria; he's not often tender, but at least you know they're related. If we had been picked up for next season, my agent was going to fight for more character development for me. I told him that the way things stood now, I could go on for five years having only two lines a week."

The few people who remember *The Paul Lynde Show* chalk up its demise to a format ill-suited to an otherwise capable comic. The Web site Jump the Shark, which tracks the point at which TV shows go bad, lists the very concept of *The Paul Lynde Show* as the moment it peaked. "It was the wrong series for him," Charlotte Rae says. "I mean, here he is, he's a wonderful guy, and they've made him like...*Father Knows Best* with a wife and kids. Well, that wasn't using him properly at all. I mean, they should have thought about it. They should have been more creative and thought of something that fitted him better so that he could show his humor better and everything. So that was unfortunate because he was so gifted."

Sam Bobrick says the failure of popular second bananas like Paul, Tim Conway, or former *Seinfeld* cast members doing own sitcoms can't be explained so simply. "You could have placed [Paul] in another formula, and he may have done worse. You never know," he says. "I don't know what the reason is, and if I did, I'd probably be living in a much bigger house."

ABC reportedly offered Paul a chance to fix the show, but he wanted nothing more to do with the character. The network came up with another idea. Its polling revealed that the public liked Paul but hated his show, while they liked *Temperatures Rising* but not its star, James Whitmore. Applying typically warped programming logic, the network wanted to fire Whitmore and replace him with Paul.

Asher and Paul hated the idea, but they both eventually agreed to the changes. "I said, 'Don't mess with [the shows] because that'll just screw them up,'" Asher says. "They said, 'Well, we've talked about it, and we've said we'd rather have one big hit instead of two.' So that's what they did, and they fucked it up." Paul told a reporter from his hometown that he only went along with the alterations to fulfill a contractual obligation and that he would much rather play a more upbeat role, like a "jolly priest."

That summer, Paul took Elizabeth Allen on another foray into Kenley territory with *My Daughter's Rated X,* a play penned by Paul's sitcom scribes Bob Fisher and Arthur Marx. Paul played the head of the Motion Picture Association of America, who finds his job in jeopardy when his daughter has an illegitimate child with a New York Yankee.

"There are reviewers who might rate this bit of nonsense G (God-awful) or even PG (Pretty Grim)," Gene Gerrard wrote. "But since I chuckled right along with the rest of the capacity audience, I'll be content to slap it with an R (Ridiculous)." Beyond bad puns, most critics found little enjoyment in the trifle. "It's a little like hearing a rerun of a two-year-old, once-topical Bob Hope monologue," wrote Gregory Jaynes of *The Atlanta Constitution*. (Linda Lovelace hoped to go legit by starring in the play in a Vegas production that closed after a week once fans realized her costumes stayed on.)

Despite his canceled TV show and a two-year absence from the Kenley Players, Paul still played to packed houses...and competed with another *Squares* regular for box office supremacy. John Davidson, a middling star of stage, TV screen, and records, turned out to be almost as popular as Paul in Kenley country when he toured there in *Oklahoma!* in 1972. He returned the next summer to perform *The Music Man* with Laurie Lea Schaefer, the Ohioan chosen as Miss America of 1972. Paul joked that he would stop coming back to his home state if Davidson ever outsold him. Davidson never did. (After the younger actor posed for a *Cosmopolitan* centerfold, Paul held up a copy on *Squares* and cracked, "You should have been the ambassador of underdeveloped countries.")

After the curtain call, Paul usually returned to the stage to field questions from the audience. That summer he began by asking one of his own. "For the past couple of hours, did you forget Watergate? That's what theater is all about." Pundit Paul considered the political scandal "the most embarrassing thing to me in my 47 years as an American." He said he watched the Senate hearings and didn't approve of the jokes made during testimony. "It's not funny at all," he said. "It's all so tragic."

Even so, the issue provided Paul with plenty of zingers:

A classic Lena Horne song of the 1930s contains these lines: "Life is bare, gloom and misery everywhere, so weary all the time, can't go on, everything I had is gone." What's the title? *"Hail to the Chief."*

According to the *Chicago Tribune,* Richard Nixon's very closest friends call him what? *From a phone booth.*

What was Julius Caesar's middle name? *Milhouse.*

According to *The Philadelphia Inquirer,* President Nixon has had something put into the executive bathtub to help him relax. What is it? *The two missing tapes.*

Pat Nixon recently confided that "nobody could sleep with Dick" because of something he does in the middle of the night. What is it he does? *I think he's digging a tunnel.*

Paul's tour obligations prevented him from being as hands-on about his new series as he wanted, though the producers frequently called him for input. At the end of the tour, he returned home to start work on the show, now called *New Temperatures Rising* and filmed audience-free in a studio adjacent to the one formerly used for *The Paul Lynde Show.* The show's makeover, spearheaded by new producers Duke Vincent and Bruce Johnson, extended beyond the name change. The show kept its time slot—Tuesdays at 8 P.M.—but most of the original cast got the heave-ho. "That was such a disaster," admitted actress Joan Van Ark, among the pink-slipped. "They kept trying to fix it up and it only got worse and worse. We started out with James Whitmore in the leading role and ended up with Paul Lynde in the part. That should give you an idea how far a field it all went."

Cleavon Little kept his job. The Tony-winning actor and future star of *Blazing Saddles* (who caught Asher's attention playing a burglar on an episode of *All in the Family*) continued playing Dr. Noland, an intern who ran bingo games and a betting parlor in the lounge during the first season but with his residency had now matured into the hospital's sole voice of reason. "I can think of *Temperatures Rising* as a spiritual contribution," Little said at the time. "Sure, it's TV comedy for the masses and therefore it's unreal. But most people don't want to see 'reality' on television. And my supermilitant black brothers are kidding themselves when they say they do. If I can make people laugh, particularly people who have to be in the hospital, then I think that's positive and life-giving."

Paul led the new cast as hospital head Dr. Paul Mercy, named as a nod to the Catholic hospital of his youth. Sudie Bond, an Obie Award–winning actress two years younger than Paul, played his demanding mother, the hypochondriac owner of the hospital. The rest of the cast included Barbara Cason as a bureaucratic desk clerk besotted with Mercy; Jennifer Darling as a sexed-up nurse, Jeff Morrow as an inept doctor, and Jerry Houser as a goofball intern. Paul's work schedule changed to the typical filming style of a Screen Gems comedy: Mondays and Tuesdays were rehearsal days, and he could sleep until seven or eight; Wednesdays, Thursdays, and Fridays were set aside for filming, which meant Paul had to be up by 5 A.M. to get to the studio in time for makeup.

Mercy's administrative duties kept him from the operating room. Instead, he dealt with ledge jumpers, striking employees, and other sitcom clichés that occurred in the "250-bed, understaffed, bilingual booby hatch." In "A

Classic Case," Mercy worries that a professional football player might sue the hospital:

> NOLAND: I can't believe this. A patient comes into this hospital in pain. An intern misdiagnoses his X-rays—drills two holes in his head, interrupts his career—and you want to let him hang up there for eight weeks when there's absolutely nothing wrong with him!
> MERCY: Precisely.
> NOLAND: Well, I'm not going to let you do it.
> MERCY: Wait a minute, Noland. You know me better than this. I wouldn't let that man suffer up there for eight weeks...
> NOLAND: I'm glad to hear that.
> MERCY: Seven weeks?
> NOLAND: One hour.
> MERCY: Noland, you're heartless.
> NOLAND: I'm on my way up to surgery. When I come down, I'm taking Belovitch out of traction. What you tell him between now and then is your business. You've got one hour.
> MERCY: Noland...Would it help if I told you that his grandfather ran a slave ship?

The writers failed at topicality as often and as miserably as those responsible for the hackneyed plots of *The Paul Lynde Show*. An episode titled "The Physical" plays the sexual revolution for laughs after Mercy thinks he has VD.

> MERCY: Who knows about this?
> NOLAND: So far, just Haskell [*the goofball intern*], you, me, and...whoever.
> MERCY: Noland, I'll get immediate treatment.... Just do me a favor: don't spread this around.
> NOLAND: I was about to tell you the same thing.

Mercy tries to steal penicillin from the hospital pharmacy. When a nurse catches him, he pretends to be looking for a sedative. She tells her overworked boss to "relax—go out and have a good time. Call a girl!" Mercy responds, "I really don't need your prescriptions. I happen to be a qualified VD...I mean MD!" (The clincher: the goofball intern made a mistake with the slides. He has the STD.)

Paul found himself still fighting censors. "For instance, in one scene, the hospital is giving physical examinations," he said. "And the doctor passes the bottle. Now, you know that any child who has ever gone to the doctor has been handed the bottle. There's no bad taste there. It's all part of hospital life. But it was nixed. Now CBS, which has all the top-rated shows, tells life like it is. I think you have to do it nowadays. You just can't have the old television situation comedies like you had ten years ago." Costar Little fought his own battles. "The worst thing was, I couldn't get them to hire black writers to write for me," he said. "It was a battle to make my dialogue real."

Reviews were mixed. *The Hollywood Reporter* thought "the show [was] really outrageous black comedy, reminiscent of a cross between *Hospital* and *Where's Poppa?*" *Variety* thought otherwise:

> The reason that the revamped *New Temperatures Rising Show* did not appear until the third week of the new season was officially listed as production delays. After seeing the initial episode, it could also be that they were very nervous.... Lynde is given more acting and less mugging chances than with his own sitcom of last year, but...[the show] seems destined to fair less effectively in the ratings area.

Network bigwigs called Asher the day after the first episode aired to tell him they'd made a mistake. After some resistance, Asher eventually agreed to take the reins from producers Vincent and Johnson and retool the show. "We understood the changes that they wanted in the show, and we just can't do that kind of work, so we had a talk with Screen Gems and decided to step down," Vincent said. "Bringing back Bill Asher was the right thing for them to do in view of the changing concept."

Asher shut down the poorly rated production for three weeks in November. Dismissing everyone in the cast but Paul and Little, Asher brought back Nancy Fox from the first season to revive her role as student nurse Ellen Turner and created the role of Nurse Amanda Kelly for Barbara Rucker. His mother among the missing, Paul now answered to a board of directors. Asher hired Alice Ghostley to play Mercy's sister, Edwina Moffitt, but the writers usually failed to create any cantankerous chemistry between the two siblings:

MOFFITT: Paul, is that all you're having, black coffee?
MERCY: It goes with my black mood.
MOFFITT: Want me to get you a hamburger with everything on it?
MERCY: Are you kidding? In this hospital, "with everything on it" means they dropped it on the floor. You know, Edwina, a man devotes his life to a noble profession, and then one day he finds out his fellow noblemen treat him like a peasant.
MOFFITT: Well, Daddy gave you your choice of going to a trade school or a med school, and you picked medicine... I think.
MERCY: I should have become a plumber.

In late November, ABC announced the schedule for its "second season" in January, sans *New Temperatures Rising*. The network had considered moving Paul's show from its

Tuesday time slot against *Maude* and a cop show called *Chase,* but ended up shelving it with assurances that it would eventually return to the schedule. Other shows that got the boot included two new series, *Adam's Rib* and *Griff,* and two long-running series: *Room 222,* which had earned Paul's friend Karen Valentine an Emmy Award, and *Love, American Style,* on which Paul had appeared three times—once as a "house bachelor." A 1950s-themed spinoff of a *Love, American Style* segment called *Happy Days* would take over Paul's time slot.

Screen Gems completed nine episodes of the third version of the show. As planned, ABC pulled the show from the air, burning off the remaining episodes over the summer. Paul packed the portrait of himself and Harry the dog that decorated his dressing room and kissed another sitcom goodbye. Despite the show's grim prognosis, Dick Gautier, Paul's Broadway costar from *Birdie,* who appeared as a country music singer in "The Healer Man," one of the summer episodes, detected little of the anxiety and strain that had marred *The Paul Lynde Show* set, "Everything was fine," he says of the taping. "We got on famously."

Robbie Rist, the jinxed cousin Oliver from *The Brady Bunch,* says he had fun working with Paul on a *New Temperatures Rising* episode titled "Kid Genius." "Paul was a total idol of mine when I was younger," he says. "So it was a really big thrill to meet him. I remember him being totally hilarious but with a sort of dark undercurrent. He had this huge painting in his dressing room of him and his dog. He cut his finger on one take when he used his fist instead of a finger to push an elevator call button, but it was definitely funnier. The man really knew funny."

Whatever ill will he spared the cast, Paul shared plenty of it with the press, becoming a TV reporter's dream interview for all his crotchety griping after the show went off the air. "When they asked me to take over *Temperatures Rising,*

I couldn't believe it," he grumbled. "If the show had been a flop before, why did they want to go on with it? I think the scripts were terrible. The only people who liked that show were people who worked in hospitals. Too many people have had bad experiences in them—the mistakes! People have died by mistakes because there is no way to take proper care of the people in hospitals…. Can you imagine what it's like to wait 20 years to finally have your own series, to be honored by having that series bear your own name—and then have it turn out to be something you're thoroughly ashamed of? Then to follow that with another unsuccessful attempt?"

Paul's finger-pointing suggests an awareness that he had painted himself into a comedy corner. Swearing off sitcoms sounded more like an admission of defeat, though he held out hope that he might at least get the kind of parts that Tony Randall scored in the 1950s and 1960s—second fiddle to bigger stars. Now the reality sank in. "In his heart of hearts, he knew that he was a little too gay for television," Jim McLernan says. "He wasn't able to change."

> PETER: True or false? Right this very minute, you are being watched by something on the moon.
> PAUL: Well, where was it when I had my series?
> PETER: Both of them!
> PAUL: That's it, rub it in.

CHAPTER 10

A LITTLE BIT OF
CHER IN ALL OF US

"When I go into a bar, it's 'Oh, look. Miss Bitch just came [in].... Who does she think she is?'"

In Ohio, Paul never let an opening-night performance for a sellout crowd—with its obligatory curtain calls, autograph line, and cast party—keep him from enjoying the local nightlife. And so it was that on the evening of August 12, 1974, with bodyguard in tow, the star found a show bar in Toledo to serve him drinks and an appreciative audience to treat him like royalty. Quickly sloshed, Paul hunkered down at a table to acquaint himself with a young fan. A woman approached them for an autograph. Paul scrawled something along the lines of his usual "Love and Laughter, Paul Lynde," but the woman complained she couldn't read it. Paul tore into her. The bartender jumped to the woman's defense, and the bodyguard to Paul's. As the altercation spun out of control, Paul's new friend suggested that the two of them get the hell out of there.

The pair wound up at the young man's apartment building in the suburbs. On his way to the front door, Paul spotted a police officer driving through the parking lot on patrol. He started screaming obscenities, and the cop stopped.

Unable to calm Paul down, the officer called for backup, but the second policeman had no luck either. They saw little choice but to haul him off to jail.

Later that morning, Ken Shaw, who, in arrangement with John Kenley, produced the play that had brought Paul and costar Elizabeth Allen to Toledo, got a call from a reporter seeking comment about the arrest. Knowing nothing but fearing the worst, Shaw asked the reporter if he could keep the story out of the paper. The reporter told him that it was too late; a popular Canadian radio had broadcast the news that morning after receiving an anonymous tip.

Shaw and his headliner had already scheduled a round of interviews to promote Paul's first appearance in town. Throughout the day, they trudged through them; Paul played off the arrest as nothing much and referred to his near-lover from the bar as "my secretary." Afterwards he asked Shaw, "Do you think anybody has heard about it outside Toledo?"

"Well, it was just on Paul Harvey," Shaw said.

A local politician offered to pull some strings and said he'd discuss the details with Paul in person after that night's performance. Paul was dubious, but figured it couldn't hurt. He and Shaw went to the official's house and found a huge party waiting for them there. The man had just wanted to show off Paul as his guest of honor.

Any Toledo resident who missed Paul's starring role that week got a free show in the local halls of justice on Wednesday afternoon. "We pull up, and the little courthouse looks like Mayberry...a typical country kind of court-house," Shaw says. "Since there's no school...the place is filled with kids and their bicycles and grandmas and moms.... Fans are throwing flowers on the car [and] Lynde is just shaking his head. He knows his whole career is going down the toilet."

Over 100 curiosity seekers filled the courtroom for the hearing, including 40 who stood in the aisles. Paul appeared visibly nervous and said nothing, save "yes" when asked if he understood the charge of public intoxication. With an audience of women and kids, the arresting officer refused to tell the judge that Paul had called him a "cocksucker."

Paul's lawyer pled no contest on his behalf. The judge imposed the maximum fine of $100, plus $10 court costs. "I think the unfavorable publicity you have received is sufficient penalty," he told the defendant. Leaving the courthouse, Paul didn't acknowledge the throng of people that came to see him. One upset member of the audience told a reporter for *The Toledo Blade,* "He wouldn't even sign autographs."

As it turned out, the publicity helped sales of *No Hard Feelings.* Demand for tickets to the Sam Bobrick and Ron Clark production—Kenley titled it *Mother Is Engaged* in his theaters—ensured a week of sellout performances, and the plight of Paul's character, a man wanted by the police after accidentally shooting his wife's new boyfriend, provided knowing laughs.

Paul had an agreement with John Kenley—or at least enough respect for him—to stay out of trouble as much as he could during his Kenley tours. As insurance, Kenley reminded police in Warren, the main location of his operation, that his shows boosted the local economy, and they usually left the star alone. Once when an officer found Paul and a friend in a compromising position in a parked car, he let them go, even after Paul spat, "This is America! You mind your business, and I'll mind mine!"

Outside Ohio, Paul lacked such protection. In Fort Lauderdale to perform *No Hard Feelings* at the end of 1974, Paul reportedly landed in trouble for soliciting young men at a bar, but the incident was covered up and didn't affect ticket sales. Paul may have left his mark in Florida another way, according to a blind item in *The Hollywood Reporter:*

> Guess which popular character-comedian has told friends he's had it with acting and plans to invest his savings in a new 'gay' bar in Fort Lauderdale? Got that hot scoop from my Hollywood Blvd. spy, Larry Limpwrist.

Less keen on the club scene in L.A., Paul usually preferred going to parties instead. Some drunks are bad drunks, others the life of the party. Paul managed both roles in the course of an evening, and hosts could count on the volatile party animal to liven up any festivities. At least once, according to friends, a plastered Paul doffed his clothes and streaked down Santa Monica Boulevard in the middle of the night. His friends had to corral him into a car to bring him home.

Paul's escapades found a more receptive audience among a revolving cast of young men who flocked to his side—and sometimes the other way around. One evening, Paul called his friend David Macklin, a struggling actor. "What are you doing?" Paul asked. "Having a party and getting smashed," Macklin said. Without a pause: "I'll be there in a jiffy." Less than an hour later, Macklin opened the door to find Paul standing there in a bathing suit, holding a half-gallon of vodka. When Macklin stumbled into the living room the next morning, Paul crawled out from under a big coffee table where he had slept to avoid Macklin's snippy dog. "Mary bit *everyone!*" Paul muttered. Macklin poured Bloody Marys down Paul's throat and sent him home in a cab dressed the same way as when he arrived.

Paul used his tongue to gut and fillet his nonfamous friends as often as he did his famous ones. But he took care to show them decency afterwards. Macklin received a rare apology of sorts from Paul after one such flare-up. "I brought my boy toy Howard to a gathering at Paul's house," he says. "Howard didn't take shit from anyone. Paul was serving drinks in some rather elegant glasses. Howard accidentally dropped one, and it shattered on his tile floor. Paul was three sheets to the wind and a bit jealous of Howard—Paul had a bit of a crush on me. He came down on him in a fury, calling him a 'drunken tramp' among other choice words. Howard picked up another of the glasses and dropped it the floor in front of a stunned Paul...then another and another until I grabbed him and got him out the door with Paul screaming as we made a hasty retreat. I called Paul the next day and apologized for my friend. Paul said, 'Don't apologize. If I had to apologize for every time I fucked up, I would be doing nothing else.' He invited us over, including Howard, and took us to his favorite junk-food place on the Strip."

Paul understood the source of his bad behavior better than anyone. "I'm cruel with the tongue," he said. "I have an instinctive sense for people's vulnerable spots, and sometimes I aim for them. I realize that's motivated by my own insecurities, and I regret it later. I don't like to hurt people.... I worry that I'm going to make an ass of myself through drinking too much. If things are going well, I'm a happy drinker; otherwise, alcohol acts as a depressant and I'm a bad drunk. The biggest mistakes of my life happened because of this." A reporter once asked Paul if his lunch cocktail was a martini. "Heavens, no, this isn't a martini," he said. "I wouldn't dare drink those. Just one martini and I'd gut this place."

Paul had one consolation: a rare long-term relationship with Pablo Rodríguez, said to be an escort whose ad he found in *The Advocate*. This "expensive hooker from Long Island," as Murray Grand remembers him, barely spoke English and knew little of Paul's fame, except that it afforded Paul the luxury of his services, which ran as high as $100 an hour.

Rodríguez got along well with the star but refused to move to Los Angeles to be with him. This may have suited Paul's solitary tendencies just fine. Paul could spend time by himself in L.A. and have a reliable companion when he visited New York or dashed away on vacation. Among other trips, the two traveled together on a *Hollywood Squares* junket to Jamaica, and Paul never once caused a scene. "You know, if he had somebody, he was an entirely different person," says Rose Marie, who also went on the trip. "He was happy."

Paul financed a gallery show in New York so Rodríguez could display his large male-nude abstracts. ("You can call it art if you want to," Grand says. "I've seen people paint fences and they were better than that.") Favors like that led some of Paul's friends to consider Rodríguez a gold digger, but others appreciated the emotional bedrock he provided. "[Paul] was a loner, except when Pablo came into the picture," Jan Forbes says. "He really cared about him.... I don't know much about his sex life because we just didn't discuss it, although he did tell me how much he loved Pablo." Paul attached a personalized license plate to his Bentley that spelled out the young man's name.

Still dead-set against pursuing another sitcom and tired of the usual plays he performed in stock, Paul planned something different for the summer of 1975: a laugh-filled evening with Paul Lynde. The stage act would feature monologues and comedy routines written by Jay Redack, now promoted to producer of *Hollywood Squares*. Guest stars would provide additional bang for the buck. "The show's all written and in an envelope," Paul told Earl Wilson. "On the envelope is written 'Open en route—preferably over Utah.' So that I won't wake up a lot of people if I scream my head off."

For years, whenever Paul attended a Vegas show, club owners picked up his tab and asked when he planned to work for them. He always declined, insisting his comedy wasn't suited for Vegas audiences. That year, with the idea of doing a show specifically tailored to his talents, the comic went so far as to announce that the tour would end on the Strip. Gnawing anxiety soon overwhelmed him, and he backed out at the last minute, primarily because of the Vegas date. "It just frightens me," he said. "Vegas is a joke town…. The jokes are timed so the audience can laugh, take a drink, and hear the next joke. I don't tell jokes."

Instead, Paul spent that summer in the comforting bosom of the Kenley Players. He chose the comedy *Stop, Thief, Stop!!* as his sixth production with the company. This effort by TV scribes Woody Kling and Robert J. Hilliard showcased Paul in the role of a cash-strapped game show producer who can't afford alimony payments and can't get his ex-wife, played by Alice Ghostley, to forfeit them. (Oft-married Mickey Rooney starred in the original version, called *Three Goats Blanket.*)

Ghostley had picked up a Tony Award in 1965 and found frequent work in television, most notably as Esmeralda on *Bewitched,* as Aunt Bea's replacement on *Mayberry R.F.D.,* and as a regular on the variety show Julie Andrews hosted on ABC. (She'd even appeared at the Oscars, accepting Maggie Smith's trophy in her absence.) She had yet to make herself an identifiable name beyond perhaps "that woman who sounds like Paul Lynde," a comparison only heightened by her role as Paul's sister on the revamped *New Temperatures Rising.* John Kenley worried that the similarities between the two would undercut their believability as ex-spouses, but in the end no one seemed to mind. One critic even assumed they had deliberately acted the same to reflect how married people take on aspects of each other's personality over time.

The local scribes, no longer so dazzled by Paul's comedy skills, gave the show a harsher reception than they had in the past. Noting the prancing about of actors playing interior designers, Donna Cherain of *The Cleveland Plain Dealer* complained, "It seems a good rule of thumb that whenever jokes about gays are introduced into a comedy, it is usually a signal that the playwrights are starved for material." Ron Pataky of the *Columbus Citizen Journal* warned, "If, like me, you're a Paul Lynde fan, count the week another must along the way. But you'd better be a Paul Lynde fan."

Tour audiences on the road still revered the summer-stock superstar. When Paul threw himself a birthday party in his hotel suite in Dallas, an adoring Texas couple showered him with expensive Western wear. Excited, Paul ran into his room to don the outfit. He emerged decked out in a Stetson hat, a Larry Mahan Western shirt, a pair of cowboy boots...and boxer shorts. "They forgot the fucking pants!" he shouted to the inebriated delight of his guests.

In prime time Paul fell back on his old standby: variety shows and specials, the latest batch hosted by the likes of Mac Davis, the Smothers Brothers, and his old boss Perry Como. Paul still wasn't thrilled with the genre, but he always managed to wrench a few laughs from the hokey proceedings. On a Sandy Duncan special in late 1974, Paul followed up John Davidson's rendition of "I Honestly Love You" by hamming it up in a "Bad, Bad Leroy Brown" production number, playing the title character of the hit song in a pimp daddy suit and telling a string of corny jokes with pure Lyndean gusto:

> I love to do mean things. I make girls walk home from my place...and I live in a submarine!

Once when I was little, I left a fake tooth under my pillow, and then I bit the tooth fairy!

Your man out front asked me to move my car off the curb, so I moved it onto his chest!

On an episode of *The Mac Davis Show* that fall, Paul delivered a send-up of the CBS *Bicentennial Minute:*

Some 200 years ago a young American officer named Nathan Hale volunteered for a dangerous mission: obtaining information about the British forces on Long Island. Disguised as a schoolmaster, he infiltrated the army and was soon sending messages back to American headquarters. Some months later, however, he was captured by the British and sentenced to be hung. To the sounds of military drums, Nathan Hale bravely mounted the gallows, and as the hangman's noose went into place, he uttered the famous words that still echo throughout the land: ring around the collar!

Recognizing the fun Paul could milk from such drivel, ABC offered him the chance to tape a comedy special–cum-pilot to air in the fall of 1975. To hedge its bets, the network made the same deal with Bill Cosby, Dan Rowan and Dick Martin, and Donny and Marie Osmond. Paul claimed he didn't mind this trial arrangement. "I'd rather do a series of specials," he said. "You need such a wealth of material to do a variety show every week. And look at the track record—it's a very fragile form.... The only difference is in who the star is, that personality difference. My personal format will allow me to be Paul Lynde more. I think the reason the network wants me is because of the way I come across on *Hollywood Squares*—and that's Paul Lynde."

As he did on other projects, Paul put his personal polish on the material, griping how he worked on scripts until 3 or 4 in the morning and wrangled with censors by day. The end result, *The Paul Lynde Comedy Hour*, aired on November 6, 1975. Paul started the show with a walk down a long runway, at the end of which he declared, simply: "There's a little bit of Cher in all of us!" Then he took questions, Carol Burnett–style, from audience members. One of the obvious plants wanted to know what bugged Paul the most, and the host had an all-too quick response at the ready:

> Everything! I'm easily annoyed. But one of the things that probably bugs me the most: If I flew a hundred times a year, I know my bag would never be the first one off the conveyer belt. But what I want to know is, whose bag is that? Nobody ever picks it up. It just keeps going round and round and round. You know what I think? I think it's a dummy bag. It doesn't belong to anybody. The airlines put it there just to drive you crazy.

The laugh track was highly amused.

Paul spent the rest of the hour yukking it up with Nancy Walker, who showed up as part of her first obligation under an ultimately unsuccessful contract with ABC. (*The Nancy Walker Show* and *Blansky's Beauties,* her two eventual sitcoms for the network, tanked.) Rich Little and Jack Albertson (the "man" of *Chico and the Man)* appeared in comedy cameos. Unable to snag a pregnant Diana Ross as his musical guest, Paul settled for the Osmond Brothers. Though past their pop idol prime, the group agreed to do the show only if Paul appeared in turn on Donny and Marie's special a few weeks later. With the inclusion of senior citizens Bob Hope and Kate Smith, the Osmond show offered something for every generation.

For all his objections with the quality of other variety show writing, Paul showed the world that he had no room to talk. In a series of uninspired skits, he portrayed a daredevil motorcyclist named Evil Weevil, a know-it-all detective (essentially Sedgewick Hawk-Styles in everything but name and locale), and a rich man who buys himself a young boy, played by Robbie Rist. He closed the show with a rousing group sing-along of The Captain and Tennille's "Love Will Keep Us Together."

Even with weak material, the variety format promised Paul a better chance at Nielsen success. As *Variety* noted, "What it all proved was that Lynde can carry the star burden in this format with more promise than the sitcom placements he's had on ABC in the past." The network ignored the trade paper's advice to "take the gamble on Lynde" and awarded the mid-season berth to the more demographically desirable Osmonds, whose special placed slightly higher in the ratings. "It takes a certain degree of boldness to put them on the air, a couple of kids, 18 and 16, who've never done a show of their own," insisted ABC president Fred Silverman.

Paul accepted the network's consolation prize: the chance to do more of his own specials, so long as he frequently appeared as a special guest star on the pop duo's weekly program. This combination—acerbic gay comic and "the Prince and Princess of entertainment"—falls just short of the infamous *Pink Lady and Jeff* as the oddest match in the history of televised variety shows, but Paul was game. Silverman hoped the siblings would recreate the ratings magic of Sonny and Cher, another act he had enticed to TV. One critic cracked that the gambit was wise if only because the Osmonds couldn't divorce each other.

ABC probably took more than a few measly ratings points into consideration when it chose the television neophytes over a performer with long-standing comedic chops. Overlooking Paul's prime-time failures and continuing arrests, scandal-shy network suits must have noticed that his homosexuality had become less of a trade secret.

Several years before, in the months before the Stonewall riots, Angelo d'Arcangelo had published *The Homosexual Handbook,* an underground paperback that included "Uncle Fudge's Grapevine Lineup," a list of famous homosexuals. The living, dead, or suspected entertainers who made the cut included Fred Astaire, Jack Benny, Rock Hudson, Bert Lahr...but not Paul Lynde. Paul didn't completely fool everyone, particularly those in the business. Freddie Roman, king of the Catskills comics, once got laughs from the guests at a Friars Club fete for Carol Burnett when he quipped, "Carol is one of the funniest ladies on TV, although Paul Lynde does come close."

Never warming to jokes that outed him, Paul did loosen up a little as the Me Decade progressed and people started growing more tolerant. While he didn't join other celebrities at *A Star-Spangled Night for Rights,* an all-star concert at the Hollywood Bowl in 1977, he at least signed the related petition in support of gay rights. He preferred acknowledging his tribal membership by more subtle means.

Paul wore caftans like a second skin. Denny Doherty of the Mamas and Papas and *Medical Center* star James Daly had donned these muumuu-like tunics in public with their machismo intact. When Paul wore his, Cliff Jahr of *The Village Voice* described it as "gaily colored," and a reporter for *People* dubbed him "Larry of Fire Island" and quoted him saying, "Someday I'm going to go onstage in a dress if I want to." He also lugged a "man purse" on so many chat shows that a curious viewer asked columnist Hy Gardner for an inventory.

When the contents of Paul's purse (which looks like a camera case with a shoulder strap) were dumped, these articles tumbled out: two pairs of glasses—one dark, one for reading—a book of American Express traveler's checks and a script for the John Kenley production in Warren, Ohio, of *Plaza Suite*. Why the purse? "Because," the comedian complains, "these days there are no pockets in men's clothes."

Archie Bunker grasped the meaning of this fashion fad on an *All in the Family* episode: "Let me spell it out for you: F-A-G...fruit." Caught on Oval Office audiotape, President Nixon insisted a character he saw on the same show was "obviously queer" for wearing a foulard, another of Paul's fashion staples.

When speaking with the press, Paul also unabashedly embraced his inner Julia Child. Though he stood by his all-American beef stew as his best dish (and once served it at a buffet for gourmet Vincent Price), Paul loved discussing fancy foods, as well as froufrou décor and diet strategies, with any reporter who asked. Even in Peggy Hudson's *TV 73*, a Scholastic Book sold to elementary school kids, Paul wouldn't shut up about food. "I went on the Olympic Ski Women's Diet," he told the author. "I can't believe they can ski on it. I could barely walk!"

The gossip pages hinted at further poof proof with headlines that carried more than one meaning:

Paul Lynde: TV's Clown With a Broken Heart—Why He Will Never Allow Himself to Love a Woman Again

Paul Lynde Tells Mystery Woman Who Saved His Life: "I'm Sorry But I Only Know One Way to Love!"

Paul Lynde's Miscast: He's a Devout Bachelor

He May Live Like a Loner, But We Found Out About All
His Women

To some people, Paul Lynde
May be just another pretty face...
But to those who really know him,
He's the man who took Errol Flynn's place.

Gossip wag Rona Barrett picked up on how much Paul
hated comparisons to Alan Sues, the gay presence on *Rowan
& Martin's Laugh-In.* In one report, she tattled:

> The *Hollywood Squares* funnyman wasn't very funny at a
> party Ruta Lee threw in Tinseltown recently. Seems some-
> one walked up to Paul and said how much they enjoyed him
> on *Laugh-In,* whereupon Paul turned at least 14 shades of
> red-hot red. Paul is one of our wittiest men, but I wish
> Paul's head wouldn't get swelled at times. If he doesn't cool
> it, I strongly suspect those ugly rumors we once heard about
> Paul might find their way to print again.

A *People* cover story about Paul in September 1976 likely
settled any lingering suspicion about "those ugly rumors" for
readers with the most remote knowledge of gay culture. In the
article, accompanied by a backstage photograph of a "chauf-
feur-bodyguard [who] doubled as his hairstylist and suite
mate" fussing over him, the comedian mused, "My following
is straight. I'm so glad. Y'know gay people killed Judy
Garland, but they're not going to kill me." The article immediately followed this odd declaration, which had been lifted
from an exposé in *The Village Voice* that had appeared a few
months earlier, with a parenthetical mention of Jim Davidson's
death plunge.

As if he had enough with the closet and the limits it placed on his career, Paul occasionally pushed the door open a crack on his own. When a Cleveland disc jockey asked why women everywhere adored him, Paul replied, "Probably because I have no interest in them at all." During a Q&A session at a Kenley curtain call, an uninformed fan asked Paul why he had never married. Standing on the stage in his caftan, Paul growled, "Do you live in a cave?"

With no other major work on the horizon in the year of America's Bicentennial, Paul overcame his fears and went out on the road with the touring show he had scrapped the previous summer. "My manager told me this year I must try making personal appearances," he explained. "Joan Rivers and Totie Fields told me [that] once I tried it I'd never go back to the theater."

In planning his show, Paul didn't want the burden of performing alone. He joked that he had his heart set on a great opening act, but he couldn't get his first choices—Barbra Streisand, Elton John, Henry Kissinger, King Kong, Betty Ford or Patty Hearst. He settled for Mimi Hines, a singer who had replaced Streisand as the star of *Funny Girl* on Broadway; Roz Clark, a young African-American vocalist whose national exposure included guest appearances on *The Tonight Show*; and Wayland Flowers and Madame. Paul had helped discover the puppeteer when he saw him perform at a gay bar in Provincetown, Massachusetts. Amused by Madame's bawdiness—"That's my name, not my profession," she'd joke—Paul convinced "that queen with the puppets" to head to Hollywood. In 1975, Flowers and his elderly charge had been featured on a summer comedy series called *Keep On Truckin'* and, thanks to Paul, would soon start appearing on *Hollywood Squares* among other shows.

Instead of entertaining the usual mob of people on the Kenley circuit, Paul opened his tour in Philadelphia in June.

"John's theater couldn't afford this package," Paul said. "He would end up making no money." Kenley once said Paul was "such a shrewd businessman that he could outwit any Yankee horse trader." Even so, Paul hated the theater-in-the-round construction of many of his venues that summer; he believed "exits make theater."

Before the premiere, Paul hit the city's clubs with a reporter for *The Village Voice* in tow. "We're appearing right over here at the theater in Valley Forge," he told patrons of one bar. "And we'd love it if you'd all come out and see us." He offered the same spiel at the next club, but, the reporter wrote, a "large woman with pendulous cleavage and a blond beehive" confronted Paul on his way back to his limo. "You son-of-a-bitch! You have the nerve to come around here after ripping us off?" she yelled. "I'm a transsexual and you're a faggot just like the rest of us." She spat at him and stormed off. Upset, Paul returned to his hotel. "I've never been spat on in my entire life," he fumed. "Oh, Jesus, that's it. I'm never coming back to Philadelphia, never. I'm getting out of this business—I mean it."

Paul went on with a show, which he opened each night "so people don't have to wait until the second half of the show to see the person they really came to see." He treated audiences to some variation of the following spectacle:

Dressed in a jacket emblazoned with iconic X's and O's, Paul walks onstage to the accompaniment of Christmas music and, once the applause dies down, launches into his opening monologue. "It's hard to get the spirit of Christmas in California," he jokes. "Santa wears hot pants." He tells the crowd he had asked for a triple Shirley Temple backstage but got a Phyllis Diller. "It's flat." Then he lights a cigarette and teases the crowd, "Eat your hearts out. Yes, I am one of the weak ones. I've even found a way to smoke in the shower."

Clark comes out and sings a few crowd-pleasers like "The

Way We Were." When she finishes, Paul reappears with a segment on teenagers. He asks for a round of applause for all the
kids who haven't assassinated a president, and, getting it,
launches into "Kids," his signature tune from *Bye Bye Birdie*.

After Flowers's act, Paul returns in a new outfit to the
instrumental accompaniment of "I Feel Pretty" from *West
Side Story*. ("I feel pretty and witty and gay!"—an inside joke
Redack would resurrect on a "costume party" episode of
Squares two years later with Paul dressed as a golden-locked
Narcissus.) "You like it?" he asks. "It's called a caftan.
They're from the Far East. This one's from my bedroom win-
dow…. If you're shy, they're great for orgies—food orgies!"

Paul launches into a talk about his problems with "The
Battle of the Bulge," which serves mostly as a plug for a certain diet plan he heard about from comedienne Ruth Buzzi:

> Of all the diets I've been on, I'd say that Weight Watchers is
> the most successful and sensible. The one thing I have
> against them is that you dirty every dish and pan in the
> house for one meal. There was a woman who always sat
> beside me at the meetings. She'd always rush in late. She'd
> still be in her apron. She always looked like my Aunt Nellie.
> She'd say, "Well, Paulie, how's it been this week?" And I'd
> say, "Well, it's the 'no booze' that's the rough part." She
> said, "Oh, honey. You mean you've been going without
> this?" And she reached into her apron pocket and handed
> me a joint. Well, I never missed another meeting after that,
> and I always made sure I saved her a seat!

Hines performs a set of "money songs" by the likes of
Elton John and Billy Joel and other standards. Then Paul
returns to the stage one last time to pull another Carol Burnett
and answer questions, some of which the road manager has
planted. As always, someone asks Paul if he plans to marry.

Paul tells the usual story about Marilyn Organ and explains how the one-who-got-away came to a performance of the show with her kids and looked "very unhappy!"

For his conclusion, Paul launches into a recitation of his most memorable "zingers" with questions prerecorded by Peter Marshall. He thanks the crowd and closes the show with a warbled rendition of the Jackson 5 chestnut "I'll Be There" and a sign-off he started using as his trademark: "Until we meet again, you stay happy and you keep well…because I sure need you."

Paul adapted the show to his environment. "This is my first time in-the-round, and I was walking on eggshells all night," he said after opening night in Philadelphia. "The contrast is frightening. I like to be blinded by the footlights." Although he admitted he was "floundering" at first, he warmed to the format and added bits to the show as the tour progressed. He treated Milwaukee audiences to old sketches like his safari bit. "I haven't done it since the early days of the Ed Sullivan television show," he said, conveniently forgetting all those subsequent years he milked the bit.

Most critics dismissed the experiment. "After a while, even most of the faithful grew tired of the strangest collection of guffaws this side of a TV laugh machine and [Paul's] whinny on the word *sex*," complained Michael H. Drew of *The Milwaukee Journal*. "And being told repeatedly how much the Star loves and needs us. (Or is it our $7.50 Lynde admires?)" Will Leonard of the *Chicago Tribune* laid into Paul as a "Liberace without a piano" in "a show of limited appeal," saving his true ire for Wayland Flowers, who he said "hauls forth the ugliest hag of a puppet we've ever seen and runs her through a raunchy monologue that brings its greatest response from a gynandrous group of chaps in section D."

Though these snipes didn't affect the brisk sale of tickets, the company knew to keep bad reviews away from the star, especially those that lavished more praise on the featured performers. When the headline of one postshow write-up read "Hines Outshines Star Lynde," the road manager had all the newspapers removed from the hotel lobby. "I don't think Paul ever saw it, God bless him," Hines says.

Paul still found reasons to fume. One night before a performance, he yelled for the road manager, and everyone hurried to the trailer that served as his dressing room. Applying his makeup with one hand, Paul crabbily waved at the far wall with the other. "I'm dressing next to this bathroom here," he said, "and this trailer smells like a cunt...I think."

Paul's manager, who also represented Hines, enlisted the singer to keep the star sober before showtime. She says she had no problem keeping him in line. "He was a pleasure to be around as far as I'm concerned," says Hines. "He would make us laugh all the time. There wasn't a day that went by when we weren't all screaming with laughter on that tour. It was so much fun."

Once a show ended, all bets were off. Paul saved his drinking for the after-hours, and the cast often tagged along with him. One night they all went to a leather bar with a clientele unimpressed by celebrities or females. "Some guy jammed a cigarette into my bare arm," Hines says. "They didn't want any women in there.... Paul got into a fight with the guy, and we all left in a huff."

The National Enquirer later misrepresented this encounter, reporting that Paul was the one who had burned Hines with the cigarette. Asked if her drunken friend may have ever used her flesh as an ashtray, Hines says, "Oh, no, he didn't burn me! Some guy in a leather armband with studs on it burned me."

For all his other disappointments, Paul could at least take comfort that he had reached a certain level of fame at this stage of his career. On an episode of *Maude,* Arthur Harmon,

Maude's conservative next-door neighbor, is expecting to meet his idol John Wayne. He arrives at Maude's house dressed as a cowboy, but she slams the door in his face:

ARTHUR *(in his best cowboy voice)*: I'm warning you, ma'am. Don't you try that again, or I'll blow this here homestead to Kingdom Come!
MAUDE: Perfect! Paul Lynde, right?

In Armistead Maupin's *Tales of the City*, a popular column that first ran in the *San Francisco Examiner*, the character Michael Tolliver offers a list of resolutions for Valentine's Day 1977, including his promise not to "do impressions of Bette Davis, Tallulah Bankhead, Mae West, or Paul Lynde."

Several entertainers—famous and otherwise—did easily recognizable impersonations of Paul. Comedian Dan Westfall borrowed heavily from Paul's clean-cut days, right down to a poem about a dead dog, in an act he took to third-rate programs like the *Rosey Grier Show* in the late 1960s. Fred Travalena, Larry Storch, and Paul's summer-stage box-office nemesis, John Davidson, did takes on him in their Vegas acts, and Richard Dawson frequently dropped Paul into his game show patter. Rich Little not only had a Paul Lynde impression—which he used as Bob Cratchit in his one-man *A Christmas Carol* for television—he also did Richard Nixon mimicking Paul. "Of all my impressions, when I do Paul Lynde it's instant recognition," he said.

When Dinah Shore devoted an hour of her daytime talker to Paul, she staged a musical interlude in which she played Peter Marshall to the passable Paul Lyndes of Alice Ghostley, Charlotte Rae, Maggie Smith and Karen Valentine. On *The Tonight Show,* Doc Severinsen got more laughs doing Paul Lynde than the visibly nervous original. Paul told host Johnny

Carson that nobody had ever aped him as well as Fred Little, Rich's brother.

Paul appreciated his many doppelgängers but considered the public's attention a more sincere form of flattery. For all his surliness with peers, Paul graciously treated his fans as "my people" throughout his career. Asked by a reporter to specifically define what he meant by "my people," Paul humbly answered, "America."

When he and his sister Helen waited at the airport for a flight home to Ohio to bury their brother Johnny, Paul put on a cheery front for passersby who recognized him. Helen asked him why. "Fans don't know I'm depressed," Paul said, "so why act that way in front of them?"

The night when Paul and "writer" met Basil Cross for dinner, another college friend unexpectedly brought along his partner, his parents, and his sister's family. Though this extra baggage spoiled what was to have been a quiet reunion of old friends, Paul put on an affable front and stayed charming all evening, even when other diners interrupted the meal for autographs.

Paul never waved to the camera on *Hollywood Squares,* but he made an exception for a special needs child whose parents had written him to say their kid connected with his humor. Paul also showered attention on a small group of young girls who idolized him. When he discovered they had driven long distances to see him perform or went out of their way to get in touch with him, he showed his appreciation by inviting them to dinner, dog shows, and other events.

Of these fans young and old, none could match the devotion of Beverly Mitchell. So grateful to Paul for encouraging her to lose 100 pounds, the grade school teacher moved to his hometown, named her German shepherd "Paula," and designated a room in her home as a Paul Lynde Museum. She took her second grade classes on tours of the houses where Paul

had lived and kept anything Paul left behind when he stopped by at Christmas—wine bottles, cigarette butts, even shoe prints in snow that she preserved in her freezer. Mitchell also spearheaded a campaign to honor Paul with signs on the way into town announcing the place as his childhood home. Paul returned for the dedication ceremony over Thanksgiving weekend 1977. Though he appreciated her devotion, Paul found Mitchell's obsession extreme and told Merv Griffin that Mount Vernon considered her the "town idiot."

All the same, Paul's craving for attention could be just as extreme. Taking a teenage fan on a limo ride in New York, Paul asked the driver to pull over. "Watch this," he said as he stuck his hand out the window. "Hey, everyone," he yelled. "It's a famous person's hand!" A crowd quickly gathered to get a look at the mystery man. Paul rolled the window down, stuck out his head, and said, "It's me...Paul Lynde!" The crowd loved it, and so did Paul.

Despite the obvious signs of his queerness—or perhaps because of them—women comprised Paul's largest fan base. For the most part, Paul preferred things this way. "I'd rather have women in the audience than men," he said. "Men don't laugh. Women are a much better audience." Sometimes, his female following pushed fanaticism to the limit. One woman from South Carolina reportedly took Paul's last name and swore they had married. Another traveled from Florida and made her daughter cry outside Paul's house to get his attention. Paul said that after he ignored her, the mother wrote letters to Harvey Korman that detailed Paul's monstrous ways.

Paul drew the occasional male worshipper as well. A foot fetishist in an autograph line wanted to take pictures of Paul's feet. John Kenley recalls that the star obliged him. But legend has it that when a blitzed fan in a gay bar asked Paul to sign his package, Paul dismissed him with a cool and simple, "I can't write that small." (Tennessee Williams and Truman Capote have also gotten credit for this comeback.) George Gobel once received a letter from a male fan that read "Dear George: I think you're cute, adorable, an altogether lovable guy, and we never miss you on *Hollywood Squares*. P.S. I'm in love with Paul Lynde."

When the Osmonds finally joined the ABC weekly lineup in January 1976, Paul lent his pissy persona to the sunshine-and-rainbow proceedings. On 30-plus episodes over the course of four seasons, he performed an assortment of comedic shorts and production numbers for the cheery pair. He offered monologues as the author of silly books like *Know Your Gorilla* and *The Arctic on $5 a Day*. He dressed in drag as "Wicked Esther" in an attempted spoof of *The Wizard of Oz* that featured Ray Bolger as the Scarecrow, Lucille Ball as the Tin Man, and Paul Williams as the Cowardly Lion. He even eked out Aretha Franklin's "Respect" while dressed as Napoleon in an unfortunate take-off of *Heaven Can Wait* with Betty White and Suzanne Somers.

The nadir of Paul's prime-time high jinks with the Osmond clan has to be an infamous 1977 *Star Wars* tribute with Kris Kristofferson, Redd Foxx, a stock actor in a Darth Vader suit, and a chorus line of lady Storm Troopers. Paul played an imperial officer determined to capture Donny's Luke, Marie's Leia, and Kristofferson's Han Solo. Foxx interjected one-liners as a floating Jedi spirit.

> IMPERIAL OFFICER: You thought you'd get away? Don't you know you'll never escape from the Farce?
> DARTH VADER: That's the Force!
> IMPERIAL OFFICER: Oh, don't bother me with grammar at a time like this!

When Chewbacca captures him, Paul yells, "Get your big ape hands off me!" Darth Vader escapes, which also miffs Paul. "Well, where does that leave me, Mr. Ungrateful?" The Wookie escorts Paul into a ship as the cast sings a few snippets of "Leaving on a Jet Plane."

The variety specials Paul made for ABC usually appeared once or twice a season, sometimes during a sweeps month. Paul resigned himself to the format, calling it the best platform for his comic style. "My forte is the belly laugh," he said.

Paul served as "ABC's answer to trick or treat" when he hosted his own Halloween special in October 1976. Unlike his first comedy hour, this one had a storyline, thanks in part to Paul's old *New Faces* compatriot Ronny Graham, who contributed material. Paul discovers that his maid, Margaret Hamilton, is actually a witch. The same iconic green make-up and outfit she wore in *The Wizard of Oz* gives her away. Hamilton's sister turns out to be Billie Hayes as Witchiepoo, the cackling hag from Sid and Marty Krofft's *H.R. Pufnstuf*. Hayes agreed to reprise the character as a favor to Paul, a friend since their *What's New* days.

The sisters want Paul to help them promote all that is good about their kind. To secure his star power, they grant him three wishes, which lead to sketches with Tim Conway and Florence Henderson, mother of *The Brady Bunch*. They also treat him to some "soothing, quiet dinner music" in the form of "Detroit Rock City" by Kiss. The well-behaved (and censored) rock group sang two additional numbers, "Beth" and "King of the Nighttime World," and bantered a little with the host. "Just what I always wanted," Paul told them, "four Kisses on the first date...I can take one look at you four and I can tell you how you got your name and how you got your act. You had a fight and your mothers told you to 'Kiss' and make up."

The evening ends in a haunted dance club, with Henderson performing a disco version of "That Old Black

Magic" and Roz "Pinky Tuscadero" Kelly (as both Paul and the announcer repeatedly identify the *Happy Days* actress) teaching everybody how to do the Hustle.

The next spring, Paul invited Cloris Leachman and Tony Randall to appear on his third special. Paul told the audience that they had all attended Northwestern University, but he was the only one who earned a degree. "As a result," he joked, "they both have their own series, while I stand around watching Donny Osmond break balloons." Among the evening's offerings—some of them written by an unknown writer named David Letterman—Paul did a couple of *New Faces*–style monologues, one as a bowler abducted by Martians, the other as a Pentagon employee trying to sweet-talk a town into accepting a nuclear laboratory.

Paul came clean about working with his college friend. "Cloris can be so difficult," he said. "We're so close—we are like brother and sister. But she is demanding, and she is always late." Leachman has her own memories of Paul's backstage behavior. "[Working with Paul] was great until he started drinking," she says. Paul may have partaken more frequently that week because he had to give up another vice. "[Leachman and Randall] are both so funny," Paul said, "but neither smokes. Tony is the worst about it. The first day he came on the set, he told everyone that no one could smoke except me, and I could only smoke because I was the star. I felt so bad about all the crew not being able to smoke that I didn't either. Tony is just impossible about the subject."

Others who performed in the smoke-free environment included K.C. and the Sunshine Band—"my favorite group," Paul insisted—and *Roots* star LeVar Burton, who participated in a Fruit of the Loom send-up in which a bunch of grapes, played by Randall, insists on using the Method to enhance his performance. *Variety* still backed Paul. "He propelled the hour almost single-handedly by the dominance of his comedy style. Lynde could front a good variety half-hour series. Might help him escape that game show cubicle."

Paul didn't seem to agree with this assessment, judging by the about-face he pulled on his fourth special, which aired during the holidays in 1977. Still dreaming of movie stardom, Paul tried to show the depth of his talents with *'Twas the Night Before Christmas*, a feel-good period piece written by Dick Clair and Jenna McMahon, who later created *The Facts of Life* and *Mama's Family*. Paul played Clark Cosgrove, a surly family man whose crazy relatives and annoying neighbors crowd his house on a Christmas Eve in the 1890s. The cast included many of Paul's showbiz friends: Anne Meara as his wife, Foster Brooks and Martha Raye as her parents, Alice Ghostley as his mother, George Gobel as a peddler, and Anson Williams (Potsie of *Happy Days*) as an annoying caroler. Paul finagled a spot in the cast for Raye. "It's my chance to repay her for all the times she used me on her NBC *Comedy Hour* back in the 1950s," he said.

Pushed to his limits after chasing a cat onto a snowy roof, Cosgrove almost tells his children he's the real person who puts the merry in their Christmas. He has a change of heart when his youngest daughter excitedly runs downstairs to see what Santa left her. Cosgrove then improvises a poem for the entire family...though it's actually Clement C. Moore's famous Christmas offering. No one on the show used cue cards because they could have distracted the children. "I had to do the poem five different times for five different camera angles," Paul explained. "If America thinks I did this with cue cards, I'll kill myself." (Paul often joked that Lucille Ball and Carol Burnett refused to teach him the art of card reading.)

Though the special received an "Award of Excellence" from the Film Advisory Board, Paul's plan to impress Hollywood didn't work. The show barely broke the top 30 in a tie with an episode of *Carter Country* and received only passable reviews. "An inept script and a subpar performance by Paul Lynde worked against the best efforts of a charming cast of characters in this ABC Yuletide special," jeered *Variety.*

Paul ended up getting better reviews that year for his commercials for a New York bank. In a survey of "star celebrities," Paul ranked third behind Abraham Lincoln hawking life insurance and Bugs Bunny shilling dental floss. His pitchman prowess beat out that of Gene Kelly, Candice Bergen, Catherine Deneuve, Speedy Alka-Seltzer, and Robert Blake. Worried about overexposure, he passed on offers to plug toothpaste in national campaigns.

Paul never expected to be loved by everyone. "Humor isn't universal," he said. "A lot of people don't find Paul Lynde funny, but that's good, because if we all laughed at the same thing, we'd let Bob Hope do it and there wouldn't be any jobs for the rest of us."

CHAPTER 11

PAUL LYNDE
GOES MA-A-A-AD

"Give me Burger King, Jack in the Box—
and my idea of real sin is a Denny's at 3 A.M."

Marilyn Organ, still married and living in Chicago, had seen Paul off and on since he'd made snarky comments at her wedding reception. She had watched him in *New Faces of 1952* when it rolled through town and had taken in his live show the previous summer. They also had fun at high school reunions, snickering together in a corner, their tumultuous (in Paul's mind, at least) past so much water under the bridge. But when she opened her door one afternoon in October 1977, Organ hardly expected to see her high school sweetheart on the other side. Standing there in expensive slippers Dean Martin had given him, looking slightly worse for wear, Paul had a story to tell. There had been a little altercation at the Burger King in Evanston.

Over the years, Northwestern had shown its appreciation to famous alum Paul with small gestures like a 1970 merit award for "reflecting credit upon the university." When the school invited the star back as grand marshal of the annual homecoming parade, he gladly accepted. Paul made a big to-do over the honor on his flight to Chicago by passing out flowers dyed with the university's purple and white colors. For its part, Northwestern planned a halftime show in which the marching band formed a grid in the shape of the tic-tac-toe board on *Hollywood Squares*.

The festivities passed uneventfully until late Saturday night, when the corked grand marshal stumbled into a local Burger King with a "bodyguard." As he waited to order, Paul launched into a string of racist comments about black people and welfare. He noticed a HELP WANTED sign behind the counter and told the only black person in line that he should apply for the job. When his turn came, Paul informed the server, "Forget the order. I'm here to see about the job." The people behind him chuckled nervously. After a mix-up with the orders, Paul pointed to the black man and said, "It's his. I don't think he understands English." The man took his bag and muttered something about a desire to "kick his motherfucking ass." Paul flipped him the bird. When his "bodyguard" tried to calm him down, Paul sneered, "That's what 'they' do to us."

James Pitts, the man on the receiving end of Paul's drunken tirade, happened to be a professor of sociology at the university. Pissed off, he went home and fired off a letter that the campus paper published on October 25. "I was so absorbed in Lynde's behavior (and the question of whether a 6-foot-9 black NU alumnus and Ph.D. employed by his alma mater can get away with beating the hell out of an intoxicated but wealthy and famous white fellow alumnus) that I didn't immediately notice that the order was mine," he wrote. A student corroborated the story in another letter printed the same day.

At first, Paul insisted the incident never happened. Then he tried to downplay it. "The blacks will try to make a big thing about it," he told the school paper a few days later, "but don't let them." When the furor showed no sign of dying down, Paul prepared a statement: "I apologize sincerely for anything

I said, but I was both physically and emotionally exhausted and upset. If I called the newspapers every time a person insulted me, I would have a severe case of laryngitis."

Paul claimed that an encounter earlier that evening had put him in a bad mood. As he left a reception on campus, he explained, two black men yelled to him, "Hey, man, who ever told you you were funny?" Paul shot back, "The American Academy of Humor." The academy had, in fact, named him the funniest man of the year in 1975, though admittedly this organization wasn't necessarily in touch with the comedic tastes of modern youth.

Crabby, hungry, and "feeling the liquor I had consumed," Paul had then headed to Burger King for some comfort food. "I have vibes for people who don't like me," he continued, "and this black, I knew immediately, was no fan of mine. I know he will probably deny it, but he gave me a very hostile grimace as an acknowledgment."

Paul only dug a deeper hole for himself when he tacked on the following observation: "At the conclusion of the parade, I mentioned to my bodyguard how disappointed I was that so few blacks were along the parade route...In the last few years, on my summer tours, I've noticed the absence of any blacks in the audience. I don't think it's just a case of economics; the blacks buy tickets when it's a black show."

The uproar fueled the ongoing racial debate at Northwestern and smoldered for weeks. Tom Roland, the director of special events, told a local reporter, "There's no question that we'll be on special guard about whom we invite [next year]." Roland regretted inviting his old friend, with whom he had previously worked in Waa-Mu and as an understudy in *New Faces of 1956*. "I hadn't seen him in 21 years," he said, "and a lot can happen to a person in all those years."

Just as that furor died down, Paul made headlines again by getting in trouble in Utah. Beginning that fall, the Osmonds taped their variety show in their own television studio near Salt Lake City. In January, after a night on the town, Paul discovered that someone had stolen a briefcase containing $1,000 from his car. He approached a police officer investigating another burglary at the time and demanded his attention by screaming the usual profanities. Yet again, Paul's cocktail mouth landed him in jail.

The Osmonds couldn't have been too surprised by Paul's shenanigans. Donny has written that Paul spared no one his nastiness, and scriptwriter Bruce Vilanch compared the frequently sloshed star to Josef Mengele. Still, the Osmonds—and the producers of *Hollywood Squares* for that matter—worried about fallout. "Of all places, Utah, to find a place to cause trouble," Jay Redack says. "Maybe because at home there's more activity, and he doesn't have to go look for it. But he gets to Utah and he has to go prowling, and he winds up in trouble....We were trying to keep it quiet. Well, you know, you didn't want bad publicity about your star. I'm pretty sure the Osmonds have a lot of weight in Utah."

Noting it was Paul's first offense in the Beehive State, the judge dropped the charge of public intoxication. Rumors spread that Paul might get kicked off the show, but the *New York Post* dismissed such talk. The Osmonds, it reported, "turned out to take him to dinner [because they] are big on Christian charity, and they're also professionals who can read the Nielsen ratings as well as the next family."

Paul kept the gig and his hosting duties on his own comedy specials, which he claimed made him the highest-paid performer on television. He also continued to accept outside work, showing up that May on *Komedy Tonite,* a comedy pilot for NBC that featured his former costar Cleavon Little. During the Burger King fracas, he said he'd soon be working with the all-black cast, as if he expected that to excuse his behavior.

Like many comedians, Paul had told his share of ethnic jokes, but he insisted he didn't particularly like racial humor. "They want me to do a lot of race put-down stuff and a lot of double entendres," he said. "I tell them, 'That's your humor, not mine…. I don't dig that.'" Still, easy laughs and *Hollywood Squares* went hand in hand:

> Your carpet is brown, your furniture is brown, your walls are brown. What does that say about you?
> *My maid exploded!*

> Benjamin Franklin once observed that before doing this your eyes should be wide open but after your eyes should be kept half shut. After doing what?
> *Impersonating Charlie Chan.*

> According to the Wonderful World of Animals, do flies make good pets? *¡Sí, senor!*

> In Italy it is traditional to throw rice at a newlywed couple, just as it is here. But it is also tradition to throw something else in Italy. What? *Soccer games and elections.*

> What do we call a cat with blue eyes; a small head; cream-colored body; and chocolate face, legs, and tail?
> *A tap dancer.*

Fans forgave these zingers, but not without some mild rebuke. "We're still going to love you," one fan told him, "but damn it, you let up on us Italians." Nevertheless, this child of the homogenous Midwest of the 1930s and 1940s, living at the high point of the Civil Rights movement, vented prejudiced comments more often as he grew older and crustier. "He said things that were politically incorrect," Cloris

Leachman says. "They were just savage. He got very bigoted, and I never saw a whisper of that at school."

Cracks like "I'm the only Gentile on the street!" might have gotten some laughs at Christmas time, but Paul's other observations about Jews didn't sound so harmless. "Paul Lynde was a despicable anti-Semite," says Skip E. Lowe, a Los Angeles public-access icon. "He hated Jews. For a long time he didn't know I was Jewish, he thought that I was 100% Italian. I'd tell him to stop being so rude and ignorant, but he just kept on with the same sick Jew-bashing, 'Hollywood's run by the fucking hook-noses. The Jews own this town, Skippy. Everything's controlled by them.' One day, sick of all his hateful ranting, I cornered him and made him listen, 'Paul, I'm Jewish.' He refused to believe it. 'Oh, fuck you, Mary. You're no Jew! I can spot those big-nosed fucks a mile away.' 'Oh, yes I am, Paul. My mother's Jewish. You're talking to a Jew, Paul, a real live Jew!' When I finally convinced him I was Jewish, he completely changed toward me. That sorry-assed bigot wouldn't even look in my direction after that. Paul wanted to be a bigger star, and he blamed his career problems and alcoholism on the Jews. Everything was the Jews' fault."

Paul placed Murray Grand in an awkward position over drinks at a restaurant one afternoon when he insulted the Jewish owner—Grand's friend—with a string of ethnic jokes that would have embarrassed Don Rickles. At a dinner party thrown by Alice Ghostley, Paul blamed "the Jews of William Morris" for the state of his career and Robert Clary, a Holocaust survivor, who had heard Paul go on like this since their *New Faces* days couldn't take it any longer. "I said to him, 'Paul, the Jews did quite well for you, so just cool it down.'" Paul insisted he'd only been joking, but Clary didn't hear it that way. Clary says he assumes Paul spared him any direct slurs or other insults out of respect for what he went through in the war. He still believes Paul was "a good person deep down."

Paul had a hard time living up to Clary's generous appraisal. His reputation for boozy obnoxiousness rose to new heights as he grew increasingly embittered and angry. He disrupted a floor show at a Palm Springs hotel by demanding that the singer, James Carpenter, return his missing wallet. Carpenter didn't appreciate the interruption of his act, nor Paul's demands that hotel security arrest him, and he sued the actor.

Sometimes, not even nightclubs would have anything to do with the troublesome star. "I witnessed Paul being dragged out of a bar on Sunset Boulevard, a place called Numbers, which was notorious for having high-price callboys and their investors," says Kevin Scullin, at the time an aspiring actor in Paul's social sphere. "[He was] swearing and cursing...[as he was] being thrown literally in the gutter.... 'You motherfuckers! How dare you do this to me! I spend enough money here to pay your wages, you pricks!' They must have thrown him down about three times until finally Paul got up swearing and staggered away."

One Lynde anecdote that has made the rounds has Paul showing up thoroughly cooked at a gay bar in New York City with his limo driver. (The actor took to hiring rides after drunken mishaps jacked up the cost of his car insurance.) The bouncer tires of the star's obnoxiousness and tosses him out. Paul returns within the hour in a sloppy disguise—his driver's uniform. The bouncer doesn't fall for the ruse.

Paul didn't let alcohol affect his efforts on behalf of the Easter Seals when he joined organizer Rose Marie in Hawaii for a 1976 telethon. But on the way to the airport for the trip back to the mainland, he couldn't resist wetting his whistle. Once aboard the private plane, Paul made a loud and persistent demand for another nip. The flight attendant refused and asked Rose Marie for help in calming him down.

"Come on, Paul, you're on a plane," Rose Marie begged.

"Well, what's the matter?" he asked. "Why can't I have another drink?"

"We can't give him another drink," the anxious attendant insisted.

"Give him another drink," advised Rose Marie. "Maybe it'll knock him out."

It did.

"We'll take care of him, don't worry," Rose Marie assured the stewardess. Paul slept through the rest of the trip, but more soundly than the crew preferred. When the flight attendant checked to make sure everyone had returned their seats to an upright position and strapped themselves in for landing, she found Paul lying on the floor with his feet propped on his chair cushion.

"Would you get him up?" she asked Rose Marie.

"Listen," said Rose Marie. "I don't sleep with him. I don't know how he gets up! He may start swinging."

Against her better judgment, Rose Marie gave it a try anyway. "Come on Paul, we're landing in ten minutes. Come on now, you've got to get up."

Not a move.

Then, remembering her friend's sense of professionalism, Rose Marie had an idea. "Paul, we've got to get to work. We've got to do *Squares*."

They wouldn't tape the show until that afternoon, and Rose Marie failed to mention it was now only 7 A.M. Yet the trick worked. Paul woke up immediately. He shook his head groggily and sobered up a little more each time he heard the phrase "We've got to go work."

Rose Marie had to beg the crew not to report Paul. When they debarked, she put the keelhauled passenger in a cab and warned the driver, "I'm gonna call in 40 minutes. He better be home."

Later that afternoon, Paul dragged himself into the makeup room for *Hollywood Squares*.

"I was bad, wasn't I?" he asked Rose Marie.

"You were very bad," she said.

Another time, on an impending flight from New York to L.A., the crew booted the would-be poster boy for air rage off the plane for shouting obscenities. Paul chalked up his plane problems to claustrophobia. "I want all flights to be 20 minutes," he said. "The pressurized cabins bother my ears."

That spring, at his local supermarket, Paul came across an article in *The National Enquirer* with the headline "Paul Lynde's Drinking Problem." Other journalists had taken occasional snipes at Paul in the past—a reporter covering a "dry party" to celebrate Alice Cooper's return from rehab suggested Paul tackle his own "serious drinking problem"—but *The Enquirer*'s jabs pissed him off. "The woman ahead of me just said, 'Oh, Paul, I never read that thing. Why should you bother?'" Paul told a more sympathetic journalist. "But I stood right there and read the whole thing. What they'd written sounded like I turned myself in to *The National Enquirer*, for God's sake, given them some kind of confession…and I never gave them an interview, not one word. I mean, I do enjoy a drink after the show because I'm under such pressure. But they blew it up like I can't wait until the show is over."

Paul failed to mention that he had worried about his booze habit for years. When he visited Barbara Blashek in Indianapolis during a stock tour, he asked her physician husband to run tests on his liver. Though the exam turned up nothing, Paul still worried, but not enough to do anything about it. He feared he would lose his comic touch if he gave up the bottle, pointing out other comedians who weren't as funny on the wagon.

If drinking made Paul funnier, the strategy was far from foolproof. At one of Karen Valentine's parties, a drunk Paul blacked out while insulting the hostess about her choice for a boyfriend: Jon Hager, one of the Hager Twins of *Hee Haw* fame. On his rapid descent to the floor, Paul hit his head on a doorjamb and passed out until paramedics revived him.

Long rejected from many Hollywood guest lists, Paul now found some of his friends abandoning him as well, especially those in the entertainment industry. "I retreated socially from him in the last few years that I represented him because I found it unbearable," Sandy Gallin says. Pablo Rodríguez also moved on, though they still visited each other as friends.

Paul's most lasting relationship, with his dog Harry, ended as well. "Harry...he was finally the special dog," Paul said shortly after putting the old pup to sleep. "He was the greatest pal I've ever had in my life. He was as close as a lover, a wife, he was all I had ever wanted anyone to be to me, but no one was."

After Harry's death, Paul swore he would never own another dog, certain that if he did, "Harry would come down and strike me dead." Eventually, he bought a black poodle while on tour in Milwaukee and named him "Torchlight Alfred Lunt," or "Alfred" for short. He then decided to relocate, a plan he had considered earlier because Harry had a tough time getting up and down the stairs. "There are some nights when I can't either," Paul said.

Paul sold the pseudo–Errol Flynn estate and bought another manse on North Palm Drive, just north of Santa Monica Boulevard in the flats of Beverly Hills. Other celebrities had lived on the street, including Jean Harlow in the 1930s and Marilyn Monroe, with husband Joe DiMaggio, in 1954. Improvements to Paul's new one-floor expanse took almost two years, with help from interior designer Reginald Adams, who had been recommended by Jim Nabors.

Once again, Paul insisted his piano and Ondine statue fit into the designs. He also revamped the dining room in red hues like the Flynn house, enclosed the porch for a solarium, swapped out the maid's quarters for a sauna, and did up the living room with raw silk and lacquer sconces with clusters of crystal, French clocks, a painted Italian chest, and a Chinese screen. "We went through what he wanted, and the comment that really stayed with me was 'I want a house that is fit for a star,'" says Adams. "That, and 'I wouldn't be unhappy if the house appeared in *Architectural Digest.*'" Adams pulled some strings and got his contacts at the magazine to tour the completed house. A feature on the redone domicile appeared in the May 1981 issue.

Paul liked to brag about the security in his new neighborhood. "The neighbors help and protect each other, which is what you've got to do these days," he said. The house's strategic position a quarter-mile west of the West Hollywood (a.k.a. Boy's Town) border didn't hurt either. Paul could keep a Beverly Hills address and still go cruising minutes from his front door. He soon found he couldn't have it both ways. He hoped to become friends with Jean Peters, the ex-wife of Howard Hughes who lived next door, but the fellow Ohioan kept her distance.

Paul's other run-in with high society didn't play well either. One night Adams took Paul to a posh restaurant for his birthday. Having knocked back a few, Paul mistook the owner for the maitre d' and dressed him down with a litany of things he didn't like about the place. Paul then shouted at Rod Stewart at the other end of the dining room. Stewart gamely shouted back at him, and the two had a lighthearted exchange that amused all the patrons—except Betsy Bloomingdale. Feeling the iciness that radiated from her, Adams warned his friend, "Paul, that's Betsy Bloomingdale next to you." In a loud, mocking voice, Paul proclaimed:

"Bet-sy Bloomingdale!" The socialite visibly stiffened and made a show of ignoring them the rest of the night.

Tricks and lowlifes never snubbed their noses at Paul, who relied more than ever on their dangerous company. Tony the Hustler, "a full-on, walking, talking, in-your-face, leather-clad whore," as he described himself in Brendan Mullen's *Lexicon Devil,* claimed Paul contacted him through an ad in *The Advocate* and became one of his best clients. "He was a freak! We'd get drunk and take his Bentley up to Fatburger with his gigantic poodle named Alfred; he'd be so drunk, I'd have to drive."

Scullin had a roommate named Marcus whom Paul kept on his payroll. "Marcus used to work as an escort on the side in addition to working as a waiter at a restaurant with me," he says. "Paul used to call him at all hours, usually drunk as a skunk.... Marcus got to a point in their friendship that he wouldn't ask Paul for money. Lynde, however, would insist...sometimes as much as $300, which was a lot then. He would call Marcus sometimes just to come and be with him. I was told there were times when Paul was extremely lonely and Marcus would just go over and sit, smoke pot, and keep him company...or he would escort Paul somewhere to keep an eye on him so that he wouldn't get himself into trouble, which Paul often did. I do remember that Paul abruptly stopped calling him... Marcus told me he assumed that they were getting too close, and Paul needed to always keep people at arm's distance."

John Kenley recalls a story told by Dean Dittman, a popular Kenley Player who became one of Paul's closest friends. Paul once refused a dinner invitation to meet Dittman's agent because he had already hired a date for the evening. Instead of taking no for an answer, Dittman set another place at the table. During dinner, the hustler excused himself only to return a few minutes later completely in the buff. "Let's get this over with," he said. Paul willingly obliged. He kept the bedroom door open, knowing that Dittman wouldn't be able to resist a peek. Sure enough, Dittman soon crept into view. Paul turned to him and shouted, "Ain't ya sorry you're not a star?"

The hero of as many tall tales as real ones, Paul—who once confessed, "I love sex as well as anyone but it's got to be clean"—practically qualifies as a pre-AIDS folk hero, a prissy and pickled Paul Bunyan for purveyors of Hollywood tawdriness. Writer Brandon Judell added a complete fiction to the Lynde canon when he pictured a kinky encounter with Paul in his short story "Hollywood Squared," included in *The Best American Erotica 1996*. After the narrator makes the mistake of closing his eyes during the act, Paul slaps him in the face and commands, "When you get fucked by Lynde, baby, you keep your eyes open." The episode sprang entirely from Judell's mind, but it *sounds* so much like Paul that it has acquired the ring of truth.

During autograph sessions, fans never failed to ask Paul why he didn't make movies. The star moped that his career on the silver screen had tanked for several reasons: Studios shunned television actors, a "small clique" of agents controlled the best scripts, and he was just too popular. "You spend half your life getting to be known," he said, "and then they contend you're too well-known."

Paul still hoped for good film roles, but if he had considered his recent spate of prime-time failures, his low-rung status as a game show personality and supporting clown for Donny and Marie, and his bad reputation for flare-ups when fricasseed, he might have stopped waiting for a miracle.

Discussions with studio executives about doing *My Fat Friend* with Barbra Streisand led nowhere, nor did director Stanley Kramer's plans to team Paul with Richard Pryor as the heads of the CIA in a comedy called *The Sheiks of Araby*.

Producer Allan Carr announced that Paul would join Nancy Walker and former New York mayor John Lindsay in *Grease,* but none of them ended up appearing in the film.

Paul had regularly turned down movie parts that were "just too gay for him," Jay Redack recalls, but the man who dreamed of Oscar ended his movie career in stock fey roles. In 1978, he played Dr. Vidal, a queeny physician, in *Rabbit Test,* a film starring Billy Crystal that Joan Rivers directed and cowrote with Redack. (The sign on the doctor's door reads ALL DELIVERIES IN THE REAR.) The film's countless cameos included George Gobel, Alice Ghostley, Charlotte Rae, and Jane Connell. The casting stunts, according to *Variety,* made "the pic seem slapdash, as if Rivers had to finish their scenes because these performers had something better to do in an hour." Still, the movie earned enough money to allow Rivers and her husband to keep the mansion they mortgaged to fund the project.

A year later, Paul played the gender-bending Chief Nervous Elk in *The Villain,* a box office flop from Hal Needham, the director of *Smokey and the Bandit.* Kirk Douglas, Ann-Margret, and a relatively unknown Arnold Schwarzenegger starred, with another cast of all-star cameos including Foster Brooks, Ruth Buzzi, Jack Elam, and Mel Tillis. Paul got to ride a horse and recite lines like "Do you want to Indian-wrestle?"

Only one film in the 1970s put Paul's talents to good use: the animated feature based on E. B. White's *Charlotte's Web.* Producer Joe Barbera decided during rehearsals that Tony Randall had "too much class for the part" of Templeton the Rat, so he turned to Paul. The project turned into a family reunion of sorts: Pamelyn Ferdin, Paul's TV daughter, played Fern, and Agnes Moorehead, Paul's *Bewitched* sibling, voiced The Goose. Paul and Moorehead even combined their vocal talents on an ode to trash called "A Veritable Smorgasbord."

Upon its release in 1973, *Charlotte's Web* quickly reached classic status, quite unlike Paul's two other animated features. *Journey Back to Oz* started production in 1962 with an all-star cast that included Milton Berle, Ethel Merman, Liza Minnelli, Mickey Rooney and Danny Thomas. Paul lent his voice as Pumpkinhead, a friend of Dorothy. The cartoon musical hit financing snags and remained incomplete for a decade. Barely released in theaters in 1971, it found a slightly better reception on TV in late 1974 and later on video. Audiences wisely stayed away from *Hugo the Hippo,* a 1976 release that teamed Paul with Burl Ives, Robert Morley, and Jimmy and Marie Osmond.

Paul sometimes blamed inflation and agents for taking more than their fair share ("When you're about to go on, they knock on the door and say 'Any problems?' I want to say, 'Yes, take this script and rewrite it and learn it and do it and give me 10%.'") Yet he didn't really need the money from these less-than-stellar projects. Noting how his summer-stock salary could reach $50,000 a week, he proclaimed, "I'm the highest paid performer onstage today, including—God help us all—Laurence Olivier."

Privately, Paul found little satisfaction in such boasts. At one of Rose Marie's dinner parties, he told Vincent Price and Steve Allen how much he despised working.

"Why do you do it if you hate it so much?" Price asked.

"For the money."

"Yes, but you're making good money. You have a gorgeous home," Price countered. "You don't need the money. Why do you do it if you hate it so much?"

"Because," Paul said, "I have no one to share it with."

Despite his aversion to work, he continued to appear onstage, largely for the escape and the paychecks. "I can earn more in Miami in two weeks than I can in over a month on

Broadway, because Broadway is so expensive and the theatres are small," he said. The tours gave him a break from Hollywood, a town "where you get up at noon, read the funnies, and if the sun's not out, you go to dirty movies until cocktail time."

Anticipating film roles that never panned out, Paul missed his usual summer jaunt in 1977, but returned to the Kenley camp a year later to tour Ohio and other environs in *The Impossible Years,* which Kenley had updated for his theaters to include topical references to *Saturday Night Fever,* Red China, and Billy Carter.

Paul played an unusual part in casting the play that summer when he replaced the actor hired as Bartholomew Smuts with his bodyguard. He had met Danny DeNoi the previous October in Palm Beach and hired him after the death of Bob Crane. "People are on drugs and all sorts of things these days," Paul said. "If they're not fans, you can be in serious trouble. I've never had any incidents since Dan has been with me." Granted, Paul hadn't experienced any incidents before DeNoi, but he found comfort knowing his protector carried a gun. "He's a good guy," Paul said. "He would take the bullet for me."

DeNoi got the acting gig after he told Paul he could do a better job than the actor actually hired for the part. Valerie Landsburg, best known for her role as Doris Schwartz on *Fame*, played Paul's younger daughter on tour. "Paul taught Danny to be OK in the role," she says. "He was very patient with him. He wasn't coming to it with a lot of experience, but he was really sort of right for the role."

DeNoi added a "touch of slime" and displayed commendable "obnoxiousness and egotism, an effective vision of leather and zippers," one critic wrote, but for some reason, either Paul or the director let the acting pupil add some "senseless and distracting" karate kicking to the action. "Paul and the director had a very good relationship. [Paul] would let him direct, but he would also suggest things," Landsburg says. "My memory is not of him directing but of [him saying] 'Try this…' because in terms of comedy, he was the best. One of the things that the director was able to do was wrangle and choreograph everyone around Paul, which is what you did with Paul."

Paul, a slightly tarnished star rehashing old material, no longer impressed the critics. Gene Gerrard, the Columbus columnist who'd considered Paul a "comic genius" when he did the same role in 1969, shared no such enthusiasm this time around. "Yes, he's still King of the Leer, master of the slow, medium, and fast burn," he opined, but "he won't take you in for a moment by hiding behind a character. Underneath that thin façade is another thin façade. Lynde walks heavily and carries a big shtick."

The critics might have been interested to learn that Paul had a more challenging role in the works for leading lady Elizabeth Allen (and not just her endless attempts to keep his bacchanals in check on the tour). "We were just discussing the other night doing *Macbeth*," he said. "She would be Macbeth and I would do Lady Macbeth. Lady Macbeth has many great scenes. She's a stronger character than Macbeth."

Paul steered well clear of Shakespeare in his final three television specials. His entry for 1978 fell short in star power (guests: Harry Morgan, Juliet Prowse, and Brenda Vaccaro), but it had its moments. "On this show, everyone's wishes come true," Paul explained in his opening monologue as studio magic turned the clothes of his guests into evening attire. Vaccaro asked if they could keep the dresses. Paul declined. "I promised my maid." In the production number "If Life Were a Musical," the cast danced and sang—or at least mimed to intentionally dubbed voices—at a gas station. Paul should have wished for more viewers; the show ranked among the five least watched programs on TV that week.

In March 1979, the comedian assembled Gary Coleman, Vicki Lawrence, Robert Urich, and Betty White for *Paul Lynde at the Movies*. The star played movie buff Maurice Dalyrimple, and he and the cast sent up then-current box office favorites such as *Grease, Invasion of the Body Snatchers,* and *Superman.* In a spoof of the horror flick *Magic*, Paul played ventriloquist to Coleman's dummy. Alfred made his television debut on the show, joining Paul's previous dogs in short entertainment careers. In the mid 1950s, Paul had hired an agent for his basset hounds, one of which appeared in a print ad for cigarettes, and he put Harry MacAfee in the promos he filmed for his first sitcom for ABC.

The ornery actor no doubt drew on personal experience for *Paul Lynde Goes Ma-a-a-ad,* "a sensational, side-splitting 'salute' to everything evil, mean, nasty and bad—as only Paul can do it," according to *TV Guide.* In turn, Charo, Vicki Lawrence, and Marie Osmond got to act out the dream of so many of Paul's victims by tying him to a gurney, covering him with face cream and motor oil, and pelting him with rotten vegetables. The May 1979 special concluded Paul's obligation to ABC, which never offered a new contract.

Paul continued to find the stage a more reliable source of income. That summer he toured again in Woody Allen's *Don't Drink the Water,* in part because he had already tested the lines, noting there was no need "to cross my eyes to make the show funny." Denise Lor was his leading lady.

The Kenley favorite had to miss two weeks of performances in Akron and Dayton when he checked into the hospital with a case of low-grade hepatitis. He recorded an apology for the opening-night audience, and his understudy replaced him with little rehearsal and a script close at hand. Rich Little offered to stand in for the ailing star during his absence. Lou Jacobi, who originated the role on Broadway, ended up taking over until Paul returned for performances in Columbus.

Paul's doctor banned alcohol from Paul's diet for six weeks, a situation that shocked an Atlanta reporter who remarked that Paul was "known in some circles as one of the most creative carousers this side of The Who." One of Paul's friends offered the same reporter a few tips before interviewing the star. "Let Paul do the talking. And for God's sake, don't mention that thing about the booze.

> PETER: Do we get any heat from stars?
> PAUL: You will, if I have to share my dressing room again.
> PETER: Who are you sharing it with?
> PAUL: Big Bird and Oscar.

In the spring of 1979, Paul finally won a Daytime Emmy for his work on *Hollywood Squares*. The overdue accolade—and his earlier nominations—didn't stop him from condemning the show. He told Earl Wilson in 1976 that people perceived him as little more than "that man in the box." Weeks later, he told Cliff Jahr of *The Village Voice,* "The longer I stay on *Hollywood Squares* and the longer I do shit on television, the further I get away from my goal." When these comments caused a minor furor among the show's fans, Paul did some hasty cleanup work. "I merely said I hated Hollywood. How could I hate *Hollywood Squares*? It's been the best greatest thing that ever happened to me, even though it ties me down…I'm not leaving, but I do wish the game shows would improve on the content of the questions. It's a way of giving the shows some purpose beyond new household appliances."

Paul may have overdone it with damage control, if the following item from a TV magazine is any indication:

Paul Lynde, who describes himself as "sweet, adorable, and cuddly," was anything but during a confrontation last week with a *People* magazine photographer backstage at a *Hollywood Squares* taping. The photographer was there taking pictures of hot new comic Billy Crystal (TV's *Soap* and the *Rabbit Test* film), when Lynde went into a shrieking, swearing, foot-stamping tirade against the magazine. He claims he was quoted incorrectly in a recent article that stated he hated *Hollywood Squares*. "And how could I," he contends, "when it has made me a household name."

The cast and crew knew that the disdain "that man in the box" felt for the game show cut much deeper, especially after libations flowed at dinner. George Gobel—who once said, "I've never been drunk, but I've often been overserved"—could drink everyone under the towering tic-tac-toe board and still control himself. Increasingly, Paul could not. (In 1975, both booze hounds appeared in their usual boxes with other *Squares* regulars to film a public service film about the responsible use of alcohol.) "By and large [Paul] was always dependable, and always ready and enthusiastic," Redack says, "except for the times when he was a little soused, and it would be, 'Here we go again.' I guess it would be true of anybody doing anything for an extended period of time…. He would still do the job but act a bit above it. 'Oh, [here comes] another one.' That kind of thing."

Content when he sat next to friends like Kaye Ballard, Suzanne Pleshette, or Lily Tomlin, Paul could get huffy with the unfamiliar faces that showed up more frequently as the long-running warhorse turned to stunt casting to boost ratings: the cast of *Dallas* and Paul; daytime soap actors and Paul; well-known athletes and Paul. The matchups went on and on. When the producers felt devilish, they deliberately sat Paul next to someone they knew would annoy him. "He would turn away from them," Redack says, "hardly acknowledging they were there."

The seating prank occasionally backfired. "The unhappiness and what not, maybe something in his private life [that] was going on...would manifest itself with some kind of tirade," Redack says. "One time we did a music show... and we had Tanya Tucker, who was sitting next to him. Either she didn't get it or she said something, and he was nasty: 'Who's she?! Who's she?!' She was almost in tears. I don't know what happened, but he was not a happy man while she was there." (In one version of this story, Paul supposedly called Tucker "a spoiled little bitch." She shot back, "You should know, queen!")

Paul threw another hissy fit when he shared the board with a bunch of pop-music stars of the day. "I came back to rebrief him, and I remember he had his dog there, and he threw his dog dish at me," Redack says. "He was pretty mad, and he had just had too much to drink to go out and we did the last two shows without him. We got K.C. of K.C. and Sunshine Band to replace Paul in the center square." The producers blamed Paul's absence on an illness.

Paul's zingers lost some of their zip when Buddy Hackett spilled the beans about their true, prewritten origin to Johnny Carson. Hackett spoke the truth, but Paul felt powerless to defend himself and grew more aggravated. "I can't go on the air and say Buddy Hackett is not allowed on the show because he is so vulgar and so rotten and so mean," he said. When asked about a system that *The New York Times* described as "legalized deception," Paul finally admitted that he had help. "People think because you're funny, you ad-lib," he said. "I'm not that secure in ad-libbing—I'm a script man. If they didn't give us some clues, we'd all sit there and say, 'Gee, I just don't know,' and you can see how entertaining that would be."

After threatening for years to vacate his box, Paul ignored the advice of friends—including Leonard Sillman who warned, "Don't ever leave it!"—and quit the show. He taped his last segments on June 12, 1979, and only notified the show's producers that he wouldn't return while in Atlanta on his stock tour. "He'd work, and he would do this and would go on the road every summer, but he sort of felt boxed in, excuse the expression, by the *Squares*," says Rose Marie. "That's why he left. He had to get away for a while."

That fall, while other TV magazines chalked up Paul's departure to work commitments or recuperation from hepatitis, *The National Enquirer* suggested the show canned its center square because of his drinking and shabby treatment of contestants. In an article titled "Paul Lynde Quits Boozing After Collapsing From Serious Disease," an unidentified "Hollywood insider" explained:

> [Paul's] career has slid almost to rock bottom. He hasn't appeared on *Hollywood Squares* for over four months. He left the show because the other stars complained. Lynde was nasty and bitchy to them on the set. He would appear at the NBC studios dead drunk on the set—and that was early in the morning!

In the past, Burt Reynolds and other Squares who'd shown up in the gossip rags had advised Paul to ignore stories about him. "Watch *Hollywood Squares* on TV and see if you don't think Paul Lynde looks wonderful," read one such item. "Yes, he's lost weight but has had his eyes and chin nipped and tucked by a plastic surgeon." Now he fought back. Inspired by Carol Burnett's legal actions against the tabloid, Paul filed a lawsuit for $10 million that December. He said that he alone had decided to leave *Squares* but had "agreed not to release the story of his withdrawing from the show in order to not bring about the loss of any of the stations that are presently carrying *Hollywood Squares*." Burnett's case went to trial almost five years after she filed hers; Paul's was dismissed after his death.

Peter Marshall says Paul's departure had nothing to do with drinking but everything to do with money. "I think someone published [that] I was making all this money, and he went crazy," he says. "He left the show for a year, and our ratings went up about two points, [and] I would send him all the ratings, so he came back."

Whatever the truth may have been, Paul's defection dealt another blow to a long-running show hobbled by years of network neglect, schedule changes, and ratings erosion. "Last season only George Gobel was a regular and found it difficult to carry the laugh burden alone," explained one reporter. "Jonathan Winters and Vincent Price made frequent appearances but the show wasn't the same without Lynde. The panel was generally filled out with lackluster daytime soap opera stars whom most nighttime viewers never heard of, borderline celebrity comics, out-of-work TV actors, Big Bird, and ventriloquists." NBC pulled the plug on the daytime staple in the spring of 1980 to make room for David Letterman's first stab at talk show glory. Paul's friend Wayland Flowers—and Madame—sat in the center square on the last episode.

During his sabbatical, Paul turned down all offers to appear on television, hoping that if he stopped showing up on the tube every day as a funnyman, he might have a chance as a serious actor. The plan failed, and he did nothing for months, save a visit to his lawyers to sue the *Enquirer* and a trip to Key West, Florida, to attend the premiere of Tennessee Williams's *Will Mr. Merriwether Return from Memphis?* Though he still lived like Hollywood royalty, Paul grew concerned. "I told my business managers something had to be done," he said. "They told me not to worry. But I worried. I didn't want to be idle because it's dangerous for a performer."

The producers of *Squares* planned to expand the syndicated nighttime version to five nights a week the following fall. To do so, they desperately needed Paul back in the center square. Playing hard to get, Paul demanded and received a few choice perks: a substantial salary, costar billing with host Peter Marshall, and an opportunity to develop a movie project through Filmways, the company that owned the show. He'd get paid whether or not he ended up making a film. Announcing Paul's impending return in late January 1980, *Variety* reported that "the signing of Lynde…is a tacit acknowledgment by Filmways that it'll be an uphill battle to get the series established as a syndicated strip for the 1980–1981 season."

Before he returned to the show, Paul focused on another summer-stock tour. He came up with a novel project: performing three acts from three different Neil Simon comedies. Friends said the playwright would never agree to the idea, but he did, and Paul prepared to tour with a *Neil Simon Suite*: the third act from *Last of the Red Hot Lovers,* the second act from *California Suite,* and the third act from *Plaza Suite.*

Beverly Sanders, well-known but not necessarily famous for countless TV commercials and an Emmy-nominated performance in *Queen of the Stardust Ballroom,* played Paul's leading lady. For the supporting parts, Paul hired Kristy Syverson—an actress, singer, and dancer who had worked with Jim Nabors—and Paul Barresi, a part-time actor with a less wholesome résumé.

A former sergeant in the Air Force, Barresi had managed a gym in Riverside, California, after his tour of duty. He happened upon a location shoot in town for *The Wild Party,* a movie starring James Coco and Raquel Welch, and started hanging out on the set. The art director of *Playgirl* noticed

him and featured him in a pictorial with Cassandra Peterson—soon to be Elvira, Mistress of the Dark—in 1975. This gig led to work as a Colt model, a cocktail waiter at the famous Backlot at Studio One, and eventually a trainer for a number of Hollywood celebrities such as David Geffen and Joan Rivers—and after avid *Playgirl* reader Dean Dittman introduced them, Paul Lynde. Notwithstanding the more famous Paul's aversion to exercise, the two became good friends.

Barresi says Paul felt safe with him (platonically) at his side. He once foiled a fan who came at Paul with a letter opener when Paul refused to give him a dictated message with his autograph. Another time Barresi threw an up-to-no-good hustler out of Paul's house. "My *hero*!" Paul cried. "I guess I won't see him again!" Later, Paul thanked Barresi for the assistance with much less sarcasm.

Paul didn't take the show to his usual Kenley stops but found new locations, including New Orleans and Toronto. By now, summer stock had lost its luster, and even John Kenley had started to scale back his operations in the face of competition from popular national touring companies. For years, Paul accepted a reasonable salary from Kenley out of friendship, though others offered to pay him much more. Now, losing thousands of dollars in Columbus each summer, Kenley may not have been able to afford even Paul's low-end salary.

On the tour, Paul spent most mornings by himself, taking his breakfast and coffee in his room. Later on, he'd mingle at the pool with his fellow actors. Nearly every night, Paul took the cast, his assistant, and other guests out to dinner. Adams visited Paul during the stop in New Orleans. On a pub crawl one night, he and the two Pauls rolled through the narrow streets of the French Quarter in a candy-red stretch limo. At one dive, autograph hunters grew too aggressive and "bitchy comments" flew back and forth. "We better get him out of here," Adams told Barresi. The angry crowd followed them outside but no one came to blows. The next day, sober Paul asked Adams, "Well, did we have fun last night?"

Paul's dutiful road manager constantly scanned the back pages of gay and alternative magazines to order evening companions for his boss. When these escorts reported for duty, Paul sometimes just paid them on the spot and sent them home. "He doesn't look anything like his picture!" Paul would complain. Of another reject, Paul observed, "He was fine until he opened his *mouth*!"

Even at this point in his career, Paul still felt the old stage insecurities. "He wanted you to see [the show], and the next day he'd ask you what you thought of the performance," says Adams. "He just didn't want to know which night you were going, even though you were staying in the same hotel and saw him every day." Barresi noticed that Paul always rehearsed his lines every night, even mouthing the words in the limo on the way to the theater.

Paul's preshow jitters may not have changed, but neither did his ability to handle obnoxious audience members. One night in Flint, Michigan, a loudmouth in the audience wouldn't stop talking. After delivering the line "Can you hear me?" Paul quipped to the audience, "I know he can't!" The audience laughed, and the man shut up.

The Neil Simon experiment—"It's like catching up on best sellers by reading *Reader's Digest* condensations," one critic wrote—earned the usual mixed reaction. Helen C. Smith of *The Atlanta Constitution* dismissed the star: "Going to see Lynde in a show is like going to Howard Johnson's for a hot dog and chowder. You know exactly what you'll get in advance. You either like his style of humor or you don't." She didn't.

Paul sometimes spoke at curtain call to inform the audience that he had been out of work for a year and would return to *Hollywood Squares* that fall. Fans excited by the news wound up disappointed. This syndicated version moved to the Riviera Hotel in Las Vegas, owned at the time by the husband of occasional panelist Pia Zadora. Beyond that, Paul's official return noticeably lacked pizzazz:

> PETER: OK, pick a star.
> CONTESTANT: Paul Smith, please.
> PETER: I'm sorry, who did you say?
> CONTESTANT: Paul Smith.
> PETER: Lynde?
> CONTESTANT: Paul Lynde!
> PAUL: Paul Smith! Thanks for the welcome back!

Paul traveled to Vegas every other week. As usual, the show taped five episodes in one day, three in the morning, two more, with a new audience, after lunch. He admitted the assignment was an "easy living," but he still found reasons to bitch. His accommodations made him mad. In a snit, he told Marshall that someone whose house had earned *Architectural Digest*'s favor couldn't live in such conditions.

The other Squares, braving similar hardships in luxurious new digs, kept the camaraderie of yore alive and well. Visiting Vegas with his friend, Barresi recalls a lunch at which Leslie Nielsen befuddled his fellow stars by walking around making fart noises with a handheld whoopee cushion. Joan Rivers then pinned down Barresi with a series of questions about workout tips. After several minutes, Paul finally interrupted: "Aw-w-w, why don't you find your own trainer, honey!"

In the off-hours, Paul took advantage of Vegas nightlife. At one casino, he lost hand after hand at blackjack, but played on because he found the dealer handsome. Finally fed up, the slightly poorer Paul walked away, turning back only once: to tell the attractive dealer, "And I hate your hair!"

The gamble on Vegas hardly moved ratings a tick. Viewers preferred newer game shows like *Family Feud, Tic Tac Dough,* and *Joker's Wild.* In some cities, even retro rockers Sha Na Na netted more viewers than Marshall and the Squares in first-run syndication.

When the Riviera didn't renew its contract, executive producers Merrill Heatter and Bob Quigley finally ended the show. (They dissolved their partnership of two decades that summer.) Paul hadn't agreed to a full season of work and didn't do the last show, but he commemorated the event with a walk-on and a wave to the audience. George Gobel sat in the hallowed center square for the finale. After 15 seasons and thousands of shows, the classic version of *Hollywood Squares* was history.

Paul's center square has been remodeled and reoccupied over the years. In 1983, *Hollywood Squares* reopened as a temporary employment agency in a one-hour format that teamed it with a remake of *Match Game.* That version lasted a year. In 1986, the show returned for another three-year gig with John Davidson as its host. Joan Rivers and then Jim J. Bullock occupied the center square. The most recent version, which started a six-year run in 1998, featured Whoopi Goldberg until 2002 in the center square and Bruce Vilanch as the resident gay wit. When she sat at the comic throne after Goldberg's departure, Ellen DeGeneres joked, "It's the power position...it did wonders for Paul Lynde." In a nod to the master, DeGeneres appeared on one show with a framed picture of Paul.

Paul has also turned up prominently on cable reruns of the original *Hollywood Squares.* Rarely seen in the two decades since it left the air, the game show's original run had been considered lost, its taped contents erased by NBC to make room for more marketable material. The Game Show Network obtained a small trove of tapes, reportedly parsed them for politically incorrect humor, and added them to its schedule, using Paul as the major selling point. One promo: "The Paul Lynde guide to humor: Rule number 1: Laugh at your own jokes. Rule number 2: Repeat."

As far back as his *Birdie* days, Paul realized the importance of dramatic career steps. Now he considered taking another. "I still think I'd be good as a sinister killer," he said. "It would have to be something extreme like that. Otherwise, no one would take me seriously." Though he often said he wanted to make an "important film" like *The Graduate,* Paul also discussed remaking some of the movies of screen villain Laird Cregar, whose body of work included *This Gun for Hire* (1942), *The Lodger* (1944), and *Hangover Square* (1945). Given film historian Gregory William Mank's assessment of Cregar, Paul may have been onto something: "An anguished homosexual, finally driven by his career hopes, private longings, and personal vanity to diet mercilessly, seek plastic surgery, and torture himself into becoming 'a beautiful man.'"

Hopes of returning to the movies in a leading role through his Filmways' deal faded quickly. Though the company had a recent box office smash with *Amityville Horror* and netted an Oscar out of Jack Lemmon's performance in 1973's *Save the Tiger,* it mainly released drive-in fare on the level of *Portrait of a Stripper* and *Flatbed Annie & Sweetie Pie: Lady Truckers.* A spokeswoman for Filmways would soon report a $66 million loss for fiscal 1981 and warn, "In future, there will be a more careful evaluation of the economic potential before we make a commitment to a picture." Apparently, the star of a canceled game show who rarely played anything but "Paul Lynde" did not live up to that economic potential.

CHAPTER 12

HIGH-STRUNG SUNDAY'S CHILD

"Truman died at 88. I'll settle for 50.
Some days I'm so tired I think, Why fight?"

Martha Raye emerged from a taxi in front of Paul's house in an emerald and satin baseball uniform. Patsy Kelly came out next in a green sequin top, followed by Betty Kean in a large muumuu the color of a vast field of grass. By their boisterous greetings—"Ho! Here we are!"—and drunken laughter, it was clear their preparations for St. Patrick's Day hadn't stopped at the color of their clothes. With a wry grin, Paul, the perfectly sober host watched the trio grow louder and more sauced as the afternoon progressed. To his friend Jan Forbes, Paul sniffed, "I didn't invite [your daughter] Meredith because I thought it'd be a little too much drinking with these ladies." The next day he told his housekeeper, Tim Noyle, "Martha lost her teeth, and thank God Alfred found them!"

Forbes had noticed Paul's good behavior, and she asked him why he rarely drank alcohol anymore. "Something happened to me," he said. "I will never touch another drop of liquor or a drug again." He gave Barresi a similar reason, explaining that he promised someone he'd stop. Barresi asked whom. "I can't tell you," Paul said. "That's something only I'm going to know."

Paul never divulged the "something" or "someone" that inspired his momentous break. Any number of public embarrassments may have forced the decision: his many outbursts chronicled in the tabloids, his verbal attacks on friends, or—perhaps most stinging of all—the snub he received from Northwestern.

In the fall of 1980, Paul's beloved alma mater marked the construction and dedication of its Theater and Interpretation Center with a gala celebration called *The Way We Were*. The school invited all but one of its distinguished alumni to participate in the televised charity event. Paul's assistant called to ask about the oversight, only to learn that the university considered the legendary Waa-Mu performer persona non grata.

All the other famous alumni participated, including Claude Akins, Ann-Margret, Robert Conrad, Charlton Heston, Carol Lawrence, Garry Marshall, Jerry Orbach, Tony Roberts, as well as Cloris Leachman, Patricia Neal, and Charlotte Rae. "Paul was very obvious by his absence because he was not invited," Basil Cross says. "He was big as any of them, except possibly Cloris and Chuck Heston and Pat Neal."

Paul didn't enter a detox program. (The Betty Ford Center opened a year after his death.) The longtime lush just quit imbibing the same way he stopped overeating to lose weight. At most, he allowed himself a glass of white wine for dinner, a drastic change for a man who once said he would happily take his firewater in a Mason jar. "It was funny because he was cold sober, and he was still very funny," Forbes says. "He was no different except that he was nice. He was still caustic and a marvelous wit." At cocktail parties Paul now observed with clear eyes, "Nobody knows what they're talking about."

"We went to dinner when he'd stopped drinking for months," recalls Reginald Adams. "I had a margarita and he said 'Oh, you son of a bitch, you get a margarita.' And I said, 'Sorry, if it makes you want liquor, I don't have to order it.' And he said, 'Oh, no, no, I don't want one margarita. I want ten margaritas!'"

Paul remained as funny as ever, but, Adams says, he just wouldn't get "to that point where he was all cranked up." Not that sobriety made Paul a saint. "One day we went to the Sav-on drugstore to buy one of those cheap instant cameras," says Tim Noyle, who kept Paul's house five days a week from 9 A.M. until 1 P.M. "We walk into the store, and this woman says to Paul, 'I figured you thinner.' Well, you know Paul, he put his hands on his hips [and said], 'I figured you *younger!*'" When the cashier mistook Paul for Jim Nabors, Paul shot back, "That's the queen on the island." (Nabors lived in Hawaii.)

Paul fibbed a bit when he said he gave up drugs as well as booze. According to some friends, he took up pot and poppers as his substances of choice. "A friend [of mine] named Larry wormed his way into Paul's life," David Macklin says. "[He] became his kind of caretaker, bodyguard, driver, et cetera. He got Paul off the bottle but into drugs."

Noyle confirms that Paul substituted hashish for hooch. "The pot—he didn't need to smoke much of it. He was just 'on'…He was very funny…and not cruel funny…. It just took the edge off." Watching his gardener's crew landscape his backyard one day, a stoned Paul opened the door and yelled, "Take off your shirts! I'll pay more money!"

Paul had worse luck with tobacco. He made a big show of inviting Adams to a graduation ceremony for the class he took to help him kick his two-packs-a-day habit. Two months later, after returning from a stock tour, he gave Adams a call. "I'm looking forward to seeing you," Paul admitted. "But I've got to tell you I'm smoking."

Noyle says he didn't notice Paul getting depressed over his stalled career. "He seemed to like what I'm going to call this marginal little life," he says. Paul spent his days swimming and spending time with friends. Dean Dittman visited frequently. "Dean was just sleazy enough for Paul," Noyle says. "He lived enough on the edge to interest Paul." Paul sometimes visited Dittman at his apartment in an L.A. high-rise, a pad that Rock Hudson used for assignations with hustlers. Paul still preferred ordering in.

Typical days for Paul began with a crossword puzzle in the morning and ended with a little television in the back patio or in his bedroom. On some mornings Barresi might come over to lead his friend through a workout. Paul let his trainer in on a little secret—he'd been wearing a girdle for some time. The extra-wide rubber sheath with elastic in the back swathed his mid section and attached with a Velcro strap. Paul said he needed the support for his back pain—surely no lie, considering how his years of obesity had left him with a tender back. Still, he also must have seen the girdle's gut-sucking capabilities as a helpful bonus.

If Paul wasn't grimacing with his hand on his lower back— his universal sign that he'd rather just talk—they'd work out. Barresi started Paul off with 15 minutes of stretching before they proceeded to various forms of calisthenics, a little weight lifting, and sometimes exercises in the pool.

One morning Paul paused in the middle of a series of sit-ups and yelled, "I've had it with this!" He grasped his copy of a Richard Simmons exercise book and waved it in his hand. The fitness guru on the cover resembled a clown-haired Pillsbury Dough Boy. "You think I want to look like that!" Paul shouted. He threw the book in the air. Its pages broke from the spine and drifted back down to Earth like confetti (soggy confetti once someone dredged them out of the pool). Paul stormed into the house without looking back.

Paul often spent nights alone, and he preferred it that way. "You'd call him at 6, 8 at night, and he was just having a little dinner," Adams says. During their conversations, a subdued Paul often spoke about how unhappy he had been growing up fat in a small town. "It was like what he had done was all to show people how far he could go," says Adams.

Free of work commitments, Paul threw occasional dinner parties. He'd do some of the work but always hired a few helpers as sobriety didn't seem to ease his hosting anxieties. Ordering groceries over the phone, Paul pulled rank when the clerk didn't recognize his name. "That's Paul Lynde, Movie Star!" If his guests rang the doorbell five minutes early, he made them wait. Noyle says Paul didn't even cut any slack for guests at a Christmas Eve get-together. "Sure enough, somebody rang the doorbell…and Paul's on the other side of these story-and-a-half double doors yelling, 'Fucking wait! It's not 6!'" Carolers came by during the dinner, but Paul wanted nothing to do with them. "We're having our dessert," he yelled. "Come back later!"

To ensure good conversation, Paul never invited more than eight guests. The mix of friends would include people from all walks of Paul's life, including his sisters on holidays. After attending enough of these gatherings over the years, Adams began to notice that Paul never invited more than one other celebrity to the table. "You could always count on a celebrity being there," he says. "You never knew who it would be, but there were never two there."

Paul hoped to use hospitality to make peace with friends he had alienated. Leachman accepted an invitation to a dinner party, and for once she had a good time, save a few tense moments when the subject of work came up and Paul got "overexcited." Alfred's presence calmed him down.

Conflicting travel plans kept Charlotte Rae, now the star of *The Facts of Life,* from attending lunch with Paul and a mutual friend. Rae called Paul upon her return, the last time she would talk to him. She commended him for sobering up. "I said, 'I love you, Paul,'" she remembers. "He chuckled and said, 'I love you too.'"

If sobriety redeemed Paul in his social circle, it didn't help him land any work. Robert Osborne speculates that Paul had reached a common stage in the cycle of an actor's life: the career downswing. "If you've been around long enough people get tired of you and they want to move on to someone else," he says. "Look at Angie Dickinson. For a while she got all those kinds of parts and then after a while they started giving them to somebody else. Then it was Stella Stevens's turn and Barbara Nichols's turn. Those things don't go on forever."

Paul considered his usual backup plan: summer stock. He mulled a tour with Bernard Slade's *Tribute,* a comedy about a Broadway press agent dying of leukemia who reconciles with his serious-minded son. Paul would have finally had the chance to be dramatic, but he decided not to do it. "Paul just looked at me one day and said, 'You know, I just don't see anything funny about a man who's dying,'" says Barresi. "He would often talk about death and his fear of death, and he would ruminate over dying before his time."

Paul also debated whether or not to do another commercial, this one for Smirnoff vodka, a company that had previously used the services of fellow tipplers Wally Cox and George Gobel. Still contemplating movie projects, Paul considered playing Lynn Belvedere, the priggish butler played memorably by Clifton Webb in three popular films at mid-century. Financial pressure didn't play a role in this decision making; Paul had the luxury to pick and choose projects by now. "Alfred and I went to the accountant," Paul told Jan Forbes one day. "We pranced all the way home with our heads held high. I never have to work again if I don't want to."

Fans still wrote to Paul, though he didn't appreciate some of the correspondence. "I would see these letters that he wouldn't open or he'd cut in half," Noyle says. "Not a whole lot of comment about them…. It suddenly hit me that unless somebody has some stalking qualities, you don't keep [writing letters] unless somebody's throwing you a little bit of salami occasionally. I think what he'd do is he'd get sauced , and he'd call [one of his fans] and he'd get to be the 'big star.' He'd kind of come to and think, *Who the fuck does she think she is?* He used her as an audience and discarded her when he could have given a shit."

When he did reply to his mail, Paul sent quick notes that made him sound busy. He included a publicity photo of himself in a red-hooded sweatshirt, toasting the camera with a glass of what looks like vodka and orange juice. "Paul was afraid of having his photo taken with the glass of juice I had made for him. He was afraid his fans would think it was booze," photographer Daphne Weld Nichols says. In the end, Paul loved the results. "Daphne," he said, "you have captured me the way I want to be remembered."

Annoyed by "the wantonness of the crimes" in Southern California, particularly the murderous doings of the Hillside Strangler and the Freeway Killer, Paul considered a change of scenery. "Paul was at a crossroads in his life," Leachman said. "He was planning to move to New York, feeling that perhaps he could find his proper place in the business there."

Paul had rekindled a love for New York and began spending his Christmases there. "I was so invigorated…that I was like a new person," he said after one visit. "I can't explain it, but I have more energy in New York than I do here. I was on the go every minute, seeing old friends and all that." Naturally, the dog went too. "He'd take Alfred with him to New York," Forbes says, "and he'd stay at the Pierre, and in those days his suite was $675 a night…. He'd have some people up for Christmas Eve and have some hors d'oeuvres and things, and Alfred would be greeting people." Paul enjoyed telling friends that "Alfred loves sweets and limousines." According to Earl Wilson, the pooch also loved the nightlife: "Paul Lynde put on a little show outside Studio 54 for those who couldn't get in, then entered with his black poodle 'Alfred Lunt,' one of the few dogs that have legged it past those portals. Brad Davis of *Midnight Express* and Robin Williams of *Mork and Mindy* made it too."

During the holidays in 1980, Paul met up with Alan King, who asked his friend to consider returning to TV as a gossip reporter in a sitcom called *Hix at Six*. Paul had warmed to the idea of a series again, especially one made in New York. Paul joked that because Alan "truly lives like a king, I'm considering it." He insisted that if he did it, "It won't be anything like the last two I was saddled with…. I've had it with those kinds of shows."

The idea of giving up show business entirely and opening a small restaurant in the Big Apple also appealed to Paul. He wanted to call the place "East Lynde" and envisioned it as "nothing extravagant…where my friends and fans can come to eat and visit. I'll be there every night. I'll be the host with the most." Paul even considered pulling a Spivy Le Voe, performing at his club if and only when he felt like it. Adams says that Paul had even found a town house in the city to buy.

In early 1982, John Kenley asked Paul to consider a return to Broadway, which Paul had long resisted. The producer wanted his most popular headliner to lead the cast of the *Greenwich Village Scandals of 1923*, an homage to the Ziegfeld extravaganzas of the 1920s and, in some ways, *New Faces of 1952*. Kenley, who had debuted as a dancer in the original run 60 years earlier, had produced a new version of the show the previous summer in Akron with Rip Taylor, Imogene Coca, and Cyd Charisse.

Paul discussed the project with the producer over the telephone on Saturday, January 9, and agreed to meet him on Paul's next visit to New York in February for the *Night of 100 Stars* charity benefit. During their talk, Paul prepared a bean dish for Paul Barresi's birthday party. He had seen Barresi the night before when they visited Barresi's friend Frank, who was interested in a job as Paul's housekeeper. Frank served lemonade and potato chips, which Paul gorged on by large handfuls. Paul had also spoken with Barresi that afternoon to tell him he'd be coming to the party. "I got your ggiiifttt!" he teased into the phone. "I met Mr. Guy." Mr. Guy was a popular clothing store in Beverly Hills.

Sunday afternoon, January 10, Jay Redack and his crew pulled a van of film equipment up to Paul's house on Palm Drive. Paul had agreed to do a segment for Redack's new pilot, *Knock Knock,* featuring celebrities pulling *Candid Camera*–esque stunts on people, but he hadn't shown up that morning. No one had answered the phone when Redack called, and now no one answered the door. *Goddamn it—of all times!* Redack thought. *He's out fucking around, or whatever he's doing!* Redack noticed the morning paper in the driveway and erroneously suspected, *Ah, shit, he never came home.* He left a note: "Paul, goddamn it, how could you do this to me! This is really crappy. I've been calling all morning. Here's our next stop. The minute you get this, call."

Dittman and Barresi worried about Paul all evening when he didn't show for the party. Sometime after 2 A.M., January 11, when all the guests had gone home, Barresi called Dittman and suggested they check up on their friend. He picked up Dittman, and they headed to Paul's house on North Palm Drive.

They arrived around 2:30 A.M. and saw no lights on. Two days worth of newspapers had accumulated on the porch. They rang the doorbell and knocked. No one answered except Alfred, who barked continually. Barresi scaled the fence to reach the driveway on the left side of the house. He knocked on Paul's bedroom window. He called "Paul, Paul." Nothing. Barresi hopped back over the fence. Dittman stood at the porch shaking and teary-eyed. "Oh, my God," Dittman said. "I hope somebody didn't kill him."

They drove eastbound on Santa Monica Boulevard to find a phone booth and call the police. Barresi was told he'd have to wait another 48 hours before the authorities could do anything. They returned to the porch for more fruitless knocking and doorbell ringing. Finally, Barresi told Dittman, "I've gotta get in there." He went to the right side of the house this time, which had a sliding door leading to the kitchen that Paul jokingly called the "servant's entrance." He broke one of the door's glass panels

to reach the knob from the inside. An earsplitting blare filled the air. Paul's Westec Security alarm had gone off. The door still wouldn't open, but Barresi kicked and battered until it did. Barresi thought the neighbors might show up to check on the noise, but none came.

With Dittman tagging along behind him, the dog running amok, and the alarm still shrieking, Barresi crept through the pitch-black house until he reached the bedroom. He saw Paul in the bed, lying on his back, his body twisted and his hand outstretched, reaching for a bedside panic button to alert Westec. His hair was neatly combed, and his blue eyes were wide open. "He had that look in his face of fear that was fixed, as if to say, 'This is the end,'" Barresi says. The body was cold and stiff.

Dittman screamed. Hysterical, he nearly threw himself on Paul's body, but Barresi held him back. As Dittman cried Paul's name over and over, Barresi noticed the death smell—decay and excrement, pungent and sour—and the white creamy corpse fluid bubbling from Paul's mouth. He took some tissue and wiped Paul's lips.

Barresi called 911 again and screamed "Paul Lynde is dead, please come" over and over. He had to scream to be heard over the alarm. They walked out into the living room to turn on the lights. Barresi noticed on the sofa a box wrapped in silver paper with a burgundy bow: his birthday gift.

Two Westec officers, alerted by the alarm, arrived before the police. Barresi and Dittman, still "a basket case," walked outside to meet them. The agents had drawn their guns. Barresi raised his hands in the air and told Dittman to do the same. They explained the situation and led the agents into the house. Three officers of the Beverly Hills police arrived soon after. The officers had Dittman and Barresi wait in the living room while they took pictures of the body until coroner's investigator Michael Shepard arrived.

The police took down Barresi's story, then gave Paul's friends permission to leave. Barresi asked the head officer if he could take his birthday present. It took a little convincing, but the officer relented. When he opened the box later, Barresi found a mohair sweater inside.

Dittman and Barresi loaded Alfred into their car and drove to Helen Lynde's upstairs apartment on Ocean Boulevard in Santa Monica. Dittman had called Helen before they left but wouldn't say why they were coming. When they arrived on her doorstep sometime between 3:30 and 4 A.M., she opened the door and asked "Paul's dead, isn't he?" Then she cried. Barresi brought Alfred in from the car. Helen later told him she gave the dog to relatives with a big backyard in the country.

Noyle heard the news from his mother in Michigan. He arrived at Paul's house around nine that morning. "[I remember] the scene in his bedroom. Someone who's had a heart attack, they've struggled…. It looked like he had struggled with the drapery on his canopy bed…. What I found interesting was that he had emergency buttons next to his bed that could notify the police department or set off the house alarm."

Reporters flocked outside Paul's house, and Noyle wasn't sure what to tell them. He called Paul's business managers for advice. They weren't much help. "I went out to make a statement…. You have to remember that the media then was nothing like the media today. Their big question to me was, 'Was Mr. Lynde aware he had a heart condition?'" Noyle said he had never come across anything in the house or overheard Paul say anything to suggest cardiac problems.

Early news reports said that Paul died of a stroke, but the coroner listed the cause of death as "acute myocardial infract"— a heart attack at 55. Officials reported that Paul suffered from a hardening of the arteries and emphysema. His recent strict regimen to counteract years of abuse may have been his undoing. "He was a perfectionist," Forbes says. "Everything had to be just right—the lighting, the colors in the home, [the] ashtray in the right place. That's really what killed him: this stress of being a perfectionist and quitting drinking and trying to quit smoking and [maintaining] his weight. When I met him he was heavy, and then it would go up and down and up and down, which was very bad on his heart." Paul's doctor reportedly told Alice Ghostley that Paul had the heart of an 85-year-old man.

Cloris Leachman said that Paul hadn't learned how to cope without alcohol. "That's the way you've handled stress, and now you can't use that way, and you haven't yet learned another way to get rid of it—you just pop," she said. "You implode! Paul was indeed a stressed person.... I think that Paul was maybe not a bitter person, but when you can't use your excellence, that's a kind of death, isn't it?"

Phyllis Diller thought Paul's moodiness played a part in his demise. "Nothing will kill you quicker than unhappiness. He really was the classic comedian who was a very sad person."

Persistent rumors have it that Paul died while having sex with a hustler—and a well-known porn actor to boot, as some theories in cyberspace like to clarify. If the hustler did take flight after Paul's heart attack with as much loot as possible, he was thoughtful enough to set Paul's security system. Barresi triggered the alarm when he broke the door, and Shepard's report mentions the officers found "no signs of foul play, or forced entry." Familiar with the house and Paul's belongings, Noyle says nothing from the house seemed to be missing, though he helped remove certain embarrassing unmentionables before Paul's family arrived. "There was very little that needed to be destroyed," he says. "What needed to be removed could be carried in one trip. Paul didn't have a house of horrors, if you will."

Two other factors may also give rise to these stories: the presence of butyl nitrate, a sexual stimulant, on Paul's bedside, and his body's apparent lack of clothing. Sometimes known as "rush" or "poppers," butyl nitrate gives a minor short-term high, making it a popular sex aid. Shepard's report describes two bottles of butyl nitrate found on Paul's nightstand, one unopened, the other nearly full. According to assistant coroner Richard Wilson, "a very small amount" of the substance turned up in Paul's system, but, he added, "We don't feel it was enough to cause the heart attack." Paul's manager told a reporter, "It's probably not his. It may belong to a friend…. It's not illegal. You buy it over the counter."

Shepard's report says Paul was naked, but Barresi says he found Paul fully dressed in pajamas and a bathrobe. This isn't the only inconsistency between the report and Barresi's memory of events (the report also states that Barresi broke in through a kitchen window instead of the sliding door, and that Barresi and Dittman called Westec at midnight before going to Paul's themselves two hours later), but to Barresi, it's a major difference.

"He wasn't unclothed," Barresi insists. "He had on his PJs, and he had his robe on." In Barresi's account, the covers were drawn over Paul's legs when he found him. Barresi says he can only speculate that police found Paul nude from the waist down and labeled him "naked" on the report.

Dittman may also have perpetuated and exaggerated the nudity angle. Kenley says Dittman told him that Paul had an erection when they found him. Possibly, Dittman wanted to impress friends with a tall tale, because a spokesperson for the investigators told reporters that the team found no indication Paul had recently engaged in sexual activity, and that medical tests supported that finding.

Paul's friends say the continuing legend surrounding the death stems from the wishful thinking of scandalmongers who equate risqué living with risqué dying. "People like to color things like that," Peter Marshall says. "They want to make a gay death into something weird." Then again, some of these same friends admit they were guilty of similar thinking at one time or another. "We always thought he'd be the last person likely to die in bed, that he'd be killed by somebody," Osborne says. The police seem to have considered similar thoughts initially. Shepard checked off "suicide" along with "natural" and "accident" in the box on his report that lists possible causes of death. He scribbled a note to himself just below that box: "Possible O.D.?"

The police officers raised the suicide question when they interviewed Barresi. He told them that Paul had been depressed about his career, "but no more than any other actor would be," says the report. Barresi also told the officers that Paul didn't have a drinking problem. Shepard noted the small springs in Paul's ears, which he described as "part of a 'stop-smoking' treatment," and package of cigarettes and a lighter on the nightstand.

Paul's obituaries rounded up bittersweet quotes from his friends and colleagues. Joan Rivers shared how she had wanted Paul to come on *The Tonight Show* when she guest-hosted at the end of January. He tried to get out of it by telling her he had nothing to talk about. "He was very down about his career at this point," she said. "He shouldn't have been because he was so talented and funny!"

"Anytime you lose a funnyman, it's a big loss to everyone under the tent," Jonathan Winters said. "I think his contributions as a funnyman were as important as anybody's. We had as good times off-camera as we did onstage. His ad-libbing was terrific. Everything came off the wall."

Leachman told columnist Shirley Eder she had stayed up most of the night after hearing about Paul's death. "All over the country his friends were calling each other to talk about Paul," she said. "We all somehow needed to be together." Their friend Forbes heard about Paul's death on the radio as she drove to an airport in Florida.

Noyle and Dittman arranged the funeral, with help from Peter Marshall. Some 250 friends, including Forbes, Dick Gautier, Ghostley, Gobel, Dody Goodman, Marshall, and Rivers attended a formal memorial service that Thursday. Bill Asher knew he wouldn't hold up, so he sent his wife, actress Joyce Bulifant.

In her eulogy, Goodman praised Paul for "his God-given wit, humor, and the ability to make people laugh." Dittman spoke next: "For Paul, although his time on Earth was comparatively short, we must rejoice! He fought and won, he was a reluctant dragon, the mouse that roared, Uncle Arthur, Harry MacAfee and Templeton the Rat, all rolled into one high-strung Sunday's child with an energy that will never be stilled. Once he belonged to the world, now he belongs to the ages, yet Paul will always be ours."

Feeling pressure about getting up in front of so many celebrities, Forbes gave her contribution a lot of thought. "The family wanted me to say something at the funeral," she says. "I thought, *Well, here I am...not a notable.... What in the world can I get up there and say?* So in the middle of the night it came to me."

Forbes read "Trouble in the Tulip Bed," one of her favorite poems that Paul had written at the start of his career. Forbes's reading of the poem—about a tulip named Blanche who saves Paul from an avalanche—provided a rare moment of levity at what some considered a maudlin memorial. "At his funeral, which should have been a warm send-off for a very funny man, there were no stories," Dick Gautier says, "only a very long, very religious ritual and mawkish songs by the Lennon Sisters. A guy as irreverent and as funny as Paul deserved a lot more. My personal take is that he would have hated it."

Paul once joked about his cremation, "Maybe they can just fly me over New York and drop me there." Instead, Helen sent his ashes to Mount Vernon. Paul had visited his hometown less frequently in the recent past. He had last returned in May 1980 to roast his childhood friend Harry Turner, then a state representative.

On Saturday, January 16, some 70 friends and family members, including Paul's siblings Grace and Richard, gathered for a service officiated by Reverend Eugene Loughran. "This afternoon on this cold, wintry day, we pause in gratitude," he said. "We remember all that is kind and good and faithful of Paul

Edward Lynde.... Whenever he appeared anywhere, we remember how Paul would frequently express a word of gratitude for this community."

Paul's ashes were to have been buried that Sunday in the family plot in Amity Cemetery, a small patch of land located a few miles north of Mount Vernon. Near-zero temperatures and strong winds delayed the internment until the weather improved. Paul now rests next to his parents; his war hero brother, Cordy; and his younger brother, Johnny. His headstone incorrectly lists his year of birth as 1927.

Paul's will, which he hadn't updated since 1965, named a former business manager as his executor. The bank assigned to serve as coexecutor spent months trying to iron out legal details. The estate employed Noyle for another year until it finalized everything.

Dittman told Kenley that Paul promised Dittman all his money, but Paul's will contains no mention of that claim. The document stipulates that his sisters Helen and Grace "share and share alike," and that his nephew Douglas Lynde receive $10,000 for college. Helen got Paul's art collection, furniture, and dog. Grace's husband got his clothing, personal effects, and jewelry. Paul specifically left nothing to his brother Richard, though he gave no reasons why. Kenley says that Paul "especially hated" his brother, but he doesn't know why.

Helen's reaction to Paul's death and refusal to accept his homosexuality outraged some of his friends. "We went immediately to Helen's apartment in Santa Monica, and we gave her the news," Barresi says. "Her whole attitude and the things that she said after the death—I mean not showing up to his wake.... It was just pretty damn appalling, as far as I'm concerned.... She never really gave her love to [Paul]; she only lent it on the best security and at the highest rate of interest." Noyle grew friendly with Helen while dealing with Paul's belongings. Once, when she started a sentence with "Now I'll be able to," Noyle expected her to say something like "take a trip to New York." Instead, she finished with "afford cable television."

Noyle talked Helen into letting some of Paul's close friends take an item from the house. Alice Ghostley asked for the first painting she bought for Paul when they were both starting out in New York. Barresi reclaimed a tiny hand-painted Chinese tray he bought for Paul as a gift. Noyle says another friend walked through all the rooms, carefully eyeing everything before claiming what seemed to be the most expensive item in the house. Noyle suspects the friend headed straight for a pawn shop.

Paul's sister Grace took the famous X's and O's shirt he frequently wore on *Hollywood Squares* and later gave it to a female fan who drove from New England to visit his grave. Noyle kept just one of Paul's iconic caftans, which he lent out one year as a Halloween costume and never got back. Jan Forbes keeps Paul's Emmy Award on her mantle.

Since Paul's death, his snide laugh continues to echo throughout pop culture. Squidward Tentacles, an easily annoyed cephalopod who sounds suspiciously like Paul, works at the Krusty Krab with SpongeBob SquarePants on the Nicktoon of the same name. Tom Kenny, who plays SpongeBob and several supporting characters, remains coy about Squidward's sexuality. Not so ambiguous, Bi-Polar Bear, a character on the Showtime series *Queer Duck,* also sounds like Paul. On *The Simpsons,* Bart's favorite superhero, Radioactive Man, takes on "the worst villain of them all," the Scoutmaster, in a send-up the campy *Batman* TV series. "Go get 'em, Scouts," the Lynde look-alike commands. "Don't be afraid to use your nails, boys!"

Writers still like to reference Paul, his many professional and personal mishaps making him a favorite punch line. *Will & Grace* has dropped his name in various jokes over the seasons: "You know, we've narrowed down the identity of Jack's father," says Karen, played by Megan Mullally. "It's either one of the 11 Black brothers of New Canaan, Connecticut, or Paul Lynde, the center square." In 1998's *The Opposite of Sex,* a character tells the smarmy, blackmailing boy-toy of his ex-lover:

> Listen to me, you little grunge faggot. I survived my family, my schoolyard, every Republican, every other Democrat, Anita Bryant, the Pope, the fucking Christian Coalition, not to mention a real son of a bitch of a virus, in case you haven't noticed, and in all that time, since Paul Lynde and Truman Capote were the only fairies in America, I've been busting my ass so you would be able to do what you want with yours!

"Paul Lynde Impersonation Lost on Daughter's Friends," a mock article in a 2002 issue of *The Onion,* shows us a glimpse of what the world will be like when future generations forget about Paul:

> Sarah Ammons, 14, expressed befuddlement Monday, when, during a ride to school, her father attempted to entertain her and several friends with an impromptu impersonation of late comedian and *Hollywood Squares* regular Paul Lynde. "The next time I have a daughter, I hope it's a boy!" Bob Ammons, 41, bleated nasally in an imitation of the once-popular pop-culture reference. "Paul Lynde." Added Ammons: "Center square, usually sat between George Gobel and Rose Marie? Voice of Templeton the Rat?" After dropping the girls off at school, Ammons stared into his car's rearview mirror at the crow's feet developing around his eyes.

This grim future approaches far too quickly. The signs proclaiming Mount Vernon as Paul Lynde's hometown stood at the city limits for two decades. They have since been replaced with new markers: DANIEL DECATUR EMMETT, AUTHOR OF "DIXIE" BORN AND BURIED HERE.

Acknowledgments

From the moment we stumbled into each other on the desolate Paul Lynde research trail and decided to work together (blissfully ignorant of the pain and suffering we were destined to cause each other), we've been indebted to several people for their gracious aid and support. These include: Angela Brown, Nick Street, and all the fine people at Alyson Books. Chris Barton, Mary Batin, Tom Beer, Pete Bell, Mickey Boardman, Fred Charleston, April Clark, Stephen Cole, Stephen Cox, Basil Cross, Frank DeCaro, Greg Dunne, Michael Ellis, David Everitt, Terri Fisher, Cathy Fitzrude, Margaret Florenski, Marleen Florenski, Ralph Florenski, Jan Forbes, John Fricke, Kristine Gable, Greg Gattuso, James Gavin, Bruce Hainley, Bill Harnsberger, Dixon Hayes, Matthew Hogan, Mike Holmes, David Huffman, Brandon Judell, Sammy Keith, Marc Kirkeby, Dominic Hamilton Little, William J. Mann, David Massello, Michael Naylor, Daphne Weld Nichols, Matt Ottinger, Bill Payne, Tim Reilly, Julie Erwin Rinaldi, Mike Sacks, Matthew Sayre, Norman Sherfield, Sidney Sheldon, Donna R. Smith, Susan Strine, Steve Suskin, Mary Lou Wallace, Dan Westerfall, and Gavin Lambert—author of the best star biography ever: *Norma Shearer: A Life*.

Special thanks to Lisa Everson at ABC News Productions who invited us to take part in the A&E Biography of Paul, a great experience that eventually led to this project, and to Scot Holmes and Erin Mayes for endless amounts of indulgence in all matters Lynde.

Much of the initial research for this book was completed at the Columbus Metropolitan Library in Columbus, Ohio, a great place to wile away endless lunch hours reading old copies of *TV Guide* and *Variety*. In addition, friendly and accommodating staff members of the following institutions provided material and support that helped put the Lynde story into focus: American Heritage Center at the University of Wyoming (Laramie, Wyoming), Beinecke Rare Book and Manuscript Library at Yale University (New Haven, Connecticut), Billy Rose Theatre Collection at the New York Public Library for the Performing Arts (New York, New York), Bowling Green State University Music Library and Sound Recordings Archives (Bowling Green, Ohio), Broward County Public Library (Fort Lauderdale, Florida), Bucks County Historical Society (Doylestown, Pennsylvania), Bucks County Playhouse (New Philadelphia, Pennsylvania), Chicago Historical Society (Chicago, Illinois), Chicago Public Library (Chicago, Illinois), Cleveland Public Library (Cleveland, Ohio), Cleveland State University (Cleveland, Ohio), Flint Public Library (Flint, Michigan), Harry Ransom Humanities Research Center at the University of Texas (Austin, Texas), Hastings Public Library (Hastings, Nebraska), Hillman Library Special Collections at the University of Pittsburgh (Pittsburgh, Pennsylvania), Jerome Lawrence & Robert E. Lee Theatre Research Institute at Ohio State University (Columbus, Ohio), Kansas City Public Library (Kansas City, Missouri), Kansas City Starlight Theatre (Kansas City, Missouri), Kent State University Libraries (Kent, Ohio), Kenyon College Archives (Gambier, Ohio), Knox County Health Department (Mount Vernon, Ohio), Knox County Historical Society (Mount Vernon, Ohio), Library of Congress, Margaret Herrick Library of the Academy of Motion Picture Arts and Sciences (Beverly Hills,

California), Museum of Broadcasting (Chicago, Illinois), Museum of Television & Radio (Los Angeles California, and New York, New York), Northwestern University Archives (Evanston, Illinois), Ohio Historical Society (Columbus, Ohio), Ohio State University Libraries (and Archives) (Columbus, Ohio), Ohioana Library (Columbus, Ohio), Public Library of Mount Vernon and Knox County (Mount Vernon, Ohio), Rauner Special Collections Library at Dartmouth College (Hanover, New Hampshire), Ray & Pat Browne Library for Popular Culture Studies at Bowling Green State University (Bowling Green, Ohio), Saratoga Springs Public Library (Saratoga Springs, New York), Southeast Steuben County Library (Corning, New York), St. Louis Mercantile Library at the University of Missouri-St. Louis (St. Louis, Missouri), St. Louis Municipal Opera (St. Louis, Missouri), State Library of Ohio (Columbus, Ohio), UCLA Film and Television Archive (Los Angeles, California), University of Iowa Libraries Special Collections (Iowa City, Iowa), University of Texas Library (Austin, Texas), Wisconsin Center for Film and Theater Research at the Wisconsin Historical Society (Madison, Wisconsin), Wright State University (Dayton, Ohio).

Special thanks to Allen Streicker of the Northwestern University Archives for research assistance above and beyond all others, and to Jim Gibson of the Knox County Historical Society for granting access to a wonderful collection of memorabilia.

Acknowledgment should also be extended to the man from Paul's hometown who insisted Paul was not a "faggot," the threatening Lynde acquaintance who kept demanding "You put me in that book!" and all the other loons left over from Paul's life who gave us a good laugh.

Index